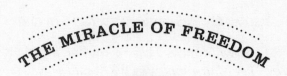

THE MIRACLE OF FREEDOM

7
TIPPING POINTS
that SAVED *the* WORLD

Chris Stewart

....

Ted Stewart

SHADOW
MOUNTAIN

ALSO BY CHRIS STEWART AND TED STEWART

Seven Miracles That Saved America:
Why They Matter and Why We Should Have Hope

Visit us at ShadowMountain.com

Library of Congress Cataloging-in-Publication Data
Stewart, Chris, author.
  The miracle of freedom : seven tipping points that saved the world / Chris Stewart and Ted Stewart.
      p. cm.
  Includes bibliographical references and index.
  Summary: Examine seven important "tipping points" in history that were instrumental in the rise of freedom in the United States and the world.
  ISBN 978-1-60641-951-9 (hardbound : alk. paper)
  1. Miracles. 2. Europe—History—Religious aspects—Christianity. I. Stewart, Ted, author. II. Title.
  D24.S785 2011
  940—dc22   2011005037

Printed in the United States of America
Publishers Printing, Salt Lake City, Utah

10 9 8 7 6 5 4 3 2 1

Contents

Preface

Many have asked us if this book is designed to be a follow-up to our previous book, *Seven Miracles That Saved America*. The truth is, it wasn't our intention to write two books that were closely tied together.

The first book was an account of events in the history of the United States, with a particular eye toward answering these questions: Were there events in the history of this nation when God literally intervened to save us? Was there a reason for these miracles? Does God have a purpose for us still?

The theme of this book is very different. Rather than looking at miracles, we wanted to examine some of the most important events in the history of the world—epic and world-changing events—all of which were indispensable stepping-stones toward the miracle of expanded freedom and democracy in this day.

But soon we began to realize that there is a string that runs through history, a common thread that ties it all together in a manner that was not so obvious to us before. We began to see a magnificent sense of purpose—a sense of *intention*—in what might otherwise be considered a series of unrelated historical events. It was as if there was a plan, as if each step in human progress was not just a matter of chance or happenstance but was supposed to be.

A second idea also became very obvious.

We believe in the idea of American Exceptionalism. We make that very clear in the first book. America is an extraordinary nation. It has played, and will continue to play, a special role in the world. But it is also clear that America wouldn't exist, indeed it *couldn't* exist, without the foundation that was laid so many millennia before. This great nation, with the freedoms that we love, owes its existence to the events that are described in this book, some of which took place in modern day, some of which played out almost three thousand years ago.

So though it wasn't our intention to write a follow-up book to *Seven Miracles That Saved America,* and in a greater sense we haven't, many of the powerful themes that run through the first book can also be found here.

Regarding the title of this book: Some may wonder what we mean by the phrase *saved the world.*

Imagine a world without any freedom. Imagine a world with no democratic governments or rule of law, without justice or equality. Imagine a world without free nations willing to stand against the tide of hate and oppression that seems to be the natural tendency of man, a world without the immeasurable good that has been brought about by democratic governments.

Now take it one step further.

Imagine a world with the means of mass destruction—nuclear warheads, biological weapons, chemical and conventional attacks—held only in the hands of despotic men and governments.

Imagine a world, for example, with another Adolf Hitler or Joseph Stalin in command of much of Europe and all of Asia. Imagine such a man holding all this power, along with all of the other potentially destructive technological developments of the past forty years, without the counterbalance of free governments like those in Western Europe and the United States that have proven willing to stand up to tyranny and oppression.

Imagine tyrannical governments with the modern-day capability to monitor, track, harass, suppress, and persecute their own people, their neighbors, their enemies, all without a group of nations willing to stand as a light of freedom against oppressive leaders. Consider what our world might be like—what our world *would* be like—without the overwhelmingly positive influence of modern democracies.

Then ask yourself this question: Have democratic governments saved this world?

A world without free nations that were willing to sacrifice their blood and treasure to support the idea that *men should be free* would be a very different world from the one we live in today.

Regarding the idea of *The Miracle of Freedom,* some may ask, "Is the existence of freedom truly a miraculous event?"

To most people, the word *miracle* conjures up images of manna from heaven, the parting of the Red Sea, Muhammad riding a horse into the seventh heaven, or Buddha creating a golden bridge out of thin air.[1] More personally, we think of miracles as those unexplainable coincidences that seem to shape the direction of our lives in subtle but powerful ways.

Yet when we consider the complicated and extraordinarily unlikely series of events that led to the existence of freedom in our day; when we consider the fact that freedom runs counter to what seems to be the natural order of men and that, as will be shown, an incredibly small percentage of human beings have had the blessing of living free; the widespread existence of freedom in our day does indeed seem to be a miraculous event.

In the following chapters, we hope to show how, at critical tipping points in world history, certain events took place so as to assure that freedom and democracy would be common in this day.

In telling these stories, we think it's important to note that cultures of the past are very different from those of our day. When large majorities of people were simply fighting for survival, the norms of their behavior were different from what we have come to accept. People. Nations. Families. War. Mercy and compassion. Justice. Expectations of behavior. All of these have changed. Because of this, it may be difficult to categorize people and events into unambiguous groups that we would say are good or bad.

Complicating our evaluation is the fact that no individual, nation, culture, or institution was always virtuous. Every leader had weaknesses. And all of them were mere men, struggling to accomplish difficult undertakings that would alter the course of history. This being the case, would we expect that there would be no mistakes? And though it would be easy to emphasize their failings or character flaws, we have tried not to let their weaknesses diminish the extraordinary role they may have played.

Parts of these stories will be told in a historically accurate context portrayed fictionally through the eyes of certain participants; parts will be told through pure historical narrative. We have chosen to tell the stories chronologically, although that is not necessarily what we would consider their ranking of importance.

Taken together, these stories show that the march toward freedom was never assured, that at any of these critical points in history, the tide of freedom might have been turned.

Note

1. It's interesting to note that a surprisingly large majority of Americans believe in miracles. A 2008 Pew Forum on Religion and Public Life study (one of the largest ever conducted, in which more than thirty-six thousand adults were interviewed) found that nearly 80 percent of Americans believed in miracles. A 2010 Pew study found nearly identical results, with 79 percent of Americans believing in miracles (see www.pewforum.org). And Christians are not alone. Muslim theology accepts the reality of miracles, as do many other world religions.

Introduction

Along the Southern Nile River
1876 BC

AKHENATEN AMSU WAS A strong man. At more than six feet and two hundred pounds, with the sharp face of his Philistine fathers and the olive skin of a mother whose ancestors had been lost in a thousand years of time, he stood above the other slaves in many uncomfortable ways. With the average Egyptian being just more than 150 pounds, it was obvious that Akhenaten Amsu had been taken care of, at least in the early part of his life, for he was not only tall but broad. And though the last few years had been terribly debilitating, he was still strong.

As he toiled, his back to the sun, the day passed exactly as the day before had passed. And though he didn't realize it, this day was his seventeenth birthday. Had he remembered, he might have taken a moment to consider the life that lay ahead. Nothing but toil and work and death. A million tons of rock to cut and shape and move. Sometime around the age of thirty, he would almost certainly be dead.

Like a calf that had been fattened at the troughs of the king before being led to the slaughter, Akhenaten Amsu had spent his youth away from his family, fed and trained and strengthened in order to prepare him to spend his life as a quarry master, extracting and shaping stone. And that was all he would do now. It was backbreaking work, as crushing as the weight of the rock around him. Eighteen hours a day. Seven days a week. The heat of the Egyptian summer. The unrelenting whip of his taskmaster—a fellow slave who had murdered and extorted his way to the coveted position of overseeing his lesser brothers.

That was all that was expected of him now: ten or fifteen years of cruel labor. Cut the stone. Build the temple. Sacrifice his body to the pharaoh and his gods.

The irony wasn't lost on Akhenaten Amsu, for he was not a stupid man. Tens of thousands of his fellow slaves would work until they died, all to build nothing but a temple in which they would bury another man.

And the reward for all his efforts? Life. Food. A little water every hour. Straw to make a bed when he was exhausted. A sparse whip if he was dedicated. A sharp-tongued crack if he was slow. Because he was strong, he would be forced to father children, all of whom would be committed to the same fate as his. All of his children and grandchildren would be born into a life of slavery and broken dreams.

Hearing sudden grunts of pain, Akhenaten Amsu lifted his eyes to see his master beating another slave. Taking advantage of the moment, he stood and stretched, twisting to lessen some of the ache in the muscle that wrapped around his spine. Looking at his hands, as rough as leather, and hearing the crack of joints up and down his back, he felt the early signs of aging. It made him cringe, seeing his body so abused.

Glancing quickly to the south, he saw a line of dust that followed the dirt road that led from the quarry to the site of the new temple, an unknown number of miles away. He hadn't seen it, and he never would, but he had heard of its magnificence, a pyramid of carefully cut rock rising over the river. Between the quarry and the temple there was nothing but sand baking in the desert heat. Closer in, if he squinted, he could just make out the wadi where they threw the bodies of his fellow slaves when they were done, the heat and desert quickly stripping them to nothing but leather and bone. Looking west, he could see that the sun was just setting. Soon the torches that would allow them to continue their endless work would be passed around and lit.

Why? Akhenaten Amsu wondered for at least the thousandth time. *Why have I been robbed of any hope?*

He looked at the setting sun again. His masters worshipped many gods, but none more than the gods of the sky, and so they had become some of the greatest astronomers the world had ever seen. Having been taught a little from the masters, Akhenaten Amsu had a sense of space and time, a sense of his place in the world. And one thing was always certain. He would die a slave.

Yet sometimes he had to wonder.

Would men always live in such a world?

He turned back to his work, never knowing that more than fifteen hundred years later, on the other side of the world, a child would ask the same question as he did.

Hangchow, China
230 BC
Just before the reign of Emperor Shih Huang Ti

ZHU RAUN SUNG WAS only twelve, but he already understood the most important lessons that life had to teach. He knew how to work. He knew how to get by on nothing but a daily bowl of rice with an occasional chicken foot or rat bone for sustenance. He knew when to talk and when to be silent, when to bow and when to run. He knew he would honor his father and their ancestors until the day that he died, just as his children would honor him even in his old age. He knew that in four years he would marry a girl he might care for or maybe not, the primary purpose of the marriage being to produce children who could labor alongside him on the ragged piece of land that they were tasked to work. He knew he would never own his own home or even an animal except for maybe a rabbit or a dog. Every piece of ground, every hut, every building, city wall, shop, water hole, and piece of furniture or food belonged to the royal family and no one else.

Most important, he knew that he and his family would always live to serve the royals and their warriors, surrendering everything they had, even providing their children as a human sacrifice if the occasion presented itself.

Had Zhu Raun been born in a more forgiving time, he might have risen to a position of favor or power, for he was handsome and intelligent and willing to take a chance. But that wasn't to be. And Zhu Raun knew it. His expectations had been adjusted to the realities of his day.

Lying on the dirt floor, a cushion of cottonwood leaves for his bed, Zhu Raun looked around the one-room shack in the early morning light. His mother and father slept beside him, his younger brother and two sisters balled together at his feet. A couple of pigs had slipped through the open door and were sleeping in the slant of sunlight shining through the cracks in the thatch roof. The shack was situated in one of a dozen small villages half a day's walk from the Great City's outer wall. Three hundred thousand people lived inside the city, a number Zhu Raun couldn't begin to comprehend, but he was not one of them. Indeed, he had been inside the city only a few times in his life. But having been inside the city, he knew that the nobles lived a life of luxury that was beyond his dreams.

Turning his head, Zhu Raun looked at the glistening goblets his father had created in the kiln that he and a hundred other farmers shared beside the communal well. His eyes grew wide as he stared at the beautiful creations. They were quite simply the most wonderful things he had ever seen. Brilliant, with red swans and purple wildflowers, the gifts represented at least a quarter of his family's total wealth.

And today they would be given to the royal family and buried with the king.

The tradition went back an unknown number of generations. When a king died, hundreds—or, if he had been particularly powerful, thousands—of slaves and peasants were sacrificed and buried with him, along with the most valuable treasures the empire's peasants could produce.

Today, along with their beautiful gifts, the village would offer up a child to be sacrificed to the king.

And though he didn't know it yet, Zhu Raun was going to be that sacrifice.

Three hours later, his head bowed, his heart racing so hard he thought it might explode, Zhu Raun had a rope tightened around his neck and was led away.

As he walked, his hands bound, the biting rope making it difficult to breathe, he built the courage to glance back at his family. His mother was on her knees, weeping into her palms. His father stood beside her, one hand on her shoulder, his chest trembling with rage. His younger brother and little sisters had already been led away, protected from the terrifying scene by the kindness of friends.

As Zhu Raun nodded to his father, a sudden thought raced through his mind. *Will it always be this way?* he wondered in fear and grief.

Then the rope was tugged and he was mercilessly pulled away.

And because the world wasn't ready yet, another eighteen hundred years would pass away.

Prague
Czech State (Bohemia)
Winter, AD 1696

THE JEWISH FATHER PULLED his son close as they huddled against the misty rain. The river was calm, as if it had stopped flowing altogether, pellets of rain creating a million tiny ripples to break the water's surface. It was cold, the early winter deep and chill, and the young boy leaned into his father, feeling for the warmth of his coat.

They stared sadly at the statue that stood over the Charles Bridge, a beautiful Gothic overpass that spanned the Old Town and *Mala Stranλ*. The great king Charles, a powerful leader who had gone on to become the Holy Roman Emperor Charles IV, had commissioned the bridge almost three hundred years before. Guarded on both ends by thick stone towers, the *KamennΥ most,* or Stone Bridge, as it had originally been called, was one of the great architectural achievements in the entire Bohemian kingdom, which had reached its crest of power now.

The father looked at the statue of the Christian god and thought of the events of the last few weeks. A leader of the Jewish neighborhood, he had been accused of blasphemy against the Holy Christ. As punishment, he had been forced to create a ring of gold-plated Hebrew letters and place them around the statue's neck. *Holy, Holy, Holy, the Lord of Hosts,* the sign read.

The sacred words, taken from the book of Isaiah, were part of a blessed Jewish prayer.

His son, he knew, shared in his humiliation. He felt the shame of his people, their history, their culture, even now their great Jehovah. The sacred words were intended for the Messiah only, not for the Christian god.

The father looked down at his son, reading the look in his eyes. "God exempts the man who is constrained," he said in a quiet voice.

The son pressed his lips together.

They had all heard the Hebrew saying far too many times before. This wasn't the first time their people had been forced to denigrate their faith.

The father shook his head, then glanced down at the crimson badge his people were forced to wear. The first Jewish ghetto had sprung up in Spain about three hundred years before, but the idea had been embraced until ghettos were common throughout all of Europe now: Madrid, Barcelona, Venice, Rome, and Prague. He thought of the accusations all of them endured. *Blood Libels,* they were called. Jews had been accused of ritual killings since the height of the Crusades, when all the heretics (Jews, Muslims, and suspicious Christians) had been forced to hide or flee. Some of his own ancestors had been accused of killing Christian children and using their blood to make unleavened bread for the Passover.

Pulling his coat against the humid chill, the father looked east, knowing the hatred from his fellow citizens was not the most dangerous of his concerns.

He thought of the brutal Cossack army that had swept through the heart of Eastern Europe not too many years before, massacring the Poles and Jews as if they were rats or wolves. Even now, he knew that nothing stood between the deadly Cossacks and the place that he called home. Nothing stood between the Jewish ghettos and the evil governments and institutions that had sent his people here. Nothing stood between the Jewish people and the superstitious hatred that had been growing for five hundred years.

His people were alone. No one would stand up to defend them. No state, no nation, no religious institution or act of man, nothing could protect them from their enemies, even if they had wanted to.

Looking at his child, he prayed for words that might give his son a little hope. Having none, he held his tongue and pulled his son close.

Office of Information
Omsk, Siberia, Union of Soviet Socialist Republics
AD 1986

THE RUSSIAN INVESTIGATOR stared at the papers scattered across his desk, then leaned back and closed his eyes, unconsciously holding his breath.

It was too much. *It simply couldn't be!* The numbers didn't make any sense!

He stared at the water-stained ceiling and exhaled, then closed his eyes again.

Forty million people in the first generation. Maybe ten or twenty million after that.

Leaning forward, he let his breath escape, then picked up a yellow page from the top of the pile and read some of the numbers that he had just compiled.

Sixty million people!

And we did this to ourselves!

Gulag. *Glavnoye Upravlyeniye Ispravityel'no-Trudovih Lagyeryey i koloniy.* Chief Administration of Corrective Labor Camps and Colonies. The word had been feared for generations now.

At one time, there had been at least five hundred separate labor, penal, or "reeducation" camps scattered throughout the Communist nation, a vast majority of them concentrated in the northern tiers, each of them containing tens of thousands of the dying and condemned. Indeed, some of the major industrial cities in northern Russia had been built entirely upon the back of prison labor. More than fourteen million people passed through the gulag in a span of only twenty years. During this same time, another six to seven million were exiled to various "unofficial" Siberian labor and reeducation camps, where they were essentially worked to death.

By the early 1960s, the Soviet government had officially disbanded the gulag camps. Or at least they had on paper. In reality, the prisons continued operating in newly renamed "colonies." For a man who had, as a Communist party member, committed his life to furthering the Stalinist cause, it was devastating for the investigator to realize how many of his countrymen the party had killed. *Millions* of Soviet citizens! Many guilty of nothing more than being orphans or not having a place to live. There were stories of starving children sent away for stealing bread. Political prisoners who let slip the wrong word or phrase. Women who had done nothing more than ask the local party leader when they could expect to get some firewood. Millions of innocent victims, condemned by a government that craved tyranny and power.

The official records indicated that only a million prisoners had died in reeducation and labor camps. The Russian scoffed. It was a joke. He knew that the common practice was to release prisoners a few days before they died, removing them from any official government list of the dead.

And though some of the gulag inmates were not political prisoners, he knew that many of them were. He glanced to a green binder on the floor. Demetrius Kosack. Age twenty-two. Married. Father of two. The young man's father had been a colonel in the Russian army during World War II. He was a loyal party member himself. It didn't matter. One morning he had whispered an antigovernment joke. He had been reported before noon, arrested before his shift was over, and on his way to a Siberian camp before the sun had set. No trial. No defense. No appeal. Sentenced to fourteen years of hard labor. Dead of tuberculosis halfway through his sentence. Buried in the Siberian snow.

And there were vaults the size of football fields with green folders just like this one.

He took another long breath and closed his eyes. Depressing as it was, he felt a shiver of relief.

Things were changing. He could feel it.

And he was right.

The Age of Freedom was finally near.

• • •

From the most ancient civilizations to modern times, across every continent and culture, from generations and kingdoms lost in the fog of history to the well-documented atrocities of modern day, stories such as those just related represent how most members of the human family have lived. As foreign as such accounts may be to our experience, and as dispiriting as they may seem, they might be told more than a hundred billion times, for they represent the vast majority of the human experience.

Indeed, these examples illustrate the common hopelessness that was pervasive in the day-to-day lives of most of the men and women who have been born into this world. Such were the only expectations they ever had for their lives. Scraping out a meager existence, many times on the brink of starvation or death. Fear. Nowhere to turn for justice. No police or local magistrates to protect them. Government the source of oppression rather than protection. No voice ever raised to protect the young, the weak, the women, those who could not protect themselves. Control the only thing that mattered. Power. Strength. The sword.

Liberty Is Not the Norm

For those of us living in the United States, a nation that has experienced more than two hundred years of unparalleled liberty, it is easy to take for granted the extraordinary gifts we have been given. And for most of us, it is much easier to become lackadaisical about these gifts than it is for the inhabitants of other nations who are forced to struggle every day in their battle for liberty. In fact, unless we are serious students of world history, or have traveled extensively, we might not recognize how unique the blessings of liberty actually are.

Throughout the age of human experience, most people have never been afforded the simple right of the freedom to choose. The great exception to this truth is the modern age—by which we mean the years since the United States of America has been in existence—and even in this modern age, with the exception of the United States, freedom and democracy are not universal and have not been of a long duration. These gifts are limited to those countries that we refer to as the West, meaning Europe and the United States of America, and those few nations scattered around the world that have emulated the Western form of political philosophy and government.

In the Beginning

As illustrated in the personal narratives above, individual freedom is an idea that has been barely recognized for most of human history. True, there are a few examples of rare cultures or extraordinary leaders who at least tried to understand the value of freedom and justice, but they are few and far between. One example would be the ancient Babylonian king Hammurabi, who in 1790 BC put forward a code that would assure "that the strong should not harm the weak."[1] In the Jewish law, as found in Leviticus 19:15, Jehovah tells the people,

"Thou shalt not respect the person of the poor, nor honor the person of the mighty: but in righteousness shalt thou judge thy neighbor."

Scattered examples of justice and acknowledgment of individual dignity aside, the fact remains that the majority of human beings have never even thought about the possibility of living under the protection of a government that would honor their individual rights or grant them freedom.

Which then raises a certain question: Are oppression, tyranny, and fear the natural order of things?

Looking over the span of human history, the answer would seem to be undeniably yes.

Nineteenth-century French philosopher Frederic Bastiat argued in his short but powerful work *The Law* that "it is injustice, instead of justice, that has an existence of its own. Justice is achieved *only when injustice is absent.*"[2]

In Bastiat's view, injustice is the norm, the instinctive way of man. He claims that, in order for justice to prevail, injustice must first be eliminated, a difficult and extraordinarily rare thing to do.

Other learned opinions—as well as historical evidence that we will discuss later—seem to agree with this view. For example, projecting what a future historian might say about our day, one distinguished American, Dr. Walter Williams, made the following observation:

> Mankind's history is one of systematic, arbitrary abuse and control by the elite. . . . It is a tragic history where hundreds of millions of unfortunate souls have been slaughtered, mostly by their *own* government. A historian writing 200 or 300 years from now might view the liberties that existed for a tiny portion of mankind's population, mostly in the western world, for only a tiny portion of its history, the last century or two, as a historical curiosity that defies explanation. That historian might also observe that the curiosity was only a temporary phenomenon and mankind reverted back to the traditional state of affairs—arbitrary control and abuse.[3]

Williams's point is hard to dismiss. This modern day we live in, with the unimaginable blessings of freedom and liberty, is the aberration, not the norm. Further, simply because freedom exists today does not guarantee this gift will survive for future generations.

The Few We Are

How unusual is it, really, in the history of all known human experience, to enjoy the blessings of living free? What are the odds of being born in such a day?

The best estimates of how many people have ever lived on the earth range from 100 to 110 billion. Freedom House estimates that approximately three billion of the earth's current population live in "free" nations.[4] Most of this is due to the fact that the number of free nations has almost doubled in the last generation.[5]

It has also been estimated that 554 million people have lived under freedom in the United States since 1780.[6] We can also postulate that perhaps another billion, or fewer, have lived under freedom in the other European nations that evolved, in fits and spurts, into free nations during the twentieth century.

Even being generous in our estimates, it seems clear that fewer than five billion of the earth's total inhabitants have ever lived under conditions that we could consider free. This would be something like 4.5 percent of people who have ever lived. And these are generous estimates. The actual numbers might be much lower than this.

Which is, as Dr. Williams said, truly a "tiny portion of mankind's population."

Even more surprising is the fact that freedom is a relatively unstable marvel. For example, in a recent work, Yale professor Robert Dahl could identify only twenty-two nations with a democracy older than fifty years. Think about that! Even now, when most of us consider free will and self-government as the norm, there are only twenty-two nations that have lived under a democratic form of government *for even a single lifetime*. (Most of the nations Dahl identified were European or English speaking, with Costa Rica being the only Latin American country, Israel the only nation in the Middle East, and Japan the only nation in Asia.)[7]

What Do We Mean By "Democracy" and "Freedom"?

Any analysis of the rarity of freedom and democracy[8] is complicated by the fact that the very definition of *freedom* is subjective and that the term *democracy* has many meanings.[9]

So how do we define those salient terms?

Perhaps we ought to start at the beginning, that is, with what our Founding Fathers considered the fundamental truths that justified their rebellion, those principles of government that, if denied, gave just cause to sever ties to their mother land and go to war:

> We hold these truths to be self–evident, That all men are created equal, That they are endowed by their Creator with certain unalienable Rights,
>
> That among these are Life, Liberty and the pursuit of Happiness.—That to secure these rights, Governments are instituted among Men,
>
> Deriving their just powers from the consent of the governed.[10]

Considering these inspired words, our own understanding of history and political philosophy, as well as the practical need to encompass a number of political values into shorthand terms, we are led to suggest definitions of freedom and democracy that include the following five characteristics:

1. Self-government. The right of the people to govern themselves, and the right of the people to form the type of government that they choose. This includes an acknowledgment that those who govern do so only by the consent of the governed. It means the right of the people to

choose those who will make and enforce the laws and the right of the people to refuse to be governed by those that are not so chosen.

2. Fundamental rights. All people are born with certain fundamental rights. It is understood that those rights include the right to life and personal liberty, and the right to keep one's property and the fruits of one's labor. These personal liberties would include freedom of speech, religion, thought, the press, and movement, among others. We believe it is understood that these rights, or liberties, are inherent and unalienable and do not come from a constitution or laws or any government, but from God.

3. All are created equal. A belief in the equality of all at birth, including the belief that a major role of government is to assure that everyone, regardless of status, is treated equally by the law and that everyone has an equal opportunity to succeed or fail.

4. Commitment to justice. By *justice* we mean that condition wherein each man or woman is rendered that to which they are entitled; that is, they should receive their earned rewards or punishments regardless of how rich or powerful they are or what class or race they may belong to.

5. Commitment to the rule of law. All people are subject to the same law—be they president or common citizen. This means that no man or woman can ignore the rightful laws of the land without being punished.

These five principles, values, or characteristics are what we mean when we make reference to *democracy* and *freedom* throughout this book.

The Importance of Economic Freedom

In addition to the freedoms listed above, our Founding Fathers clearly understood the importance of, and sought for the protection of, our economic freedom. One of the foundational freedoms mentioned in the Declaration of Independence is the right to the "pursuit of happiness," which would include the right to receive the reward of our work or actions. Our Constitution also guarantees the right of private property.

Recently it has become fashionable to demonize successful individuals, as if their accomplishments were attributable to nothing more than being the lucky winners on an uneven playing field. In fact, some national leaders have become so critical of wealth and success that they actually seek to implement policies that would lead to overall *decreases* in wealth and technology.[11] But there is no doubt that economic freedom has led to the greater common good, including less poverty, hunger, disease, illiteracy, and oppression of the defenseless.

Recent studies also show that many leading measures of environmental quality are closely tied to improvements in national incomes.[12] For example, twenty-three of the top twenty-five most polluted sites in the world are found in current or former Communist nations—governments that, by definition, do not honor economic freedom.[13]

Recent studies by the National Bureau of Economic Research also indicate a strong correlation between economic freedom and the significant decrease in world poverty that has taken place over the past forty years.[14] Other well-respected studies show a strong link between a country's wealth and other significant measures of well-being, including innovation and expanded economic opportunities.[15]

Considering the benefits that are attributable to economic freedom, is it any wonder that it is one of the first of our freedoms that our enemies seek to destroy?

Why Did Freedom Happen?

Why has the West produced such a rare, and historically counter-intuitive, commitment to democracy and freedom? What extraordinary events in history worked in concert to create circumstances in which we—a fraction of the people who have lived on the earth—could enjoy self-government, belief in the equality of man, the rule of law, pursuit of justice, and a focus on personal liberty? How are we so lucky? To what do we owe this great blessing?

Many scholars confidently assert that it was the Greeks who gave birth to these beliefs, which were then nourished by Christianity in such a way as to make possible modern-day concepts of freedom and democracy. Rodney Stark, one of the most notable authorities of the impact of Christianity upon Western thinking, has written extensively on the subject. In one of his several books on the subject, he explains:

> While the other world religions emphasized mystery and intuition, Christianity alone embraced reason and logic as the primary guide to religious truth. Christian faith in reason was influenced by Greek philosophy. . . . But from the early days, the church fathers taught that reason was the supreme gift from God. . . . Faith in the power of reason infused Western culture, stimulating the pursuit of science and the evolution of democratic theory and practice. The rise of capitalism was also a victory for church-inspired reason.[16]

Throughout his works, Stark argues persuasively that the rise of Western thought in Europe, based upon reason, faith in progress, personal freedom, and capitalism, was the direct result of Christian theology.[17]

Without doubt, the greatest achievement of Western thought was the birth of the United States of America. The United States is the cradle of self-government, freedom, and liberty. From its inception, it has provided the best evidence that democracy and freedom can not only work but prosper.

The values of equality and justice clearly flourished in this land. Belief in the rule of law was first proven to succeed in America and, for more than two hundred years, this nation has been the primary example of—and inspiration for—these values throughout the world.

How Did It Happen?

It seems that misery wasn't the outcome that God intended for this world, for over millennia of time a miracle took place. It happened so slowly and so sporadically that in most cases the progress went completely unnoticed, so much so that even with the benefit of hindsight some of these steps of progress are difficult to identify and understand. But they *did* take place. Over centuries of human development, things changed.

A deeper look at the human record reveals a series of critical events, obvious forks in the road leading to *very* different outcomes, that resulted in this extraordinary period in which we live. These tipping points—foundational events that allowed for the marriage of Greek philosophy and Judeo-Christian theology—laid the bedrock for democracy and freedom in our modern age.

Seven of the most important of these historical tipping points would be:

1. The defeat of the Assyrians in their quest to destroy the kingdom of Judah

As recorded in the Old Testament (as well as in nonbiblical sources), after the Assyrian army had defeated the kingdom of Israel and dispersed the Ten Tribes "to the north," the Assyrian king sought to do the same thing to the kingdom of Judah. Suddenly, and uncharacteristically, the king changed his mind, deciding not to annihilate the kingdom of Judah—including the capital city of Jerusalem—but instead turning his armies and leaving the city in peace. The result was critical to the development of the modern world, for had Assyria succeeded in destroying Judah and Jerusalem, its population would have been "lost," as were the Ten Tribes before. Had this happened, there would have been no Jewish state in which to plant Christianity.

2. The victory of the Greeks over the Persians at Thermopylae and Salamis

Had the Persians succeeded in defeating the Greek city-states, Greek philosophy, with its emphasis on individual rights and its experimentation with democracy, as well as Greek advances in science and culture, would not have survived. If that had happened, there would have been no Alexander the Great to spread the Greek culture throughout the Middle and Near East (generally those nations between the Mediterranean Sea and present-day Iran). Without the Greek influence bestowed by Alexander, Rome would have been a very different type of empire. Without the overwhelming influence of Rome, Europe would have evolved into a different place, far more the product of Eastern culture than those Western principles steeped in Greek philosophy and beliefs.

3. Roman Emperor Constantine's conversion to Christianity

For both good and bad, the early history of Christianity was intimately tied to the Roman Empire. For several hundred years after the death of Christ, Christianity was deemed to be subversive, the Christians persecuted to the point of death. However, the conversion of Constantine to Christianity (in about AD 312) and his subsequent adoption of Christianity as the official religion of the Roman Empire allowed that religion not just to survive but to flourish and spread until it became the dominant religion of Europe. Had Christianity not survived, Europe, and then America, would have developed with very different attitudes about self-government, free will, and human rights.

4. The defeat of the armies of Islam at Poitiers

In AD 732, Charles Martel defeated a powerful and seemingly unstoppable Islamic army in what was to become known as the Battle of Poitiers. This battle, which the Arab people refer to as *ma'arakat Balâ ash-Shuhadâ* or the Battle of the Court of the Martyrs, took place in central France and is considered by many historians as the turning point in the defense of Christianity in Europe. Though the fight to keep Islamic armies from conquering Europe continued intermittently for another nine hundred years, the Battle of Poitiers was unquestionably the high point in the Muslim conquest of Western Europe. Had the Franks not succeeded there, the armies of Islam would have continued their impassioned effort to conquer the world in the name of Muhammad. Had that been the case, respect for religious freedom, minority rights, women's rights, and governments based on reason and democracy would surely not exist.

5. The failure of the Mongols in their effort to conquer Europe in AD 1241

After sweeping through Asia, the savage and uncivilized Mongols were poised to overcome the weakened, corrupt, and disorganized European states. Then, just as the Mongols arrived at the gates of Vienna, they suffered the death of their great leader. As a result, the Mongols withdrew their attack, never to return—allowing Europe to continue its development unhindered by the brutal and destructive Mongol hordes.

6. The discovery of the New World

With its wealth in gold, silver, and other natural resources, along with new food sources and its ability to fire the imagination and thirst to explore, the discovery of the New World ushered in a new and golden era throughout Europe. The great wealth that was created with the discovery of the Americas gave rise to European nations with sufficient power to defeat the repressive and brutal Islamic army that was again knocking on the doors of European capitals. The discovery of the New World also spawned critical developments in science, navigation, architecture, military tactics, weapons, and human resources, all of which secured the future of Europe as the rising empire in the world. Most important, it allowed Europe to evolve into the home of Western political philosophy and thought.

7. The Battle of Britain in World War II

In May 1940, the pagan and tyrannical government of Nazi Germany threatened to bring all of Europe under its dark rule. Britain was the last free European government that stood in its way. Though they faced what seemed to be certain annihilation, the British mustered the courage to make a final stand against the overwhelming power of the Third Reich. Winston Churchill and the people of Great Britain refused to surrender—thereby preserving democracy and freedom for generations yet to come.

All of these critical events in history will be explored in the following chapters.

It is important to understand that, in and of themselves, none of these events created the gift of freedom that we enjoy today. However, each of them proved to be a critical tipping point in which the future of the world was altered, creating the cradle in which the gift of democracy could be born and flourish in our day. (And yes, there are many other events that would make this story more complete, but time and space must limit our effort to just these seven.)

Simply put, the case that we intend to make is this:

- Freedom and democracy are extraordinarily rare events in human history. Indeed, only a tiny fraction of humans have been given the opportunity of living in a free land.
- Throughout history, critical tipping points have occurred upon which the foundational elements of democracy and free governments have been laid. Many of these critical forks in the road occurred thousands of years before the event would bear the fruit of freedom. Some have happened in modern day. All of them were necessary for the world to enjoy the sudden expansion of free governments that we see today.
- It wasn't inevitable that the Free Age would evolve as it did. The outcomes that generated this wave of freedom were never assured, and world history would have been

dramatically altered if any one of these events had turned out differently, making the golden age of freedom impossible in our day.

The first steps taken toward creating an environment where freedom and democracy could sprout took place more than 2,700 years ago. Two hundred years later, another step was taken. Eight hundred years after that, another step. The journey has been long and tiresome, the quiet march to freedom taking millennia to complete. Yet each of these steps has proven critical to the incalculable blessing of freedom that so many citizens of the world enjoy today.

A Final Word of Warning

It is important to note that democracy and freedom are very fleeting—they can be possessed and then lost. A nation might be democratic for a period of time and then, through spasms of internal strife or war, revert to despotism. Over the past 225 years this has been shown again and again to be true, the tides of democracy causing many nations to sample and then lose the great gifts of freedom and democracy. The experience of Germany prior to World War I, immediately thereafter, and then during the reign of Hitler is a graphic example of this truth.

In a recently published book entitled *Democratization,* the authors point out that from 1783 until 1828 the United States stood entirely alone—the only free republic in the world. Then, from 1828 to 1926, there was a move of freedom when a small number of nations in Western Europe joined the United States as democratic governments. But, like a wave receding upon the shore, many of these fledgling free nations stepped back into fascist and repressive regimes when a storm of antidemocratic forces permeated much of the world during the period from 1922 to 1942. Italy. Germany. Spain. Many nations turned away from freedom. The end of World War II brought on another wave of free republics that lasted until 1962, when a second wave of regression occurred, swallowing infant democracies once again. Beginning in 1974, a third surge of democracy and freedom took place.[18]

Is it possible that another reverse wave of tyranny and oppression may follow? Will some—or many—of the fledgling democracies that briefly tilted against the winds of the natural state of men fall back into repressive governments?

One would have to ignore the trends of history to assume it couldn't be so.

In fact, it is arguable that we are already witnessing another wave of repression.

Many of the nations that took significant steps toward democracy after the fall of the Berlin Wall have reverted back to despotism. In a 2010 study, Freedom House determined that fourteen of the twenty-nine countries from the former Soviet Union or Warsaw Pact saw their freedoms eroding.[19] And they are not alone; upheavals throughout the Mediterranean, Iberian Peninsula, and Central America show that the fragility of democracy extends far beyond the former Soviet or Warsaw Pact nations.

Speaking on this loss of democracy, Freedom House reported what they called a "global political recession," explaining that more nations are currently experiencing declines in freedom than there are nations that are experiencing gains.[20] Even some stable and formerly friendly democracies have adopted a seemingly bitter view of the West, festering with anti-Americanism that cracks at the partnerships that have defended democracies for the last sixty years. All this while powerful nations such as China, Russia, and Venezuela, along with aggressively repressive regimes like North Korea and Iran, seek to expand their influence.

Considering these troubling facts, is there any doubt that history is capable of repeating itself?

The rarity of freedom is matched only by its fragility, its ebbs and flows unpredictable and unsure. And though it is impossible to know the future, this one thing is certain: If we do not appreciate the delicate nature of those singular events that resulted in this enlightened and blessed sliver of world history, it is much more likely that the norm of tyranny will be reestablished.

It's entirely possible that our children or grandchildren might once again live under the abusive hands of powerful and vicious tyrants.

If that were to happen, that precious thing we call liberty would become nothing but a memory.

Notes

1. http://avalon.law.yale.edu/ancient/hamframe.asp. July 1, 2010.
2. Bastiat, *Law,* 25; emphasis added.
3. Walter E. Williams, in Bastiat, *Law,* vi; emphasis in original.
4. *Freedom in the World Country Ratings,* January 8, 2010, http://www.freedomhouse.org.
5. In 1981, 51 nations were deemed to be "free." In 2009, the number had increased to 89 nations (out of a total of 193).
6. Extrapolation of U.S. Census figures (assumes a 130 percent growth rate and a new generation definition of every 20 years), http://www.census.gov/population/censusdata/table-4.pdf.
7. See Dahl, *How Democratic,* 43.
8. We understand that the United States of America is not a democracy, but a republic. However, we use the term *democracy* and its application to the United States, as well as other nations with a republican form of government, because of its broader and more generally understood meaning.
9. The chief characteristic and distinguishing feature of a Democracy is: Rule by Omnipotent Majority. In a Democracy, The Individual, and any group of Individuals composing any Minority, have no protection against the unlimited power of The Majority. It is a case of Majority-over-Man. . . . A Republic, on the other hand, has a very different purpose and an entirely different *form,* or system, of government. Its purpose is to control The Majority strictly, as well as all others among the people, primarily to protect The Individual's God-given, unalienable rights and therefore for the protection of the rights of The Minority, of all minorities, and the liberties of people in general" (Long, *American Ideal of 1776;* emphasis in original. See also http://www.lexrex.com/enlightened/AmericanIdeal/aspects/demrep.hmtl).
10. Thomas Jefferson, *Declaration of Independence.*
11. For example, John P. Holdren, President Obama's Director for Science and Technology Policy, has pioneered the formula I=PAT (negative environmental

impacts = the population multiplied by the affluence of the population multiplied by the technology of the population). Simply stated, this formula purports that the richer and more populous we are, the more environmental havoc we cause. Using this formula, government leaders would seek to reduce national wealth, technology, and population (see Tierney, "Use Energy, Get Rich, and Save the Planet").

12. See Yandle, Bhattarai, and Vijayaraghavan, *Environmental Kuznets Curves,* 1.

13. *The World's Worst Polluted Places,* The Blacksmith Institute, New York City, 2006. http://www.blacksmithinstitute.org/top10/10worst2.pdf.

14. See Cropper, Jiang, Alberini, Baur, *Getting Cars Off the Road.*

15. *Economic Opportunity and Prosperity,* The 2010 Index of Economic Freedom, Heritage Foundation and the Wall Street Journal, New York City, 2010.

16. Stark, *Victory of Reason,* x–xi.

17. See ibid., x–xiii.

18. See Haerpfer, Bernhagen, Inglehart, and Wetzel, *Democratization,* 41–54. These authors identify those periods or "waves" where democracy was on the ascent and spreading, and those "reverse waves" where the number of countries enjoying democracy contracted.

19. *Nations in Transit 2010,* Freedom House, 2010. http://freedomhouse.org.

20. Tom Melia, quoted in Hiatt, "Around the World, Freedom Is in Peril."

Chapter 1

Two Gods at War

As for Hezekiah the Judahite, who did not submit to my yoke:
forty-six of his strong, walled cities, as well as the small towns in their area,
which were without number, by leveling with battering-rams and by bringing
up siege-engines, and by attacking and storming on foot, by mines, tunnels, and
breeches, I besieged and took them. 200,150 people, great and small, male
and female, horses, mules, asses, camels, cattle and sheep without number,
I brought away from them and counted as spoil.

PRISM OF SENNACHERIB

Eastern Judah Plain
25 Miles Southwest of Jerusalem
About 701 BC

THE GREAT CITY WAS GOING TO DIE. There was no longer any doubt.

No, that wasn't quite right. There had never *been* any doubt, and the Assyrian general quickly corrected himself. The destruction of the city had always been as certain as the rising of the sun or the coming of the moon. Anu, the king of gods, had demanded it of them. There was no longer any choice. Victory being their sacred obligation, they could no more deny their religious duty to expand the kingdom than they could command the wind to stand still. And with their gods before them—Qingu, the battle leader; Ashur, the personal god of Assyria; Adad, the storm god; Mammetum, mother of destiny and fate; and other gods unspoken—there was never **any** doubt that the general and his soldiers would claim the city as their own.

Indeed, the Assyrian army could hardly be defeated, for they were the mightiest and most brutal army in the world. That being true, there was no conceivable alternative other than to destroy the city once the order had been given, its obliteration having been determined by the Great King Sennacherib himself.

General Rabshakeh,[1] the supreme commander of the Assyrian army, stood on the fertile Judah plains and looked out on Lachish, the great city on the hill. Second only to the Jewish capital of Jerusalem, Lachish was one of the most thoughtfully fortified cities in the entire Jewish kingdom. The hill that the city had been built upon rose several hundred feet into the air. A buttress of natural rock jutted on the south side, the outer wall rising above it. To the right was the main access to the city, a set of stairs and natural rock platforms that would leave his men completely unprotected from the assaults of arrows and stones that would come raining from above. Knowing there was no way to assault the city from the heavily defended trail, his army had spent weeks building an enormous dirt ramp, tons of earth moved by hand and dumped beside one corner of the hill, a ramp they would use to assault the outer walls once the battle had begun. Inside the outer ring, General Rabshakeh knew there was another rock wall, then a maze of residences, shops, wells, barns, and city buildings, then finally the great palace, a massive structure in the center of the walled city.

Sitting high above the fertile plain, surrounded by thick rock walls and manned by some of Judah's bravest and most skilled warriors, the city looked to be impenetrable.

But the general had seen and conquered many of the great cities in his world, including many that were much greater than this insolent Jewish collection of stone walls and rock homes. Lachish was formidable, that was obvious, and ten thousand of his men might be killed in the attack, but it would be foolish to doubt the outcome. With the gods walking before him, his warriors fighting beside him, and the Great King commanding from behind, he knew he would prevail, sweeping aside the people of Lachish as dry reeds before a flame.

In the moment of reflection, he turned and looked north, thinking of his home—Nineveh, the capital of Assyria. The greatest city in the world. His wife and children lived there. His concubines, slaves, friends, and cousins lived there too. His master, the Great King Sennacherib, lived there in the greatest palace of them all. He thought of the capital with its massive walls, beautiful gardens, and irrigation canals; its snow-white temples, granite palaces, and government buildings; its terraced olive gardens and swan-filled lakes. How he longed to be there. To smell the mountain air and coming rains. To feel the warmth of his woman's embrace and the coolness of the granite temple floors beneath his feet.

Nineveh. City of his fathers. Cradle of the gods.

That was a city worth dying for.

But Lachish, this . . . this *city,* if he called it that, was hardly worthy of his men.

The second greatest city in all of the kingdom of Judah would shortly be defeated. The arrogance of the people of Judah simply had to be contained. Contained and destroyed. A proper example set. If not, other impertinent kingdoms might try to follow suit.

The general was a large man: tall, straight, strong as the ironwood trees in Mesopotamia, with a tightly curled beard and hair that hung below his shoulders, also tightly braided. He had a broad face and strong arms, with metal bands around his enormous biceps that were designed to show them off. His people worshiped many things. Power. Blood. Gold. The sword. Beauty was certainly among the things they worshipped, and the general was as handsome as he was cruel. And he had not become captain of the army by being stupid, weak, or kind.

He glanced once more to the north, muttered a quick prayer to Qingu, then turned to his lieutenant and gave the signal.

Seconds later, the battle for Lachish began.

• • •

The general watched from atop his mighty warhorse, a black mount with flanks high as the shoulders of a man.

The campaign against Lachish followed a fairly simple plan, one that had proven successful a dozen times before. Heavy infantry carried the brunt of the attack, moving up the earthen ramp they had spent the last five weeks constructing in backbreaking work. A wooden bridge to span the final gap between the ramp and the city walls was ready to be hauled into place. Opposite the ramp, the narrow stairs that led up to the city were already flooded with his men. Forty thousand infantry were ready to die in this battle, with another hundred thousand held in immediate reserve.

Hundreds of his men went down in the first ten minutes of the attack, some of their bodies pierced with a dozen arrows, their blood pouring on the smooth stones like water from a spring, turning the moss-covered steps slippery as ice. Their bodies were quickly pushed aside as other Assyrian warriors moved in to take their places. The general watched and listened to the sound of battle from two hundred yards away, near enough to hear the cries of pain, near enough to feel the thumping of the wheels of the enormous battery rams as they were lugged toward the city walls, the aroma of battle filling the air and swirling with the gritty dust against his teeth.

He watched and smelled and looked and listened, counting in his mind the number of his soldiers as they fell. He watched the battle plan play out, slowly at first, the initial steps more deliberate to develop, then falling more quickly into place. It was strategy. It was fortune. It was the will of the god of war. Watching his men die, he felt a rush of rage and pride that brought tears to his eyes. Battle was beautiful and stark and horrible and lovely. He fiercely spurred his horse and rode closer, watching the battle mature as his strategy took hold.

The main thrust of infantry was beginning to make its way toward the city walls. The eastern and southern flanks were holding steady as infantry units leapfrogged each other to create fighting space. Two thousand archers covered their approach, arrows falling upon the Jewish defenses like deadly raindrops from the skies. He spurred his horse again and moved closer, feeling his mount's hot breath upon his bare knees. He had to pull the reins, for she was anxious to run toward the battle, and his heart swelled with affection for the animal. If he turned his head and concentrated, he could hear the cries of Jewish soldiers from behind the city walls. They were dying by the score there, and he smiled in satisfaction. The number of rocks and arrows coming at his own men had noticeably lessened now. Turning, he could see that his slingers were moving forward, pounding the Jewish defenses with sharpened stones. The leather-covered battering rams were almost to the gate now and he spurred his horse even closer.

The battle raged. The sun moved. The afternoon grew long. As night fell, reinforcements were moved into position, the Assyrian army able to throw a seemingly unending number of men into the fray. The exhausted men of the first assault pulled back and he estimated their casualties as they formed up in line, the commanders leading their bleeding and depleted soldiers to the valley floor for food and rest. He had lost many men, he could see that, and his black heart turned cold.

But the Jews would pay the price. For every soldier that he lost, two Jewish soldiers would be skinned alive, their legs nailed spread-eagle upon a board and long strips of flesh peeled from their chests and faces and backs until they finally bled out or died of shock.

Through the night the battle raged. The twang of bow strings. The *thiiirrr* of arrows. The *THUMP* of the battery rams upon the city gates, the sound vibrating along the rocky walls. The moon was near full, the stars bright—at one point the soldiers had enough light to continue fighting without the use of torches. And fight they did, never letting up or slowing down. It was an integral part of their battle strategy. Wear the enemy down. Exhaust them. Demoralize them from heart-wrenching fatigue.

For three days and two nights, the general didn't sleep, by which time the battle was winding down, the outcome then assured. Exhausted, he handed command to his primary lieutenant and fell upon the downy bed inside the inner chamber of his massive leather tent.

Four days later, the Assyrian army led the Jewish captives along the blood-drenched road that wound down from the city. At the foot of the road, dozens of civilian, religious, and military leaders sat tied together, their backs bent in a long, unbroken row of defeated men. Some looked around in terror, but most of them stared blankly at the mud. They knew what was going to happen to them. Stories of the brutality of the Assyrian army had been broadcast for many years, their brothers to the north having tasted its bitter fruit when the kingdom of Israel had been destroyed some eighteen years before. General Rabshakeh watched as his soldiers moved down the line of men, slitting each of their throats, their gurgled breath filling the remaining Jews with greater terror than they had ever felt before. As the leaders were assassinated, their families were forced to watch. Even the youngest of the children were too terrified to cry.

When the work of death was finished, the blood was so thick it gathered in small pools that were already drawing flies. The surviving inhabitants of the city were then marched past the trail of slit-throated men. At the end of the line, the bodies of the Jewish soldiers killed in battle were stacked in piles, the survivors forced to walk among the rotting bodies of their fathers, husbands, brothers, and sons. The religious leaders of the Jews were treated with particular scorn, having their stomachs split open, their bowels left to spill upon the ground.

The general stared at the mutilated corpses and smiled with satisfaction.

Was there any doubt whose god held the greater power now?

The reserve Assyrian soldiers, those who had not been tasked to join in the front line of the battle, were commanded to herd the remaining inhabitants of Lachish north into the heart of the Assyrian kingdom, where they would be turned into slaves and scattered among the far regions of the Assyrian Empire. The fortunate old ones, the general knew, would live a short time. The unfortunate children would live far too long.

Watching the survivors, General Rabshakeh pushed his feet against his stirrups and looked east.

Jerusalem, the capital of the Jewish kingdom, was out there, little more than a two-day ride away. Once he had taken that last city, the entire kingdom would be subjected once again to the Assyrians' control.

Turning to one of his lesser lieutenants, he commanded in a dry voice, "Identify the highest leaders among the dead. Take off their heads, cut off their lips, gouge out their eyes. I want at least a hundred heads. Pack them up and send them with my emissary to Jerusalem. I want those fools in Jerusalem to understand what fate awaits them!"

Death Comes to Lachish

For people living in the Near East seven hundred years before the birth of Jesus Christ, the cry, "The Assyrians are coming!" would have caused hearts to tremble and blood to rise in fear.

From the beginning of the first millennium BC through late in the seventh century BC, the Assyrians dominated the Near East. Though the extent of their empire would expand and retract through the normal give and take of empire building and maintaining, at its zenith the Assyrian domain extended from western Iran to the Mediterranean, from modern-day Turkey to the Nile. Within this kingdom were areas that included not only Assyria but Babylonia, Armenia, Media, Palestine, Syria, Phoenicia, Sumeria, Elam, and Egypt.

To describe the Assyrians as "militaristic" would be a grave understatement. Brutality and power were at the heart of everything they did. For one thing, their kings were required to go warring every year. Their gods expected it. Their noblemen and people did as well. They had a long history of nearly brilliant and very strong-willed kings, all of whom eagerly certified their aggressiveness by recording stories of their campaigns in stone.

But the Assyrians didn't set out to rule the world just to appease their gods. Some of their motives were far less pure. Like most empires before and after them, the Assyrians conquered for land, wealth, slaves, and power. In order to sustain their military campaigns, all Assyrian men were subject to conscription. The people they conquered were expected to supply men and supplies to facilitate their campaigns. And when it came to army building, the Assyrians were extremely effective. It is estimated that even a small Assyrian army would put forward fifty thousand men, their larger armies having more than two hundred thousand soldiers.

One of the leading authorities on the period describes the Assyrians this way:

> Their circumstances, however, forbade them to indulge in the effeminate ease of Babylon; from beginning to end they were a race of warriors, mighty in muscle and courage, abounding in proud hair and beard, standing straight, stern and solid on their monuments, and bestriding with tremendous feet the east-Mediterranean world. Their history is one of kings and slaves, wars and conquests, bloody victories and sudden defeat.[2]

If the term *terrorism* could apply to any regime, it certainly could apply to the Assyrian method of conquest, for they were as savage as any regime known in the history of man. Their policy, described with a bit of understated passiveness as "calculated frightfulness," had proven very effective. Yet it was fairly straightforward. In order to weaken a nation's major cities or capitals, its smaller towns and lesser cities were assaulted. (Note the Assyrian record quoted at the beginning of this chapter describing the "forty-six of [Hezekiah's] strong, walled cities, as well as the small towns in their area" that were destroyed before their army fell upon Jerusalem.) Brutality then reigned:

> A captured city was usually plundered and burnt to the ground, and its site was deliberately denuded by killing its trees. The loyalty of the troops was secured by dividing a large part of the spoils among them; their bravery was ensured by the general rule of the Near East that all captives in war might be enslaved or slain. Soldiers were rewarded for every severed head they brought in from the field, so that the aftermath of a victory generally witnessed the wholesale decapitation of fallen foes. Most often the prisoners, who would have consumed much food in a long campaign, and would have constituted a danger and nuisance in the rear, were dispatched after the battle; they knelt with their backs

to their captors, who beat their heads in with clubs, or cut them off with cutlasses. Scribes stood by to count the number of prisoners taken and killed by each soldier, and apportioned the booty accordingly; the king, if time permitted, presided at the slaughter. The nobles among the defeated were given more special treatment: their ears, noses, hands and feet were sliced off, or they were thrown from high towers, or they and their children were beheaded, or flayed alive, or roasted over a slow fire. . . .

Ashurbanipal boasts that "I burned three thousand captives with fire, I left not a single one among them alive to serve as a hostage." Another of his inscriptions reads: "These warriors who had sinned against Ashur and had plotted evil against me . . . from their hostile mouths have I torn their tongues, and I have compassed their destruction. As for the others who remained alive, I offered them as a funerary sacrifice; . . . their lacerated members have I given unto the dogs, the swine, the wolves. . . . By accomplishing these deeds I have rejoiced the heart of the great gods." Another monarch instructs his artisans to engrave upon the bricks these claims on the admiration of posterity: "My war chariots crush men and beasts. . . . The monuments which I erect are made of human corpses from which I have cut the head and limbs. I cut off the hands of all those whom I capture alive." Reliefs at Nineveh show men being impaled or flayed, or having their tongues torn out; one shows a king gouging out the eyes of prisoners with a lance while he holds their heads conveniently in place with a cord passed through their lips.[3]

With this carnage on full display, an emissary would then be sent to the targeted capital or other major city with the Assyrian king's demands for capitulation and the terms of homage demanded. While making their demands, these emissaries were known to stand upon the city walls and speak in the native tongue so that the local populations would be certain to hear of the savagery the Assyrian army was about to wreak upon them. The besieged people were often reminded that no gods had been able to protect their people from the Assyrian attacks, the list of kingdoms they had destroyed being long and impressive. Finally, the emissaries would remind their targets that those who capitulated at least had the hope of further life, while those who had the arrogance to refute them only doomed themselves to destruction.

Often (and understandably, with the terror such images would convey) this was all that was necessary for the surrender of the larger cities. If a city was foolish enough to reject the terms of surrender, the Assyrian army would attack.

And what of the people of the conquered cities and lands? As already stated, many times the entire population was killed. When not killed, in order for the victims to be rendered totally impotent they were removed en masse from their native home and relocated throughout the Assyrian kingdom. Under this policy, literally millions of victims were scattered throughout the Assyrian Empire. The reasons for this mass deportation were several. Foremost was the fact that deported peoples were extremely valuable assets, working as slaves to fulfill the never-ending demands of empire building: laborers, agricultural workers, household servants, warrior-slaves—whatever and wherever manpower for the kingdom was needed. Also, the transplanting of potentially rebellious peoples away from the borders of the Assyrian kingdom resulted in less need for military occupation or policing, saving the Assyrian leaders from having to guard so closely their captive kingdoms. Finally, once the defeated populations had been separated from their own people and relocated to strange lands, scattered, weakened, and disoriented by defeat and the brutality they had suffered, they found themselves entirely dependent upon the Assyrian king for protection from their new and often hostile neighbors. This left them with little chance of escaping from the distant, unfriendly, and unknown territories, their desperate circumstances making effective prisons.[4]

Such were the prospects that King Sennacherib's emissaries were about to present to the terrified people at Jerusalem.

Nineveh, Assyria
About 701 BC

GENERAL RABSHAKEH SAT atop his powerful warhorse and looked across the river at the *exceeding great city,* as it had become known. After a thousand years of existence yet a hundred years of neglect, Nineveh had been reclaimed by his master, the Great King Sennacherib, who had rebuilt it to become one of the greatest cities in the world. It was magnificent now, and he praised the gods for bringing him home.

The city sat along the only highway that stretched between the Indian Ocean and the Mediterranean Sea, its strategic location bringing it fabulous wealth. To his left, the Khosr River flowed through the city and merged into the Tigris outside the Water Gate. Before him, the mighty Tigris ran along the western walls, the city rising in a multitude of levels more than a hundred feet above the river. Blues. Greens. Pinks. Light browns. The colors of the city walls and the Palace of Sennacherib glinted in the morning light. Perhaps 150,000 inhabitants lived within the city, though the true number was not known. It was a multiday journey to walk around its mighty walls.

Fifteen great gates penetrated the city walls, most of them housing armories of the Assyrian army. Within the city, eighteen canals brought fresh water from the hills more than forty miles away, providing the inhabitants with lush ponds and a cleaner source of water than the Tigris and Khosr could provide. Built upon the fertile plain, wheat and oat fields waved golden in the light, the wind moving across them in unpredictable waves. Orchards dotted the distance, and vineyards scented the dry air. Within the city, the Assyrians had built magnificent temples to the gods: Sin, Nergal, Samas, Ishtar, and Nabiu. But none of the temples were any match for the Palace of Sennacherib. The general knew the statistics well: 1,650 feet long, almost 800 feet wide. More than 160 million bricks had been used in the palace foundation alone, as the king had once famously pointed out to a group of government leaders who had no concept of what a million even meant. Atop the deep foundations were eighty rooms, most of them guarded by magnificent rock figures, thirty-ton sculptures of winged lions and bulls with human heads. Throughout the mighty palace, the stone walls were inscribed with the stories of various military campaigns.[5]

And that was why the general had come—to report on Lachish and Jerusalem. And to explain to the king what he was going to do next.

He stared at the city a long moment, knowing his wife and children were waiting for him. But first he had to see the king. Indeed, he knew it was unlikely that he would get to see his family on this visit, not with unfinished business in the south.

Forty minutes later, he was escorted into the inner sanctum of the Royal Palace, a location few living men had ever seen.

The king was waiting for him.

General Rabshakeh began his report.

• • •

The king was clearly losing patience, but the general stood his ground, though his heart slammed with fear inside his chest. Although the king was not a god, he was just a breath away, for he was chosen by the gods, he was their spokesman, their emissary, their voice and heart and soul here on earth. There were only a handful of men in the world who dared to have anything close to a frank conversation with the king, for to take a stand against him was just a hair short of standing against the very gods themselves. But the general had no choice. His only purpose in life was to serve the gods through service to the king, and he was wise enough to know that he would fail in that purpose if he wasn't honest with the king.

"How could they be so insolent!" the king cried. "How dare they stand before me! Think of other nations I have scattered. Yet they defy me now!"

General Rabshakeh stared through the narrow windows that looked out on the river, not seeing the small ships with their multicolored sails or the waving fields beyond the riverbanks. He knew what he had to say, but the words were slow to come. Finally, he offered carefully, "The Jewish king believes his God will save them."

Sennacherib snorted. "Knows he not what I and my fathers have done in other lands? Have any of the gods of other nations delivered their people from my hand? Where are the gods of Hamath? The gods of Arpad? Where are the gods of Sepharvaim, Hena, or Ivah? All of them defied me! All of them have been destroyed! Are there any nations that have been protected by their armies *or their gods!* Didn't the suffering of Lachish teach anything to the Jewish king?"

Rabshakeh brought his eyes away from the window. The smell of smoke and salt and fish permeated the palace air. Among the odors was the scent of his own skin, tart and sweet, like fear. "Hezekiah is a young king," he offered the master. "With youth sometimes comes obstinacy . . ."

"Young or not, he is a fool!"

"He believes he has spent his entire reign preparing for this moment. He has purged heresy from his people, bringing them back to their true religion. He believes that he is called of their god, Jehovah. This has given him moral power, which brings him foolish courage, I am afraid. But that is not all, my king. He has fortified the city, built underground aqueducts and canals. He has prepared men of arms. Rebuilt the walls and towers. He has prepared darts. Bows. Arrows. Slings and shields. He has prepared for war."

The king's eyes grew dark. "Do you think he is the first one to prepare?"

General Rabshakeh shook his head. "Of course he is not, my king." But there he hesitated, for there was something about the Jewish king that weighed upon him. Something he didn't understand. He thought of the words King Hezekiah had told his people: "Be strong. Be courageous. Be not afraid or dismayed of the king of Assyria or his army *for there be more with us than with them.*"[6]

How could that be?

The general took a long breath, then shook his head. "He rallies his people," was all he said.

The angry king leaned forward on his chair. "He is lying to his people. He cannot withstand us and he knows it. They will only be destroyed." The king was not used to being defied and it showed in his face. Very few cities would have failed to capitulate after they had observed the fate of Lachish.

The general watched his master carefully. "Hezekiah *has* committed to paying homage," he reminded him. "He has ransacked his own palace and their temple to raise the gold and silver sufficient to save the city."

King Sennacherib didn't answer. The general knew he didn't care. This was no longer just another military campaign. This was pride. This was rage and fury. This was about showing the insolent Jews whom to fear.

The two men sat in silence a short moment, the general staring at his feet. There was something else that he wanted to tell his master, but he couldn't find the words, the idea so troubling that he had decided to keep it to himself.

The Jews, he had been informed, had a talisman. An oracle. They said he could divine the will of God. This was something new for the Assyrians, for even their royal king was left to wonder if he had sufficiently predicted the will of the gods. And Rabshakeh had been told that King Hezekiah had counseled with this prophet, and the prophet had talked to God. Then the seer had told the king to stand against Assyria, to hold their ground. The words of the prophet came back to him again: *There be more with us than with them.*

• • •

Sennacherib stared at the general, then wet his lips. It seemed Rabshakeh had more to say, but when he held his tongue the great master turned away and thought.

The hard truth was, he *had* to take Jerusalem. It was the only thing that stood between his empire and the growing power of the Egyptian army. How long now had the Egyptians vexed him? And they had grown powerful once again. Their armies were rising, growing restless, their generals eager to expend some energy, their men lusting to taste spoils, their pharaoh thirsting for more power. And though the kingdom of Judah was small and insignificant, there was always this one thing: It stood along the land bridge between Assyria and the Nile.

To the west was the great ocean, to the east the desert stretched for miles. Because of its strategic location, Judah was a natural buffer, the only thing that stood between Assyria and the powerful kingdom along the Nile. And the insolent Jews had already formed an alliance with the hated Egyptians. Alliances with the Phoenician sailors and the Syrians as well.

No. He *had* to take Jerusalem. It was absolutely necessary to protect his southern border.

He turned and leaned toward Rabshakeh, his eyes burning with rage. "I want you to take Jerusalem. I want you to bring it to its knees. My fathers have already destroyed the northern kingdom. Surely, you can do the same in the south. I want every Jew to be taken, their city leveled and burned with fire. Do you understand me, general! I want to scatter their entire people as the chaff before the wind. Like a hundred other gods before it, let the name of Jehovah be lost in time."

He paused and took an angry breath, his nostrils flaring, his dark cheeks tense above his braided beard. "Have I ever undertaken to destroy a city, then changed my mind and let it be? Never have I, general. Not once! You understand? And I certainly don't intend to start such a habit now, especially with such a weak and insolent people as the Jews. You will destroy them. You will kill them. You will scatter their people to the far corners of the world. Then the memory of their religion will die with them, the world forgetting the God of Israel before my son is old enough sit upon this throne."

A Reason to Fight

Powerful as it was—and it was very powerful—Assyria was not alone as an empire in the Near East in this era. As history has proven, few empires have the luxury of sitting atop the pile, preeminent and unchallenged, for long periods of time, for by definition their status breeds the contempt and jealousy that give rise to other powers. During the time of the siege at Jerusalem, Babylon was an emerging menace in the southeast. Most threatening, however, was the kingdom of Egypt in the southwest.

At one time, in between the two major powers of Assyria and Egypt were located the small kingdoms of Israel and Judah. Once a united and relatively powerful nation, the kingdom of David split soon after the death of Solomon (about 928 BC). The resulting kingdoms, known as the kingdom of Israel in the north and the kingdom of Judah in the south, were occasional allies but more often enemies in the two hundred years after Solomon's death. Judah's capital was Jerusalem and Israel's capital was Samaria.

Both Judah and Israel possessed certain strengths. Judah controlled copper and iron resources. Israel had better rainfall and more fertile land, especially in the Jordan and Jezreel valleys. More important than these assets was the fact that, together, they controlled the land bridge between Mesopotamia (Assyria) and Egypt. This position brought them considerable wealth through the invaluable trade routes that existed between these major nations. More important, they became a natural buffer—or a battle zone, depending on the situation—between the rival kingdoms.

In addition to their value geographically, both kingdoms were players in the ongoing drama of nations allied with or against the Assyrians and Egyptians. Sometimes the two kingdoms would unite with neighbors to combat the Assyrians, joining with the nations of Syria or Phoenicia to claim a greater degree of independence. As an example, in the year 853 BC, Assyrian King Shalmaneser III fought a major battle at Qarqar against an army made up of Syrians, Egyptians, and various other nations and city-states, with Israel being the major contributor— two thousand chariots and ten thousand troops.[7] But though engaged in a constant struggle for survival and independence, both kingdoms were relatively powerless against the far greater nations to their north and south.

In addition to their constant struggle for survival, both nations also suffered from internal rivalries for power.

The northern kingdom of Israel had a particularly violent history. From the time of Solomon until their destruction by the Assyrians, twenty monarchs ruled the northern kingdom, most of them reckless and idol-worshipping men. Five family dynasties were instituted, all of which came to short-lived and violent ends, it being common for a new king to kill all of the descendants of a previous leader as well as to murder any of his other rivals. For these and other reasons, neither kingdom ever attained to any degree of significance on the world stage, the rivalry between them keeping them far weaker than they otherwise might have been.[8]

In short, during the two-hundred-plus years of their independent existence after Solomon's death, both of the kingdoms experienced periods of ascent and decline, independence and vassal status. During this time, both kingdoms spent some time allied with, and paying tribute to, Assyria as well as some time allied with, and paying tribute to, the kingdom of Egypt. Occasionally they were allied together, but more frequently they were at war with one another, some of their battles being bloody, bitter affairs. In addition to their rivalry, they also had to contend with their immediate neighbors, Syria being a particular thorn in their sides.

And though the exclusivity of their religion and the elitist nature of their culture predisposed them to a national pride far beyond their apparent eminence, very often they were reminded that they were no more than pawns in a world chess game neither of them could control.

In 722 BC, the nation of Israel came to an epic and violent end when their King Hoshea decided to rebel against his Assyrian master. After he stopped paying tribute to Assyria and sought alliance with Egypt, Assyria's King Shalmaneser V decided to remove the troublesome little kingdom once and for all. He undertook a campaign that ended with the brutal siege of Samaria. Though the three-year battle was long and bloody, ultimately he was successful. Samaria was destroyed. The kingdom of Israel was depopulated. Shalmaneser's successor, Sargon II, turned Israel into an Assyrian province, repopulating the territory with various peoples from throughout the vast Assyrian Empire. Eventually, Samaria was rebuilt and used as the home of the new Assyrian governor and governing elite and bureaucrats. Assyrian became the written language used in most transactions.

History records that the former inhabitants of the kingdom of Israel were scattered throughout the Assyrian Empire: from northern Syria to Helah in the east. Tens of thousands were taken as far away as Media in the Zargos Mountains, 745 miles across the Mesopotamian plain.

By the time King Shalmaneser V was finished, the kingdom of Israel had ceased to exist.

To the outside world, the tribes of Israel that made up the population of the kingdom of Israel had lost their identity as a distinct people and have since been referred to as the "Ten Lost Tribes."[9]

After the destruction of the northern kingdom, Judah remained a vassal of Assyria. Having witnessed the total and extraordinarily brutal destruction of Samaria, Judah's King Hezekiah was a compliant vassal—for a time. But freedom was in his heart. In 705, the Assyrian King Sargon II died in battle. Believing the time was right for the Jews to reclaim their independence, Hezekiah seized the moment and organized Judah, Syria, and Phoenicia into a broad revolt. Hoping to weaken their enemy, Egypt promised support for the rebellious little nations.

Hezekiah prepared Judah for the inevitable Assyrian response. The wall around Jerusalem was extended. Towers were rebuilt and strengthened. Men were armed, preparations for war extending throughout the kingdom. Perhaps most important, a massive 1,750-foot tunnel was constructed to bring water from the Gihon Spring into the city of Jerusalem, assuring the inhabitants of a source of water during a long siege while denying the Assyrians access to the water they would need to keep their massive armies alive.

Sargon's successor, Sennacherib, waited for a few years to address the rebellion. But when he acted, he did so decisively. Sennacherib marched and quickly overcame the rebellious Syrian and Phoenician city-states that had joined with Hezekiah. Egypt sent an army to aid the rebels, but the mighty Assyrian army quickly dispatched it to the wind.

Sennacherib then turned his fury upon Judah.

The Assyrian records state that he conquered forty-six of Judah's fortified cities and their smaller surrounding towns, though Sennacherib seems to be particularly proud of the destruction at Lachish. In the walls of the Assyrian capital of Nineveh is a relief that depicts the assault on that city, portraying in great detail the assault machinery used to conquer the city, citizens impaled on stakes, and the survivors being marched into captivity. Sennacherib's records claim the Assyrians took more than two hundred thousand slaves as booty from Lachish.

Having dispatched the second greatest city in the kingdom, Sennacherib then laid siege on Jerusalem.

Assyrian envoys demanded capitulation, threatening the citizens of Jerusalem with the same fate as those of the cities already captured. The primary emissary, Rabshakeh, stood within the city walls and spoke in the local language so that the common people could understand his threats. He reminded the people of the greatness of the Assyrian army. He listed the cities they had already destroyed. He listed the gods that had been called upon to save the inhabitants of the cities that the Assyrian army had defeated, pointing out the futility of their misplaced faith in lesser gods. He commanded the people not to trust their own leaders, especially the naïve king, stating that neither Hezekiah nor their Lord could deliver them out of the Assyrians' hands. He even promised the people of Jerusalem that they would be taken care of, assuring them with the lie that Sennacherib would send them to another good land like unto their own, one filled with olive oil and honey.

Hearing such statements left the city in shock.

The situation was more than desperate. They stood alone, all of their neighbors already defeated, their Egyptian allies having been cast back across the border to their south. All of Judah's satellite cities and towns had been destroyed, their brothers to the north having been taken away a generation before. Their capital was under siege, entirely surrounded by the greatest and most brutal army in the world.

The Jews were trapped, their king shut up, in the words of Sennacherib's own scribes, "like a bird in a cage."[10]

And though there is some dispute as to what exactly followed, this much seems clear: no one expected Jerusalem to survive. The last of the Jews' cities, along with their culture, their religion, their government, their people, and their faith in the great Jehovah was about to be destroyed.

But the battle didn't go as everyone would have predicted.

Sometimes history takes a dramatic turn.

Outside the Jerusalem Gates

THE LINE OF MEN stretched for miles, a thousand horsemen riding beside them, their weary feet kicking up a thick cloud of dust that choked their brother soldiers in the last half of the somber column. The men walked with their heads low, shields and swords slung around their shoulders, arms hanging loosely at their sides, their eyes looking only at the ground, all of them considering the frustrating walk ahead of them, the miles and miles they had to go.

Weeks of marching lay before them. And for everything that they had suffered, they had nothing to take back home!

The mighty Assyrian army that had been assembled to take Jerusalem—one of the most fearsome fighting forces the world had ever seen, the army that was able to strike terror in the hearts of every adversary at the mere call of their approach—was marching back to Nineveh with *not a thing to show*. Not an ounce of treasure. Not a single piece of gold or silver. No old men to haul their satchels. No days of rape and pillage to earn their soldiers' loyalty. No horses, rams, or cattle. No sheep or calves to eat along the way. No slaves.

An army of young and violent men is like a coiled spring; it can only remain wound tight for so long. At some point the tension built inside it must be allowed to spring. And the Assyrian soldiers were as tight, frustrated, and angry as they had ever been. Tension seethed throughout the columns. Fights broke out at every turn. Their captains had to ride the soldiers hard and close. More than a few angry and disappointed soldiers had already been disciplined, the rebuke of their officers as hard and unbending toward their own men as it would have been toward the captives they would have taken if the battle had been fought.

Atop his mighty horse, General Rabshakeh watched his soldiers as they marched north. Inside, he raged with fury. Any way he looked at it, he was returning with a defeated army. An unknown number of his men lay unburied on the plains of Judah, seemingly forgotten by their gods. Such risks were the cost of raising and maintaining armies, and it was not the first time his ranks had taken ill. But that wasn't the thing that killed him. It was the fact that King Sennacherib had ordered him to abandon the siege against the arrogant little city of Jerusalem . . . *that* was the thing that tore at his warrior heart.

He turned and glanced back, seeing the undamaged walls of the Jewish city glinting in the evening sun. Through the dust, the mighty walls seemed to rise above him, as if taunting his retreat.

Forcing himself to swallow the bile inside his throat, he turned his horse toward Nineveh and spurred it hard.

The Sword of an Angel?

Biblical sources assert that after Rabshakeh blasphemed against Jehovah, a horrible plague beset the Assyrian army and 185,000 soldiers died.[11] A hundred and eighty-five thousand soldiers killed in a single night! And though this seems like a self-serving account from Judah's side of history, other reliable histories have also made the same report.[12] If true, the Assyrian army could not have sustained such a loss and remained combat effective. Their assault against the highly defended city would certainly have been met with defeat.

The fact that there are no Assyrian records to support the plague story is not surprising, for the Assyrian records were largely propaganda meant to aggrandize the Assyrian king, not to provide an unbiased or accurate historical account. This being the case, it would not be surprising if the Assyrians depicted the battle of Jerusalem in a self-aggrandizing manner, it being critically important for them to defend the reputations and preeminence of their gods.

And though there are conflicting accounts in this history (as there almost always are), this much is clear: For whatever reason, the mightiest and most brutal army in the world did not take Jerusalem. They left the people of the kingdom of Judah, with their religion and culture, intact. To the Jews, this event was proof that Jehovah was mightier than the gods of the Assyrians, for he was responsible for smiting the most powerful army on the earth. To the Assyrians, it must have encouraged their adversaries on both the south and east.

If the plague did happen, modern-day scholars assert that it was likely the result of the Gihon Spring project undertaken by Hezekiah that diverted the local water supply into Jerusalem and deprived the Assyrian army of the clean water that was vital to sustaining such a massive army on the Judean plain. If so, it wouldn't have been the first time an army had been decimated by the plague.

A Second Explanation

Assyrian records indicated that Sennacherib simply negotiated a deal with Hezekiah and, having done that, decided to spare the city. But this seems exceedingly unlikely for several reasons. For one thing, it left their southern border exposed to a vassal state that had already allied itself with other Assyrian enemies. It also demonstrated uncharacteristic timidness against a small and belligerent kingdom that had openly rebelled against them, showing a sign of deadly weakness to the Assyrians' rivals. Perhaps most puzzling is this question: Having already destroyed so much of the kingdom of Judah, why would Sennacherib leave the capital city unharmed? Such an action was contrary to everything the Assyrians had demonstrated in their history and culture.

But even if it is true that Sennacherib decided of his own accord to leave Jerusalem unharmed, that was no less remarkable. Indeed, it was stunning! As one scholar declared:

> Later generations, looking back on the attack on Judah
> in that year, viewed it as perhaps the most fateful event in
> the kingdom's three-hundred-year history to that point.
> Had Jerusalem fallen, Judah would have gone the way of

the northern kingdom of Israel and especially its capital, Samaria—to exile and extinction. That Sennacherib struck a compromise with Hezekiah, given the strategic upper hand held by Assyrian army throughout the land, seemed inconceivable. Sennacherib was not beyond the most ruthless punishment of rebellious cities: a decade or so later he would literally wipe Babylon from the map.[13]

As noted here, Sennacherib's ruthless nature was on full display in 690 BC when he undertook a siege of the rebelling city of Babylon. After a siege that lasted fifteen months, his records reveal the destruction of the city, the razing of its temples and houses, looting of its wealth, and deportation of its population.[14]

Compare this outcome with what happened to Jerusalem, and the question lingers with even greater uncertainty.

But whether it was because of plague or simply an astonishing change of heart, the fact remains that Jerusalem was saved.

The Struggle Goes On

The Assyrian army marched away and the kingdom of Judah was permitted to survive as a vassal state, which it remained until the Assyrian Empire began to lose its hold over the Near East.[15] But that was not, by any means, the end of the Jewish struggle for survival.

As Assyria fought to hold on to its expansive empire, the kingdom of Babylon continued rising in the east. By late in the sixth century BC, the reign of Assyria finally came to its end.

Will Durant, one of the preeminent scholars on the era, suggests part of the reason for the fall of the Assyrian Empire:

> The qualities of body and character that had helped to make the Assyrian armies invincible were weakened by the very victories that they won; in each victory it was the strongest and bravest who died, while the infirm and cautious survived to multiply their kind; it was a dysgenic

[biologically defective] process that perhaps made for civilization by weeding out the more brutal types, but undermined the biological basis upon which Assyria had risen to power.

Durant goes on to provide further explanations for Assyria's fall:

> The extent of her conquests had helped to weaken her; not only had they depopulated her fields to feed insatiate Mars [the god of war], but they had brought into Assyria, as captives, millions of destitute aliens who bred with the fertility of the hopeless, destroyed all national unity of character and blood, and became by their growing numbers a hostile and disintegrating force in the very midst of the conquerors. More and more the army itself was filled by these men of other lands, while semi-barbarous marauders harassed every border, and exhausted the resources of the country in an endless defense of its unnatural frontiers.[16]

Sensing Assyria's weakness, in 612 BC Babylon attacked the Assyrian capital of Nineveh, sacked it, and burned it utterly to the ground.

Assyria was no more.

With the king of Babylon now the power to be feared in the Near East—along with the enduring Egyptian pharaoh in the south—once again Judah found itself in the middle of a great struggle for power. With the Assyrian capital in flames, the Egyptians became intent on taking control of Assyria's former territories in the region, including Judah. Upon the death of King Josiah about 610 BC, Judah fell under Egyptian domination, becoming a vassal state of the empire along the Nile.

Josiah's successor, Jehoiakim, was installed by the Egyptian pharaoh, Neco. For the next decade, Judah shifted to and fro in its loyalty to Egypt and the new guy on the block, Babylon. However, when Egypt was delivered a decisive defeat in 605 at the hands of the rising prince of Babylon, Nebuchadrezzar (sometimes referred to in the Bible as Nebuchadnezzar), and was forced to retreat to defend its homeland, Judah and its neighbors were surrendered up to the Babylonian juggernaut.

In 601, Nebuchadrezzar failed in his attempt to invade Egypt and was forced to retreat and expend time and treasure to recover. This failed campaign resulted in Judah aligning with Egypt once again. The Babylonians were not amused. In 598, a siege of Jerusalem was undertaken. After a year of desperate struggle, the city and her citizens were forced to capitulate. As punishment, the king of Judah was sent into exile and a puppet king, Zedekiah, who was only twenty-one years old at the time but willing to swear allegiance to Nebuchadrezzar, was put in his place. Joining the defeated Jewish king on the long road to Babylonian captivity were other members of his household, military officers, elite fighting units, and skilled workmen and craftsmen, all to be utilized by the Babylonian Empire where their talents were most needed. Loot from the city, including from King Solomon's Temple, accompanied these royal survivors on their sad journey into the heart of Babylon.

Though he owed his position to the king of Babylon, the puppet-king Zedekiah was not particularly loyal to the liege who had installed him on the throne. Over the next ten years, his rebellious nature evidenced itself in various acts of defiance. Then, when Nebuchadrezzar was distracted with serious challenges elsewhere in his empire, Zedekiah decided it was time to act. He sought to unite his neighbors in a rebellion, but nothing came from the effort—primarily because Egypt was busy securing its southern border and refused to support the effort.

In 592, however, Egypt reappeared and made a surge into Judah and its environs. Believing that Egypt was the more powerful of the two, Zedekiah broke with Babylon, a decision that proved deadly. Within a very short time, Judah was invaded and conquered by the Babylonians. Jerusalem was again laid to siege. This time, the Egyptians did not come to Judah's aid. Nor was the king of Babylon satisfied with only replacing the Jewish king and making prisoners of his palace elites. In 586, Jerusalem was taken, the city burned, nearly every building torn to the ground, a great number of its inhabitants killed or enslaved. King Zedekiah tried to escape the city. Though he was able to slip through the gates, he was later captured on the Jericho plains. As punishment for his rebellion, he was forced to watch as his sons were murdered; then his own eyes were gouged out.

The Babylonians, however, did not follow the tradition of the Assyrians in depopulating Judah and scattering the exiled slaves. A Judean from a prominent, if not royal, family was even appointed as governor of Judah. Most important, many of the rural citizens were allowed to remain in the outlying parts of the kingdom, farming the land and tending to their vineyards. So it was that a substantial Jewish population remained in Judah. These were the survivors who rose up to greet the first group of exiles when they were allowed to return to their homeland from Babylon.

Of great importance was the nature of the Jewish exile under the Babylonians. Unlike with the Assyrians, those Jews who were taken captive by King Nebuchadrezzar were settled in a single geographic area inside the Babylonian Empire. While in exile, they were allowed the autonomy of largely ruling themselves, including the freedom to practice their religion. As Babylon began to fail, to be replaced by yet another rising power (this time the Persians), hope ran high among the Jews that they might be allowed to return to the kingdom of Judah. The biblical record states that after a period of about fifty years, the exiles began to return.[17]

Did the Battle for Jerusalem Change the World?

Even with the end of the reign of Babylon and the Israelites' return to their homeland, the travails of the Jewish kingdom did not abate, for they were subsequently conquered by the Greeks and then the Romans. Yet through all this, the kingdom of Judah remained a viable community of Jews (as well as other assorted members of the

Hebrew tribes), its identity as a nation and religion remaining largely intact, until shortly after the death of Christ.

One of the reasons the Jews were able to remain an enduring community was their unbending faith in their God, Jehovah, who they believed had saved them from the Assyrians. Much of their later self-perception pivoted on this event. Having lived through this terrifying and yet comforting experience, they had come to the conclusion that their God was powerful. More, this incident, along with the foundation of their monotheistic religion, gave them the confidence to argue that their God had power over the entire world. Everything that happened was in accordance with His will. Looking back on the destruction of the northern kingdom of Israel, Jewish religious leaders exhorted their followers that if their brothers had not abandoned the true religion, they would not have been destroyed and lost.

Their ancestors had been warned, they were constantly reminded, for had not Jehovah's prophets foretold just such an outcome?

Yet the fact that a large number of the citizens of Judah survived their exile into Babylon and were eventually allowed to return to their homeland was evidence of God's desire that the Jewish nation should survive.

One historian described the powerful and positive resurgence the Jews experienced while in exile:

> As we all know, this was not the end of Jewish history, for the exiled people of Judah did not pine away. Instead they flourished by the waters of Babylon, and reorganized their scriptures to create an unambiguously monotheistic, congregational religion, independent of place and emancipated from the rites of Solomon's destroyed temple in Jerusalem. Moreover, the revised Jewish faith, tempered in exile, subsequently gave birth to Christianity and Islam, the two most powerful religions of our age, and of course also retains its own, distinctive following around the world and especially in the contemporary state of Israel.[18]

This historian also declares that if Jerusalem had met the same fate as the nation of Israel, "Judaism would have disappeared from the face of the earth and the two daughter religions of Christianity and Islam could not possibly have come into existence. In short, our world would be profoundly different in ways we cannot really imagine."[19]

One eminent American scholar of the Near and Middle East, Bernard Lewis, reached this same conclusion:

> The advent and triumph of Islam in the seventh century was preceded and in a sense made possible by the rise and spread of Christianity, which itself was deeply indebted to its religious and philosophic predecessors. Both Christian and Islamic civilization have common roots in the encounter and interaction in the ancient Middle East of three universalist traditions—those of the Jews, the Persians, and the Greeks.[20]

In short, the survival of Jerusalem and Judaism was essential for the ultimate birth of Christianity into the world.

Regarding the importance of the Assyrian battle for Jerusalem and its subsequent impact upon world history, the *Quarterly Journal of Military History* asked thirty-seven historians to identify the single most important military battle in history. Many critical battles were mentioned: the Greek navy's victory over Persia in the Battle of Salamis in 480 BC, England's defeat of the Spanish Armada in 1588, and many others. But one preeminent scholar, William H. McNeill, author of *Rise of the West* (for which he was awarded the National Book Award for History), believes the Assyrian battle for Jerusalem exceeds them all in importance. Believing that the nation of Judah was saved by an unexplained plague, and while writing for the journal and representing the historians' collective view, Mr. McNeill states:

> Had the Assyrian army remained healthy in 701 [BC], Jerusalem would probably have been captured and its people dispersed, as had happened to Samaria only 20 years before.

Think of what that would mean! For without Judaism, both Christianity and Islam become inconceivable. And without these faiths, the world as we know it becomes unrecognizable: profoundly, utterly different.[21]

Why Jerusalem and the culture of Judaism survived was because of either a mysterious plague or the softened heart of a brutal Assyrian king. Either way, it doesn't matter. Both were miraculous and unexplainable events. Further, the fact that the Jewish religion survived clearly paved the way for the birth of Christianity. And as we will explain in subsequent chapters, without the foundation of Christianity, the freedom and democracy that we enjoy in this golden age would not have been possible.

Little did the people living in the days of the Assyrians comprehend the critical role that Sennacherib, Hezekiah, and the retreat of the Assyrian army back to Nineveh would play in the development of freedom and democracy during the centuries yet to come.

Notes

1. The use of this name is based upon the Biblical account in Isaiah and the works of Josephus. It is not certain from either the biblical account or the historians whether this was a proper name or a title. For ease of use, we will use it as a proper name. There is also dispute among historians as to whether Sennacherib himself was involved in the siege of Judah and Jerusalem or whether he remained in Nineveh or was engaged in a campaign against the Egyptians. For purposes of this account, we have accepted the version that has the king remain in his capital city.
2. Durant, *Our Oriental Heritage,* 266.
3. Ibid., 271, 275–76.
4. For information regarding the Assyrian Empire and its military might and tactics, see Coogan, *Oxford History,* 236–58; De Mieroop, *History of the Ancient Near East,* 229–33; *Interpreter's Dictionary of the Bible,* 1:272; and Rizza, *Assyrians and the Babylonians,* 130–98.
5. For information regarding the ancient city Nineveh, see Russell, *Final Sack of Nineveh,* 2, 16–17, 66–67; www.britannica.com; www.bible-history.com /assyria_archaeology; www.associatedcontent.com/article/447190/history_of_ the_ancient_city_of_nineveh.html.

6. For information regarding the battle for Jerusalem, see 2 Kings 18–19; 2 Chronicles 32.

7. See De Mieroop, *History of the Ancient Near East,* 227.

8. For information about the kingdoms of Israel and Judah and their kings, see Thiele, *Mysterious Numbers of the Hebrew Kings.*

9. For information about the fall of the kingdom of Israel, see Coogan, *Oxford History,* 206–40, 256; De Mieroop, *History of the Ancient Near East,* 233, 251; Josephus, *Works of Flavius Josephus,* 262–63.

10. Cowley, *What If?* 3.

11. This account is contained in the King James Version of the Old Testament at 2 Kings 18–19, 2 Chronicles 32, and Isaiah 36–37.

12. See Josephus, *Works of Flavius Josephus,* 265.

13. Coogan, *Oxford History,* 252.

14. See De Mieroop, *History of the Ancient Near East,* 255.

15. For information about the Assyrian assault on Judah, see Coogan, *Oxford History,* 244–56; Josephus, *Works of Flavius Josephus,* 264–66; Cowley, *What If?* 3–12.

16. Durant, *Our Oriental Heritage,* 1:283.

17. For information about the fall of the kingdom of Judah and its exile, see Coogan, *Oxford History,* 258–86.

18. Cowley, *What If?* 5.

19. Ibid., 5–6.

20. Lewis, *Middle East,* 26.

21. Quoted in Henry T. Auben, "The Rescue of Jerusalem," *Assyrian Campaigns: Ancient Mesopotamia,* http://joseph_berrigan.tripod.com/ancientbabylon/id21.html.

Chapter 2

How the Greeks
Saved the West

And dying, died not.

Simonides, the Greek poet, in his epitaph to the
Greek warriors who died in the battles against the Persians

The world is a warring place. It is a jarring, unforgiving, and violent place, with power and riches going mainly to the strong. In
its long history, there have been thousands of battles fought. Millions
of soldiers and civilians have died. Tyrants have been defeated. Heroes
have been made.

But none of these battles affected the future of the human race
more, or created greater heroes, than did the two battles fought between the Greeks and the unconquerable Persians at Thermopylae and
Salamis, in the nation of the Greeks.

Western Persia Kingdom
March, 480 BC

He was a king. He was a Spartan. He was a warrior and a leader of
the most advanced civilization on the earth.

Or at least he used to be.

Now he was something else.

He was a traitor. A collaborator. A man whose lust for power was greater than even his love for kin. For a chance to reclaim his old crown—or for even a few cities, it would seem—he would betray his own people.

The Persian king knew what kind of man the dethroned Spartan had become, for that had been established when the Spartan had first approached him and offered to be his guide. They may have haggled over the price, but what the blackness in the old Spartan's heart had led him to was not in question anymore. After a short time, they had agreed on the coastal cities of Pergamum, Teuthrania, and Halisarna, a small price to pay in order for the Persian ruler to own the former Spartan king.

Knowing what he was, King Xerxes understood he could never trust the man completely. So, though he listened to him, he was cautious in accepting what he heard.

Demaratus, the Spartan, lifted his head bravely to the Persian king, daring to look upon his face. Xerxes was incredibly intimidating—dark and tall and strong. He sat on a massive wood and gold throne, mobile (for he intended to travel with his army), but only barely, for it took many men to lift the enormous chair. The spoils of war around him represented the Persians' unbelievable wealth and power: gold from the Phoenicians, emeralds from the mines in the Azbek highlands, pearls from the mouth of the Nile, red sandalwood from the jungles of eastern India—the display of wealth dazzled like the sun.

The granite slabs beneath the king's feet were from the territories of the Black Sea to the north, the slaves from the fallen cities of Babylon, from whence the most beautiful women in the world were known to come. The tent was high and strong, large as any Greek temple, with the exception of the Athena Polias that looked down on Athens. Around the fearsome king, the Immortals stood—large men in thick armor that held the scratches, dents, and bloodstains from many battles, the warriors leaving the chinks intact as a memory of every conquest they had made.

Xerxes leaned forward. "Tell me about your brother Spartans," he commanded.

Demaratus hesitated. "O King, forgive me, but I must know. Do I speak of things as you wish they were? Or do you want to hear truth?"

Xerxes shrugged as if it didn't matter, then answered, "As they are, Demaratus."

The dethroned king, loser of a bitter power struggle in his old home of Sparta, lifted his head. "Spartans do not fight for a king or empire, my lord. They do not fight for riches or captured booty. They will not fight under the sting of the whip or the threat of blood. They do not fight for greed or lust or power. They fight for something very different." He stopped and took a breath. When he continued, his voice was as soft as the night breeze that moved outside the thick tent walls. "They fight for each other. For their families. For the idea that men should live free."

Xerxes scoffed. *Freedom! Liberty!* Greek words, foreign to him. There was nothing in his language that came close to explaining what the Spartan even meant.

Demaratus saw the uncertainty in the Persian's face and knew he had to seize the moment or he would lose the king. And it didn't matter much if he sounded like a fool. It was the truth. All he could do was tell it. Let Xerxes decide what to do with what he was about to say. "One against one, they are as good as anyone in the world. But when they fight in a body, they are the best of all. For though they are free men, they are not entirely free. They accept law as their master. And they respect this master more than your subjects respect you." The Spartan paused. "Whatever the law commands, they do. And that command never changes: It forbids them to flee in battle, whatever the number of their foes. It requires them to stand firm—to conquer or die."[1]

Xerxes' eyes narrowed and he thought a long moment. He was the most powerful man in the world, maybe the most powerful man who had ever lived. A million men would live or die by a single word he said. But his fathers had taught him to listen and deliberate before he settled on a plan.

"But these Spartans, they are not many," he volleyed back.

"True, lord. But the Spartan soldiers are not like anything you have ever faced before. They believe they are the master race. Six hundred years of unpolluted Spartan lineage must be proven before a man-child is brought into the circle of Spartan warriors. Once selected, a child is taken from his mother and trained to be nothing but a master of war. They dedicate their lives, steeling themselves to die in battle if that is their cause. They grow their hair long, work their bodies into muscle, keep their spirits lean, their stomachs hungry. They are fearless when committed. And they will be committed now."

Xerxes was unimpressed. "All men are committed when faced with certain death," he said. "The sword of Persia brings out commitment. Believe me, Demaratus, I have defeated many committed men before."

"You haven't fought against free men," Demaratus answered simply.

The great one moved forward on his throne. "What is the difference?" he sneered. "Rule of law? Rule of an emperor? Show me a single place or time in history when the rule of law meant anything to anyone!"

Demaratus didn't answer. There was no example he could call upon. The Greeks were first. That was why it was impossible for the king to understand.

The two men were silent for a moment. The entire court had fallen still. The slaves stayed in the background, nearly bare bodies hovering behind the heavy draperies upon the walls, ready to spring forward if the king showed even the slightest need or desire. The Immortals eyed the Spartan traitor most carefully. As the king's personal warriors, they knew that, for a man who sought the favor of the king, Demaratus spoke much too loudly. Too honestly. Much too full of confidence. Those who were wise enough to see that were interested by it, for it seemed to prove his point. Even as a fallen Spartan, Demaratus was still poised and much too proud.

"Will they really fight against us?" King Xerxes asked for the final time.

Demaratus didn't hesitate. "I can't speak for the Athenians, but this much I know: Sparta will never accept your terms. They will die a thousand times before they accept *earth and water,* for to do so would reduce them all to slavery, a thing they could never do. Even if all of Greece were to lie down before your army, the Spartans would stand and fight. It matters not how many or how few. If only a thousand should take the battle before your army of a million, they will stand and fight."

"You think too highly of your people," Xerxes shot back. "Time will show that you are a braggart and your crowing will prove weak. We outnumber them fifty, maybe a hundred, maybe a thousand to one! Yet you say that they will stand before me!"

"I am certain that they will! And remember, Great King, I speak not out of love for Sparta. They have robbed me of my rank and my honors, left me in exile, put my name and lineage under shame. But mark my words, O King, and make me not an enemy for speaking the truth. They will stand and fight you if there is but one Spartan warrior left. It is their law. It is their honor. It is the reason they were born. They will stand to stop you. And though you may destroy them, you will also pay the price."

● ● ●

Two hundred miles across the Aegean Sea, the Spartan king, Leonidas, watched the sun crest the mountains to the east, the light sparkling atop the heavy dew on the tips of the spring grass. He sucked a breath and held it as he stood on the wooden portico that surrounded his home. Behind him, his wife was sleeping, his children too. As he listened to the calm of the morning, he felt a sudden surge of fear. Leonidas was a warrior, but he was no fool. He loved life. He loved his family. He loved his people, sometimes weak though they were. He wanted to live.

He was by nature a good man, and the times and challenges that befell him were not something he would have sought.

But such were his days and he would not turn away.

Tall. Dark-skinned. Dark-eyed. Thick arms. Leonidas was the epitome of everything a Spartan warrior was supposed to be. Strong as oak. Quick with a sword. Fearless. Intelligent. Beyond the reach of pain. Hardened by a lifetime of preparation to fight and kill and die in war.

He felt a sudden surge of energy as he looked out on the land he loved. Greece. Home of the gods. He turned, taking in the narrow valleys and steep mountains that rose around him, the greenery broken by random outcroppings of granite slabs that jutted from the ground. The mountains were thick with low shrubs and thistle. The air was cool and smelled of juniper, and he took another long breath, holding it in his lungs.

He thought again of the words the oracle of Apollo had told them: The fate of Sparta was to see their great city destroyed, or to see the death of a great king.

Which of the two it was to be, he did not know. No one did. But of this much he was certain: War was coming. The messengers from Xerxes had made that very clear. Which meant they had to stand against an army so large that it was said that when they stopped to drink, they would drain the rivers dry!

His people were not ready. And that frightened him to the core.

The Seed of a Republic

A little less than a century after the brutal Assyrians faced the city walls at Jerusalem and walked away without victory (as noted in the previous chapter), the Assyrians met their demise at the hands of the Babylonians. In 612 BC, those lands that had once been controlled by the Assyrians were divided between the Median Empire to the north and the Babylonians to the south. In 540 BC, the center of power suddenly shifted once again when Babylon fell under the rising Persian power. King Cyrus and his Persian army conquered not only Babylon but all of Asia Minor.

Cyrus, who had no bone to pick with the small and relatively unimportant kingdom of Judah, had allowed the Jews to return to their homeland, something that happened only a few decades after they had been taken captive into Babylon. (Throughout his reign, Cyrus the

Great was known for his tolerance of the religions of the people, his treatment of the Jews being only one example.)

During all of this upheaval, primarily because of their relatively protected location away from the warring empires, the Greek city-states had progressed beyond any other culture or society in the ancient world. By any standard, their achievements were remarkable, and few if any societies can claim such a long-standing and positive influence on cultures or nations yet to come. In so many critical human endeavors, the Greeks stood alone. United by a common language, religion, and alphabet, and with the rise of the Roman Empire still a few centuries in the future, the Greeks

> . . . created a literature which is still living, still read: laid the basis, through Pythagoras, Euclid, Archimedes and others, of nearly 2000 years of geometry: commenced, with Herodotus and Thucydides, history as we both know and practise it: created diverse schools of philosophy which still exercise the minds of men: invented political science: laid the foundations of biology: created geography and extended cosmology: developed medicine far beyond anything previously known to the ancient world. And these were but a few of their achievements which can be rivalled in this period of human history by none.[2]

Yet none of these great achievements could occur if the Greeks were to be defeated by the mighty Persian army, for most of them wouldn't be achieved until *after* the battles at Thermopylae and Salamis were fought.

Who Were the Greeks?

Though the emergence of their culture can be traced back to the eighth century BC, the Greeks exerted their greatest and longest-lasting influence on the world during their Classical and Hellenistic periods, dating roughly from 500 BC until shortly after they were overcome by the Roman Empire in 146 BC.

For all their achievements in so many noble fields of human endeavor, the greatest contribution of the ancient Greeks was their experimentation and success in establishing the concepts of the rights of the individual, personal liberty, and self-government or democracy.

One of the primary reasons for the phenomenal progress of the Greeks, not just in democratic thinking but in so many other areas, was their early adoption of the city-state form of government. The Greeks organized themselves around their local cities. Adjoining areas were considered part of the city-state; for example, the city-state of Athens included the entire Attica peninsula, roughly a thousand square miles.

On occasion, the city-states would unite together in leagues, primarily for mutual protection through military alliances, but also to enrich themselves through trade. But these leagues were always limited in scope and subject to shifting membership. Indeed, they were so fleeting that they could often not be relied upon, for the fiercely independent Greeks were determined not to become just another small part of someone else's greater kingdom or empire.

Although their resistance to uniting made them vulnerable to more powerful forces, the Greeks' city-state form of government had many significant advantages. Each city-state was small, locally governed, and in vibrant competition with its fellow Greek city-states. Each set its own priorities and its own agenda. This facilitated innovation and creative genius. One scholar declared them to be examples of "extreme chauvinism . . . highly individualistic and autonomous . . . all that had allowed the creation and growth of a free landowning citizenry like none other."[3]

Other scholars have noted:

> From the close of the Greek Middle Age (*ca.* 750 B.C.) Greek civilization developed with remarkable rapidity. No other Indo-European or Oriental people has achieved results comparable to those of the next centuries. The one

institution more responsible for this extraordinary achievement than any other was the city-state (*polis*). . . .

. . . [T]he city-state made possible boundless versatility
in the fields of literature, art, and philosophy. Perhaps its
most precious contribution to civilization is republican government, which the Greeks devised in endless variety and
which assured to the citizens a varying degree of liberty and
self-government.[4]

Although not alone, the city-state most active in experimenting
with self-government was Athens. Over decades its government evolved
from a kingship, to a king with a council made up of aristocrats, to
rule by a broad collection of aristocrats, to a representative government
of all citizens. This evolution was not without its failures and the occasional tyrant or two, but for the quarter century before 480 BC, the
city-state of Athens had tested the limits of democracy and found it
acceptable. After 480, it continued to experiment and achieved an even
higher degree of self-government.[5]

Of the Athenians it was said, "They bow to no man and are no
man's slaves."[6]

Noted historian Victor Davis Hanson has commented on how unusual the Greek experimentation truly was by pointing out what was at
stake when Persia invaded Greece in 480 BC:

First, we should remember that the decade-long Persian
Wars . . . offered the East the last real chance to check
Western culture in its embryonic state, before the Greeks'
radically dynamic menu of constitutional government, private property, broad-based militias, civilian control of military forces, free scientific inquiry, rationalism, and separation
between political and religious authority would spread to
Italy, and thus via the Roman Empire to most of northern
Europe and the western Mediterranean. Indeed, the words
freedom and citizen did not exist in the vocabulary of any

other Mediterranean culture, which were either tribal monarchies, or theocracies.[7]

With its culture that valued freedom, individual liberty, and self-government, the Greek city-state was critical to the future development of the Western world. And although it is impossible to know how the history of Europe would have unfolded, this much is surely true: had the Greeks been defeated at Salamis—had their people been conquered by a power for whom the concepts of *freedom* and *citizen* did not even exist—history would have unfolded much differently.

Who Were the Persians?

Much of the early history of the Persian Empire remains obscured by the fog of time. Still, from a murky genesis sprang one of the most powerful empires the world has ever known. Encompassing almost three million square miles, the Persian Empire stretched across three continents: Asia, Africa, and Europe. It included an extremely diverse group of peoples: Persians, Medes, Egyptians, Greeks, Scythians, Babylonians, Bactrians, and Indians, among others. At its zenith, the Persian Empire controlled territories that spanned from northern India across Central Asia and Asia Minor, stretching as far north as what is now known as Uzbekistan and the Black Sea coastal areas to the Mediterranean Sea in the west and as far south as Egypt and Libya in northern Africa. And all of these people paid tribute to the Persian king, making the empire enormously wealthy.

Cyrus founded the empire by conquering the Median kingdom, bringing together the Medes and the Persians, then building twin capital cities at Pasargadae and Persepolis. (As conquerors of the Medes, the Persians are sometimes referred to by historians as the Medes. We will refer to them as Persians here.) Cyrus continued conquering new territory throughout his reign, the most important conquest being the defeat of Babylon, a victory that brought all of the former Babylonian Empire under his control, pushing his western border to the Mediterranean Sea.

After the death of Cyrus in 530 BC, his son Cambyses made significant gains in Egypt. His reign was short-lived, however, and only eight years after the death of Cyrus, Darius (whom many consider the greatest of the Persian kings, although his claim on the royal line was tenuous) fought his way to power.

Darius started a series of brilliant military, engineering, and governmental campaigns. He initiated the construction of a canal between the Nile River and the Red Sea (the forerunner of the Suez Canal), and construction of the Royal Road, a great highway stretching for more than a thousand miles between Mesopotamia and the Aegean Sea. Among his other achievements, he made acceptable the use of coinage, spread the Old Persian language, and greatly increased government and military efficiency.

His immediate successor, Xerxes, ruled from 486 to 465 BC. Cunning and incredibly ambitious, Xerxes was intent on expanding his empire west, determined to bring all of Europe under his domain. He dreamed of an empire that stretched from the hills and swamps of India to the rocky Atlantic shores. Looking across the Aegean Sea, he saw the magnificence of the Greek culture, knowing he would have to conquer the territories of Greece before he could venture any farther west.[8]

The First Invasion of Greece

Xerxes was not the first of the Persian rulers to lust after Greece. His predecessor on the throne, Darius, had also looked longingly at the city-states of Greece. Convinced that they were weak and ready to be plundered because of their continual inter-city conflict and unwillingness to agree upon mutual defense, Darius considered them easy targets for invasion.

> The Persian Empire was predatory and seemed to set no limit to its growth, and there was now no reason why it should not spread across the Aegean to the Balkan peninsula. Booty, tribute, and the hope of excelling his predecessor

in the glory of triumphant war no doubt attracted Darius.
. . . What should Darius' policy be toward those Greeks not
within his empire? Absorption was a likely answer.[9]

The Greeks were not unaware of Darius's intentions. Quite the
opposite—they knew that he had already made one conquest in Europe
when Thrace, a sometime ally to the north of Greece, fell under the
Persian hand. As the Greeks watched Darius reach into the Western
world, they realized that he would surely come for them.

Among all the city-states of Greece, the people of Athens were particularly perceptive of Darius's intentions. In 492 BC, they elected a
man named Themistocles to become their leader. This was a decision
that would prove to be one of the most significant in the long history
of Athens.

In preparing for the coming battle, Themistocles came to a critical
conclusion: Hellespont was the key.

Located in modern-day Turkey, Hellespont, or what is now called
the Dardanelles, is the narrow strait of water that connects the Aegean
and the Black Seas. Long recognized as the boundary line between Asia
and Europe, it is, at its most narrow point, less than one mile wide.[10]
The Persians would have to move their massive army across Hellespont
before they could begin to track west and then south toward the rugged
mountains that made up most of Greece.

Themistocles realized that once the Persians had crossed at
Hellespont, their army could be resupplied only by sea. Understanding
this, he made a strategic—but very risky—decision, convincing his fellow Athenians to shift their resources to building a navy to counter the
Persian fleet.

When Darius had positioned his army and was ready to attack, he
sent his emissaries to the Greek city-states, demanding "earth and water"—the Persian term for unconditional surrender. Many of the Greek
city-states in the Aegean Islands surrendered. The situation looked
bleak. The Greeks' tradition of independence, which had proven to
be one of their great strengths, now appeared to be their potential

undoing. Standing alone as independent city-states, the Greeks could not hope to withstand the might of the Persian army.

Many of the city-states in Greece were ready to capitulate. Most were unsure of the best course of action. But the Athenians, under the inspired leadership of Themistocles, ramped up their preparations for war.

The first confrontation of what would become known as the Greco-Persian Wars occurred in 490 BC at Marathon. A Persian army under the command of Darius's nephew sailed across the Aegean with the intent of subduing two city-states, Athens and Eretria. Eretria fell quickly and was sacked, its people taken captive.

Within Athens, the debate raged on: surrender or fight against impossible odds? Their warrior neighbors were called on for help, but in a great irony of history, the devout Spartans were unable to come to the assistance of the Athenians due to the Carneia Festival. During this sacred holiday, for fear of offending their gods, all Spartan male citizens had to be purified. More important, the Spartan army was forbidden to leave the territory or fight in any kind of military campaign.

Amid the chaos, and without the help of the Spartans, Athens was barely able to muster ten thousand men. The Persians had an army at least three times that number.

On the plain of Marathon, the Athenians faced their mortal enemy. Terribly outnumbered, inexperienced in combat, and uncertain even of the sanity of their decision, they didn't wait for the mighty Persian army to march forward. Instead, the brave Athenians initiated the attack. Running in fury toward their enemy over a distance of almost one mile, they engaged the Persians. Relying on such courage, as well as a variety of brilliant military tactics, the Athenians routed the Persians. Much of the invading army was destroyed and the survivors sent scurrying across the Aegean in utter shame.

Just as the battle was winding down, with their religious rites finally complete, the Spartans eagerly marched onto the scene, arriving just in time to inspect the dead Persians scattered across the plains of Marathon.

Although only the first skirmish in what was to prove to be a brutal and protracted war, the battle of Marathon was significant for two reasons. First, it proved to the Athenians that they were better warriors than any had believed, giving them a jolt of confidence. It also proved that the Persians could be defeated. They were not indomitable. Soon, the story of the Athenian victory in the battle at Marathon was whispered throughout the Persian Empire. The shocking revelation that the Persians were not invincible led to revolts in Babylon and Egypt, the people rising up against their Persian masters.

From the Persian perspective, the defeat at Marathon led to a hardening of their resolve, altering the dynamic within the royal court. No longer was the conquest of Greece seen as just a military option. To the rulers of Persia, it had become vital to maintaining a firm grip upon their expansive empire.

Prelude to Invasion

Although the victory at Marathon had been a land battle, the Athenians continued to concentrate on building their navy, for two facts had become even more apparent: first, the Persians would attack them again, and this time nothing would be held back; and second, in order to defeat the Persians, the outnumbered Greeks had to defeat the Persian navy so as to sever their army's source of supply.

On the other side of the Aegean Sea, Darius spent several years amassing men, equipment, sailors, and ships for a second and decisive attack upon the Greeks. But he died in 486 before he could fulfill his great ambition.

His oldest son, Xerxes, set out to finish the task. After crushing the various rebellions within his kingdom, he turned his attention back to the upcoming invasion of Greece. His plan was to defeat the tiresome Greeks and then continue marching west until he had conquered all of Europe. It was a monumental task, and he knew it. He spent years in preparation, amassing an incomparable army to guarantee that the invasion would be unstoppable.

The Hellespont was conquered by the construction of a bridge consisting of 674 boats.

Once he had crossed onto the European continent, Xerxes commanded the digging of a massive canal across the entire peninsula at the base of Mount Athos.

It took an untold number of men, standing on ladders while lifting bucket after bucket of rock and dirt, to build this canal. Part military necessity, part a statement of pride and power, Xerxes spent nearly three years in this effort. It would have been a massive undertaking in any age, but for the era of the Persians and Greeks, it was a wonder—especially considering that its only purpose was to avoid a dangerous and stormy area of the Aegean Sea where his father's navy had suffered severe losses ten years before.

This mighty effort spoke clearly of the simple truth that Xerxes knew that his invasion would succeed or fail based upon the ability of his navy to supply his immense army.

Vast stores of supplies were then laid up along the route that Xerxes' army was to follow. His army was immense. The Greek historian Herodotus claimed that it had five million soldiers and more than 1,200 ships. This was certainly an exaggeration. Modern historians estimate the army to have been between 150,000 and 500,000 soldiers—some say as high as 800,000—with a navy of 700 to 1,200 warships.

Regardless of the actual number, this is clear: It was the largest combined invasion force Europe was to witness until the D-Day invasion of World War II.[11]

The Armies and Navies Compared

Greece is a mountainous region, its land extremely unconducive to warring (as was rediscovered during World War II). Not only are the mountains steep and rugged, with sharp and pointed rocks, but the undergrowth is very thorny. In many locations, the hills and mountains are covered with high, thick bushes. It is almost impossible to traverse them except over established trails, making it infeasible to fight anywhere in Greece except for on its plains, which make up only about one-fifth of the country. This physical characteristic dictated the makeup of the army.

The core of the Greek army consisted of the hoplites—heavily armored citizen-soldiers. They wore bronze helmets, the rest of their upper bodies covered with bronze and leather. They carried round shields, about three feet across, made of wood with a bronze covering, called hoplons, from which the hoplites received their name. Their primary weapon was the spear, about six feet long, with a wood shaft and iron tip. A short sword completed their personal arsenal. Bows and arrows were rarely used.

Neither the Spartans nor the Athenians were ever able to muster armies of more than a few thousand soldiers—in the case of Sparta, never more than eight thousand. Being greatly outnumbered, the Greeks were forced to rely on disciplined mass to overcome their enemies. They fought shoulder to shoulder, with shields touching, spears held out in front to rip the Persians apart. Once their spears were hacked to pieces, the soldiers would fight to the death with their swords. Standing brother to brother, the entire unit depended upon the courage and resolve of each and every soldier. As one historian has noted, the hoplites would be expected to be "'standing foot to foot, shield pressed on shield, crest to crest and helmet to helmet, chest to chest engage your man.'"[12]

For the Persians, bows and arrows were weapons of first choice. For close-in combat, they used daggers and short javelins that could be thrown, unlike the Greek spears that would be wielded. Only the personal bodyguards of Xerxes, the "Immortals," wore armor approaching the quality of that worn by the Greeks. The rest of the Persians were lightly armored, their shields made of wicker, not bronze.

But what the Persians lacked in armaments, they more than made up for in the vast number of soldiers that they could throw into the battle.[13]

Both the Persian and Greek naval vessels were called triremes. Captained by a master, each trireme was fairly large, the Greek versions being about 130 feet long and 30 feet wide with the oars extended. They had three levels, or banks, of oarsmen. The top level had 31 oars on each side. The two lower levels each had 27. With one oarsman per oar, there were a total of 170 men pulling on each boat. In addition to the oarsmen, there were fifteen deckhands and a contingent of marines, some of whom were archers.

Each trireme had one small mast and sail that could propel the ship, but only under perfect conditions. Generally the trireme was dependent upon the toil of the oarsmen to drive it forward. In battle, the oarsmen were the only means of propulsion. Manning an oar was harsh and backbreaking work, the opportunity to rest very rare.

Once in the open water, the combat tactics used by both sides were simple: either ram an enemy ship with the ram positioned below the waterline to sink it, or run alongside of the enemy ship to break off the oars and kill the oarsmen, and then either capture or sink the boat at your leisure. Both maneuvers required speed and mobility, a fact that was to prove fateful to the Greeks.[14]

The Only Hope for a Greek Defense

Before the command to invade Greece was given, Xerxes sent heralds to the various city-states, demanding they surrender. Then, in a show of supreme confidence, he allowed Greek spies to observe the mustering and maneuvers of his military forces, knowing fear would play a significant role in the Greek decision as to whether it was worth the cost to stand and fight.

There was precious little unity among the Greeks. Seeing the massive invasion force, some of the city-states surrendered "earth and water." Others, out of lingering anger for past defeats and injuries, refused to align with certain neighbors within the emerging defense league. Still, the impeding threat was so obvious, the fear of utter destruction so great, that it spurred a greater unity and sense of "being Greek" than had ever existed among the city-states before.

Sparta had historically been the strongest of the Greek city-states and was again looked to for leadership. In a meeting held in 481 BC, the city-states that had decided to fight agreed to Sparta's overall command and to the adoption of a comprehensive strategy.

As Themistocles had so persuasively argued, the navy was the key. Athens and its allies now had a fleet of almost three hundred ships. If it could defeat or at least inflict major damage on the navy of Xerxes, his army would be left without the means of adequate resupply. Without the ability to supply his massive army, Xerxes would be forced to withdraw.

But before the Greeks could engage the Persian navy, the Persian army had to be slowed on its long march south. The Greeks hoped not only to give the citizens of Athens time to evacuate their city but also to limit the inevitable death and destruction that would shadow the approach of Xerxes' masses.

But where to engage the massive Persian army that was approaching from the north?

The defenders had to find a strategic spot where whatever small army they could muster could have some hope of blocking Xerxes' immense horde.

Battlegrounds to the far north were out of the question. Too many of the city-states in Macedonia, Thrace, and Thessaly had already surrendered.

Another consideration was the fact that the farther south Xerxes marched, the more stretched his supply lines would become, making him more dependent upon his navy for resupply.

The critical decision as to where the tiny nation of Greece could engage the mighty Persians was not an insignificant one, for not only was the freedom of the Greeks at risk, but the future of the entire Western world hung in the balance.

• • •

Xerxes' plan depended on close coordination between his army and his navy. As the army marched south, the navy sailed with it, hugging the coast, slipping through the canal at Athos, always keeping abreast of the main thrust of Persian forces.

The Greek leaders, watching and studying the advancing enemy, realized that their initial assumptions regarding the critical interdependence between the Persian army and the navy were holding true. After days of debate, it was finally decided to confront both of them simultaneously. Themistocles always believed this first sea battle would be a holding action. He chose to meet the Persian navy at the narrow strait at Artemisium, hoping to inflict enough damage to weaken it and also to gain intelligence about Persia's naval capabilities before the main sea battle would be fought farther to the south, at Salamis.

As for the land battle, the choice of where to engage the Persians was of much greater importance. The Greeks were terribly outmanned. In the end, they sent an army of seven thousand to meet Xerxes' horde of no fewer than twenty times that number, and perhaps thirty times or even more.

Where could the Greeks stand to fight?

Thermopylae was the only choice.[15]

Some hundred miles northwest of Athens, Thermopylae was a critical choke point through which the entire Persian army would have to pass. Edged by steep mountains and the sea, the narrow passage was only about twenty yards wide. There was also an ancient wall that could be rebuilt quickly. With the sea protecting the Greeks' flank to the right and the steep, sheer base of Mount Kallidromos protecting their left, the advantage of the innumerable Persians would be mitigated at the pass.

So it was that, at this narrow neck of land tucked between the mountain and the sea, King Leonidas, three hundred of his Spartans, and a few thousand other Greek hoplites would make their last stand.

The Spartan Warriors

Unlike Athens and most other Greek city-states, Sparta did not rely on citizen-soldiers. In the Spartan social structure, only descendants of those who were part of the original group that had conquered the southern tip of Greece some six hundred years before could be full citizens. For the last two hundred years, the rulers of the Spartan "master race" had developed a set of very strict rules regarding its military class: weak or defective newborns were killed; at age eight, selected males were to be separated from other citizens in camps called messes; no ownership of gold or silver was allowed by those selected, nor were trading, farming, arts, or a profession; these men-children were immersed in military training, focusing entirely on becoming skilled and physically strong warriors. Everyone ate the same food at the messes, and it was a "Spartan meal" insufficient to satisfy hunger, so thievery was encouraged. But one should never be caught, so cleverness and cunning were developed. To further distinguish the warriors, they were encouraged to grow their hair long. Women were revered, good manners and order in families were demanded, strong marriages were admired.

Sparta sustained this warrior class through the efforts of the other citizens who engaged in all those fields forbidden to the warriors. Its form of governance was not like that of any other Greek city-state, for it was a strange mixture of monarchy, aristocracy, and democracy.[16]

The Spartan life required the strictest adherence to religious formality, which explained why the Spartans had showed up late for the battle at Marathon. (Odd though it seems, such restraint was a sign of the discipline and strength of the Spartan warrior.) Yet once again, during the summer of 480, the approach of the Persian army coincided with a sacred holiday. But the enemy forces that approached this year could not be ignored. Despite the religious prohibition against doing so, three hundred warriors were assembled. Under the command of King Leonidas, the tiny army was dispatched to Thermopylae.

As the Spartans started marching toward the narrow pass, the Greek fleet (consisting primarily of Athenian ships) also sailed north.

The collision of East and West was drawing near.

The War Begins

If history shows us anything, it shows that Xerxes, the man who presided over one of the largest kingdoms in world history, was not a weak or foolish man.

In May of 480 BC, his giant army, with soldiers from at least forty-six nations, crossed the Hellespont.

It took a week for the throng of men and animals (seventy-five thousand horses, mules, and camels) to cross over the bridge of boats. Building a road before them, these so-called barbarians (a title attached by the Greeks to anyone not of Greek blood) proved to be quite marvelous in planning for, and skilled in the unfolding of, an invasion. Creating the bridge across the Hellespont, building the Athos Canal to avoid the dangerous seas around Mount Athos, managing a supply of water for such a huge number of men and animals, supplying the men and animals with sufficient food in an area that barely sustained its own population, buying or frightening off the local population to avoid unnecessary fighting on the march south—all of these showed the genius, preparation, and skills of King Xerxes and his royal court.

Xerxes possessed a confidence born of planning, preparation, and an unparalleled history of military success. He fully expected to easily sweep through all of Greece just as he had just swept through the north of that country.

But, unknown to the Persian leader, King Leonidas and his tiny band of long-haired, scarlet-cloaked warriors were marching north to meet them.

As soon as their most holy of festivals was over, the rest of the Spartan army would follow. But all knew that it would be too late. The marching Spartan soldiers were on a suicide mission. Knowing this, Leonidas selected for his army only those Spartans who had living sons who could carry on their family names once their fathers had been killed.

While the Spartans marched, the Greek navy struggled toward Artemisium, their ships fighting the prevailing currents and wind.

Xerxes was taking his time moving south, enjoying the beginnings of his European conquest. His navy was able to sail faster than his army could march. That created a problem for his naval captains, who knew that the longer they lingered, the higher was the risk of encountering dangerous storms in this temperamental area of the Aegean Sea. The fact that Darius's navy had been wiped out ten years before, not far from where they now toiled under the summer sun, was not forgotten by Xerxes' naval commanders. Their fears proved justified, for, while waiting for the army, the navy was hit by a three-day storm, and a large number of ships were lost off the coast of Euboea.

As the Spartans marched north toward Thermopylae, they gathered additional soldiers: seven hundred from Thespia, four hundred from Thebes, a few hundred here and a few hundred more there, from cities large and townships small. By the time he reached Thermopylae, Leonidas had perhaps seven thousand hoplites.

One must wonder at the willingness of these men who joined this doomed army. All of the solders knew what type of terror was descending from the north. Many of their fellow Greeks had already surrendered in fear. Others had betrayed their homeland for Persian coin. But whatever the reason, there was something different about these men. Willingly, they left their homes, their families, their peaceful lives, and joined in the valiant but hopeless effort to defend Greece.

Leonidas must have considered the last words he is reported to have said to his wife, the queen, upon his leaving. Looking at him for the last time, she had pleaded, "Leonidas, Leonidas, what am I to do?"

He had answered her simply. "Marry a good man and bear good children."[17]

Such willingness to sacrifice on behalf of all Greece would prove to be the key to the battles that lay ahead.

Thermopylae Pass
Ninety-Eight Miles Northwest of Athens

KING LEONIDAS STOOD upon the rock and looked out on the narrow valley that lay on the other side of the pass. Sand. Broken shale. Mountains on his left; steep rock, thick with trees and thorny brush. To his right, the deep waters of the Gulf of Malis, the shoreline abrupt and craggy.

Four days now. Four days and four nights. That was how long he had been watching as the Persian army flowed into the narrow gorge between the mountain and the sea. Four full days just to amass and organize the army. The crowd of men and horses was so vast it created a thunder throughout the ground and there was a nearly constant glint of flashing swords in the setting sun, the clouds against the mountain bathing the scene in filtered light. Columns of men. Thousands of tents. It seemed a million horses. Looking at them, he had to force himself to breathe. Amid the army, a massive portable building—was it really just a tent?—rose out of the flatness of the plain. The mobile palace of the mighty Xerxes. Leonidas forced himself to breathe again.

His tiny army waited on the south side of the wall. He turned to look down upon them.

How does one wait to die? he wondered as he stared down at his men.

He was standing where the man-made wall met a natural out-cropping of stone. His Spartans were the closest to him, closest to the enemy, just where they should be. Most of them were bare above the waist, exercising, eating, sharpening their short swords, washing their long hair. Behind them, the hoplites stood in disorganized ranks, milling here and there. They were good men all, and he didn't doubt their hearts, but none of them were warriors, and their ability to carry out the work of war was an unanswered question in his mind. Yes, they would fight, but would their fighting be effective? And would any of them live?

His lieutenants stood on the wall beside him, watching his eyes.

Behind them, the sounds of the mighty Persian army seemed to fill the air, the mass of so many men and animals concentrated so close together creating a constant commotion in their ears. Dust drifted up from the roads that followed along the beach. Still more soldiers coming in.

The Spartan warriors turned to their king. One of them spoke, his voice uncertain. "I wonder, lord . . . how can so few hope to stand against so many?"

Leonidas lifted his chin. "If numbers are what matters, then all of Greece cannot match even a small part of this army," he said. "But if courage is what counts, then our number is sufficient."[18]

The Spartan warrior thought, then nodded.

Leonidas nodded gently to the hoplites and his Spartan brothers. "I have plenty of men," he seemed to whisper to himself, "since they are all to be slain."

The other Spartans watched, heavy with the burden of the coming battle, but thrilled to be there all the same. The king frowned, then looked across the wall.

A party of horsemen were riding toward them, their horses kicking up the sand. They were dressed in long black robes and jeweled headdresses—their coats flowing behind them, reaching almost to their horses' knees, created the impression of dark ghosts floating in the wind. The riders rode quickly, pulling up their horses at the wall. Only their eyes could be seen above the black veils across their faces. Dark pupils. Powerful expressions. No fear or doubt or concern were evident in either their eyes or body language.

The lead horseman reached up to pull aside his veil. "We come in the name of our lord, King Xerxes," he shouted, his voice harsh and arrogant.

Leonidas stepped up a few paces, taking a position higher on the outcropping of rock against the wall.

The horseman waited for an answer, then shouted once again, "We come in the name of Xerxes!"

Leonidas pointed at the land of Greece behind him. "You are not welcome here," he said.

The horseman seemed to freeze upon his saddle, then cracked a thin smile. "We go where we go, Spartan!"

Leonidas motioned to the magnificent tent of Xerxes, the banners, the trumpets, the slaves, unnumbered wagons filled with food, the mounts and herds of animals, the majesty of the greatest army in the world. "Persians must be greedy," he said. "Look at all you have. Yet you come to take our barley cakes."

The emissary studied him a long moment. "We go where we go, Spartan," he repeated. "And we take what we take."

Jerking on the leather reins, he pulled his horse around, the animal snorting in pain against the bit. Then he nodded to his escorts, who seemed to gather nearer. "Our lord demands that you surrender your arms!" he sneered.

Leonidas watched him, his eyes narrowing in disgust. A Spartan moved his hand toward his spear, but Leonidas held him back with a lift of his finger.

A puff of hot wind blew, lifting dust into the air. None of the Spartans answered.

The messenger waited, his face dark, his jaw growing tight. "My lord will spare you and your men," he shouted. "You may go in peace. And you will go much richer. My master is a kind and generous man. You will live a life of luxury. Or you can die here on this day. Those are your choices, Spartan. Surrender this fight, and live to see another day! Or die against the pitiful wall that you have built here. There is no other way!"

Still Leonidas didn't answer. The burn in his eyes said everything.

The emissary stretched against his stirrups and lifted up his sword. "Surrender now your weapons!" he screamed into the wind.

"Come and take them!" Leonidas shouted back, his voice dripping with disdain.

The emissary sat back into his saddle, his horse pawing at the ground. He stared at the Spartan king in disbelief. Heat lifted off the brown earth and a salty breeze blew in. Turning in rage, he pointed to his right. Ten thousand blue and gray tents were positioned on the high ground against Mount Kallidromos, up where the hills rose out of the plains but before the scag trees grew. "Do you see that?" he screamed in anger. "Do you see that, king of Sparta? Thousands of the best archers in the world stand there with their weapons, waiting for the command from Xerxes to bring your world to an end. They alone can do it; we won't even need our army. Do you understand that, king of Sparta? Our archers will darken the sky with our arrows!"

Leonidas smiled. "So much the better. We shall fight in the shade."[19]

The Persian shook his head. Never had he seen such insolence! Such pride! Shifting in his saddle, he spat on the ground, pulled on his reins, and cut his spurs into his horse's side. The animal lifted to its rear legs and pawed the air, a trickle of dark blood running down its flank.

The emissary spat again toward Leonidas, then turned and rode away.

Day One

Herodotus recounts that, while his army was assembling for combat, Xerxes sent one of his horsemen forward to try to determine how many Greeks they faced. The narrowness of the pass, plus the wall that had been rebuilt, made it impossible for this scout to see much, but he returned with an unusual report: Some of the vaunted Spartan warriors were stripped and exercising. Others were combing their long hair. Xerxes was apparently amused to hear this report, though his Greek spies, including the former Spartan king, Demaratus, surely could have warned him not to be misled by the lackadaisical approach of the Spartans to the impending combat.

While Xerxes was doing his spying, Leonidas was gathering intelligence as well. During this time he became aware of a potentially fatal Achilles heel of his location.

A deadly trap lay to his west. Something that could change the outcome of the battle.

Did Xerxes also know of the deadly possibility on the mountain?

Only time would tell.

• • •

On August 18, Xerxes decided he could not wait any longer. His navy had not yet crushed the Greek navy, and his chain of resupply was unsure. Because of this, he needed the provisions that awaited him in the cities and countryside on the other side of the small group of hoplites and the wall.

The assault on the Greeks began.

As promised, the Persian archers filled the air with arrows. Then Xerxes ordered his army forward. Lightly armored with their wicker shields, short javelins, and daggers, they moved through the impossibly narrow pass toward the Greek wall of spears and bronze shields and helmets.

As the Persians charged, their ranks were torn apart by the long spears of the Greeks. They fell by the hundreds, only to be replaced by other soldiers. The slaughter was immense. The Persians were forced to withdraw.

Frustrated, Xerxes ordered the men from Susa forward. Forced to clamber over or around the mass of broken bodies, they struggled toward the enemy, only to be met by the bronze-protected Greeks and their long and deadly spears.

The discipline of the Greeks was frightening. If a Greek soldier fell in the stalwart line, another would rush forward to fill his place. Despite their overwhelming numbers, the men of Susa began to fail. Facing annihilation, they were forced to retreat.

Xerxes was furious. Enough of this humiliation at the hand of the tiny band of Greeks! In a rage, he called for the Immortals, his personal bodyguards, ten thousand men strong. Xerxes watched the battle carefully, expecting the Greeks to be quickly and unmercifully swept aside by the extensively trained and heavily armed elite troops.

And a slaughter did unfold. But to Xerxes' horror, it was the Immortals who fell, their bodies added to the pile of dead Persian and Susa soldiers.

A humiliating retreat was sounded, and the Persians fell back to lick their wounds.

The first day had gone to the Greeks. Some had died. Many had been wounded.

But they had not given any ground.

War at Sea

While the mighty Persian army was beginning to realize that the Greeks might be something more than a bump in the road on their inevitable conquest of Europe—on that same day, in fact—to the east, in the Gulf of Malis, the Greeks instigated their first assault on the powerful Persian navy.

The Persians had suffered significant losses during the three-day storm off the coast of Euboea, so much so that they had been forced to disperse their large fleet along the long and rugged coastline. Themistocles tried to convince the hesitant members of his navy to take advantage of the disorder. The Greeks were outnumbered more than two to one, however, and most of them were terrified of engaging the Persians in open battle. Themistocles persisted and finally convinced them it was time to attack.

Late in the afternoon they struck, sinking several Persian ships and capturing thirty more. Despite their overwhelming numbers (plus the fact that Xerxes had promised a great reward to any crew that sank a Greek vessel), the Persians were unable to capture a single enemy ship. As darkness approached, the two navies retreated to the protection of their respective shorelines.

The Greek attack was not intended to confront the enemy in full force—its main purpose was to measure the strengths and weaknesses of each side. During the brief engagement, the Greeks learned several important lessons. First, the superior number of Persian ships was a disadvantage that the Greeks would not surmount easily, especially because their own ships were slower than the Persian vessels. In battle on the open sea, the Persians could envelop and decimate the Greeks. But the Greeks also learned that, if they acted with cunning and courage, they could be formidable foes in ship-to-ship warfare.

That night the Persians made a secret effort to surround the small Greek navy and destroy it. After they had moved away from the safety of the coast, however, another horrible gale struck. Two hundred Persian vessels were caught at sea. Most of them were lost.

The gods of war were not smiling on the Persian forces. The first day of battle had been a humiliating defeat on the land and sea.

The night would have been a hard one for the soldiers and the sailors. The gale raged for hours. The wind and rain would have made sleep nearly impossible, and a day of blood and killing cannot be followed by peaceful dreams, especially when it is known that the next day will be the same.

Thermopylae Pass
Ninety-Eight Miles Northwest of Athens

THE GREEK WAS NOT loyal to the king of Sparta, or Athens, or any other city-state. He was not motivated by love of country or freedom or any other abstract concept.

The things that motivated him were far more tangible. Life. Money. Power. The favor of the king of Persia, a man who could give him the things that he most desired. Xerxes would certainly win this battle. The Greek had to gain his favor now.

He crept along the outskirts of the massive army, searching, prodding, looking for the right location, trying to find the best place to make his move. He had to do it right or they would surely kill him. After making contact, he would have to say the right things. Grovel at the right time and stand proud at the next. He would get only one chance and he had to get it right.

Finally, just as the moon was dipping toward the eastern sky and Mars was falling behind a low bank of clouds hanging over the cold waters of the sea, he found what he was looking for: a small band of Persians standing around the dying embers of a fire. Golden headbands and oval shields. Immortals standing guard.

The traitor took a deep breath. This was it! It was death or riches.

Moving from the shadows, he disarmed himself, dropping his

father's small dagger, the only weapon he had. Then he called out to the Immortals who stood around the dying fire, their spears sticking in the sand. "Persians," he hissed through the darkness. "My brothers, I come in peace."

The Persian soldiers sprang to life. Grabbing their swords and spears, they moved toward the sound of the man's voice.

The dim moon cast enough light to show his shadow upon the ground. He knelt, his hands atop his head, his face staring at the dirt. "I come in the name of your leader, even the Great King Xerxes," he cried in a desperate voice. "I must speak to him . . . he must hear me. There is something he must know."

The leader of the Persian soldiers raced toward the cowering Greek. Standing over him, he raised his sword. The Greek pushed himself even lower, pressing his face into the sand. He closed his eyes and kept on talking, praying to his gods that the Persian would listen to him before he sliced off his head. "There is a mountain pass. A goat trail!" he cried.

The Persian seemed to hold his weapon in midair.

"High up on the mountain! I know it! I could show it! I have walked it many times. It will take your soldiers around the Greek wall, behind the Spartans. You could surround them in a short time!"

The Immortal held his sword in a strike position a long moment, then slowly lowered it and nodded to one of his men. The second soldier grabbed the intruder by his neck and jerked him off the ground. "Say what you will!" he demanded.

"This battle could be over," the Greek stammered. "I can show you the way. But my lord . . ." here he seemed to straighten, "I do not work for free."

What the Greek traitor said was true. There was a goat trail that began a few miles in front of Leonidas's position. Sheer and treacherous, the trail worked its way across Mount Kallidromos before ending up a mile to the rear of the Greeks. And though it was small and isolated, it was still potentially deadly.

The Persians could use it to pass around the Greek army.

Leonidas would be surrounded.

All the Greeks would fall.

Upon learning of the great danger the mountain trail represented to his men, Leonidas had sent a thousand soldiers from a local city-state to stand guard on the trail.

Foolishly, as he would learn, he failed to send even a single Spartan to assure that the pass would be properly defended.

The Second Day

The second day of the battle at Thermopylae unfolded like the first.

Thinking the Greeks would be exhausted, Xerxes sent in fresh troops. But it did not matter—the slaughter of his forces proceeded much as it had the day before. Worse, resentment and rebellion started growing in his ranks. Having watched the previous day's carnage, his troops had no desire to be sent to the front line. So terrified were they of the Spartan soldiers, Persian commanders had to use whips to drive some of them forward.

The day ended as had the day before.

At sea, Themistocles and his navy attacked the Persian fleet in another late afternoon hit-and-run effort. The Persians, having been battered by the storm the night before, were slow to respond, and heavy losses were once again inflicted.

Xerxes must have been frustrated as he reflected on the fortitude of the Greeks. His army had fought mightily, but had nothing to show for it. Not a yard of progress. Nothing but bodies scattered across the ground. Thousands of his men had died, maybe tens of thousands. Equally exasperating, his navy, so essential to the entire effort, was being decimated by storms and Greek maneuvers.

At this moment of frustration, the mighty Xerxes was finally brought good news. A Greek was brought before his throne. He told the king his secret. There was a pass through Mount Kallidromos. He was willing to guide the Persians. He could take them on a secret march that would bring them to the rear of Leonidas's Greeks.

Xerxes commanded his Immortals to follow the traitor. The Immortals, who had suffered such a severe blow to their pride the day before, were thrilled at the prospect. Not only was their commander giving them the opportunity to have their pride restored, but they had the prospect of sweet revenge upon the Greeks.

The Immortals waited until dark to begin their ascent to the pass, not wanting to give away their intentions. They did not know whether the pass was guarded, but they were prepared to fight their way through whatever force they encountered.

Foolishly, without the leadership of a single Spartan, the one thousand local soldiers sent by Leonidas to guard the pass were completely unprepared. Discovered asleep, unarmed, without even guards at watch, they were taken by surprise. With the Immortals approaching up the trail, they dashed to a nearby hillside. Whether they were seeking higher ground as the best spot to defend or were simply cowards, it is not known. Either way, it did not matter. The Immortals simply passed them by and continued their march through the night.

The Final Day at Thermopylae

Leonidas was alerted by a runner of the Immortals' approach. Knowing he was about to be surrounded, he gathered his commanders in a desperate council.

Some of the Greeks argued that the cause was now lost and a quick retreat was the only course. Others refused to give up the fight, committed to defending the pass.

In the end, most of the Greeks fled. Some, it seems, may have been commanded by the king to go in order that they might live to fight another day. One Spartan, upon being told to go back to tell their story, answered simply, "I came with the army, not to carry messages, but to fight." Another answered, "I should be a better man if I stayed here."[20] In the end, only Leonidas and what remained of his three hundred Spartans stayed, along with a few others who were committed to defending Greece to the bitter end—perhaps two thousand men.

Knowing that the end was near, Leonidas ordered his soldiers away from the wall and out to a broader area of the pass, leaving themselves completely unprotected. If they were doomed, he wanted his forces to have access to as many Persians as was possible.

What must the Persians have thought as they watched the hopelessly outnumbered Greeks, in utter disregard for their own safety, position themselves to inflict the greatest kill?

Even knowing that the Immortals would soon be attacking from the rear of the Greeks, the Persians did not go forth to battle with any eagerness. Indeed, Herodotus records that the Persian soldiers had to be driven again under the sting of their commanders' whips. In addition, "Many of them were pushed into the sea and drowned; far more were trampled alive by each other, with no regard for who perished."[21]

With the Immortals still somewhere on the mountain pass, the Persian slaughter commenced as it had during the two previous mornings.

At some point during the bloody melee, Leonidas was killed. A fierce battle ensued over possession of his body. The Persians wanted it as a trophy. But the Greeks were not going to easily give up the dead body of their noble king. Four times the Persians fought their way toward the body. Four times the fearless Greeks pushed them back. How many died in the fight for the remains of the fallen warrior-king is unknown, but it was many. In the end, the Greeks retained possession of their king's body.

As the battle raged, the Immortals finally appeared, having ended their hurried march along the mountain pass. A handful of soldiers from Thebes separated themselves from the battle and surrendered. All of the others fought on. The Immortals surged forward, fighting from the rear. Surrounded, the Greeks made a courageous last stand. Most of their spears had now been hacked to pieces. They fought on with sword and shield. In the end, they were finally overcome by an onslaught of arrows—the Persians unwilling to finish the task in hand-to-hand combat.

The slaughter lasted but a few hours. Virtually all of the Greeks were killed.

As King Leonidas and his men were being slain in their courageous stand, the Persian navy was again attacking the Greek fleet. Their hope—and expectation—was to claim an identical decisive victory at sea. Yet, despite the fact that the Greeks were so outnumbered, the battle was a draw.

Upon learning of the massacre of Leonidas and his hoplites, the Greek leader Themistocles was forced to withdraw his navy from Artemisium. He sent them south to Salamis, a tiny island in the Saronic Gulf, just west of Athens.[22]

The narrow pass of Thermopylae was finally open. Not only that, but the Persian navy was now free of Greek resistance. Xerxes had reason to rejoice. The lands and resources to the south were within easy marching distance. But looking at the carnage around him, did Xerxes feel any joy? Or did he have to wonder how many bloody fights like this one lay ahead?

For What Purpose?

Other than the slaughter of three hundred Spartans, several thousand other brave Greeks, and maybe twenty thousand Persian soldiers, what had the three fateful days at Thermopylae accomplished?

The significance—and, despite the disheartening outcome, the battle *was* significant—was twofold:

First, the presence of Leonidas's army at Thermopylae permitted the navy of Themistocles to operate at Artemisium. During those several days of storms and brief but fierce battles, the Persians lost hundreds of their ships. The success that the Greeks had in fighting the Persians confirmed that, were it not for the overwhelming advantage in Persian numbers, their ships and sailors were capable of defeating them. That advantage of numbers was at least somewhat narrowed after the debacle at Artemisium.

After witnessing the bravery and skill of the Spartan warriors, Xerxes was greatly sobered. And how could he not be? A handful of Greeks had humiliated his mighty army, striking such fear as to force him to drive his solders forward or into the sea under the crack of Persian whips.

Mulling the gloomy outcome of his victory, he asked his Spartan turncoat, Demaratus, how he could possibly defeat a large army of such courageous men. Demaratus told him that he had to divide his fleet and send three hundred ships around Greece to attack the Peloponnesian Peninsula where the city-state of Sparta was located. If those ships could roam freely around the peninsula, bringing terror, the Spartans would be forced to defend their homeland. Without the Spartans, the rest of the Greeks could easily be conquered. Once Sparta stood alone, they could then be defeated.

And the traitor was certainly right. But it did not matter any longer. After the devastating losses on the seas around Artemisium, Xerxes did not possess the naval forces for such a strategy to succeed. His fleet had been diminished to the point that dividing it was no longer possible.

Second, the battle at Thermopylae was by proper measure not a defeat; rather, it was a clear-cut case of sacrifice for a greater good. To that end, it was successful:

> The death of Leonidas and of the three hundred chosen men from Lacedaemon was seen at the time for what it was: a torch, not to light a funeral pyre, but to light the hitherto divided and irresolute Greek people. . . . Without Thermopylae, there would hardly have been that extraordinary surge of pride throughout Greece which produced the spirit that was to lead to Salamis and Plataea. For the first time in their history a distinct sense of "Greekness" far overriding the almost eternal (and fratricidal) squabbles of their city-states served to unite this brilliant people.[23]

With the fire of Thermopylae burning in their hearts, and knowing that Greeks from throughout the entire peninsula had died in defense of all of Greece, the Persian War of 480 took on an entirely new dimension. Word spread quickly that the Greek army had been wiped out, the great Spartan king killed in a heroic battle at Thermopylae. With the sense that all of Greece was now in real jeopardy, a unity emerged that had never been seen before. United around the memory of those men who had died in defense of all of Greece, former bitter enemies put aside their differences. Some opened their gates to welcome Athenian refugees. Others volunteered their services to Themistocles.

Maybe for the first time in history, something that approached a *national* movement of free men stood together, voluntarily unifying to fight against an empire that sought to take their free will from them.

The Battle Turns upon the Sea

Xerxes and his army passed through Thermopylae, his navy following him along the coast. Determined to make an example for the rest of the Greeks to mull upon, Xerxes' soldiers engaged in wholesale slaughter, rape, and destruction of everything in the little province of Phocis that lay south of Thermopylae. Many city-states, unwilling to endure the fate of Phocis, joined with Xerxes.

Weeks before, Themistocles had told the citizens of Athens to evacuate. Many had followed his advice. As the Persian army approached, panic spread among those that remained, most of them fleeing the city. Three months after crossing the Hellespont, Xerxes came to within sight of Athens, his navy covering his eastern flank. The city was mostly deserted, though a few stalwarts had stayed to defend the Acropolis, the high rock edifice that rises above the rest of the city, home of the gods of Greece. By the first week in September, those brave men had been slaughtered, the sacred site destroyed, the flames illuminating the city like a torch upon the hill.

One must wonder what Xerxes was then thinking, with Athens, deemed to be the capital of the Mediterranean West, smoldering in ruin. It was clear from the beginning of his invasion that his goal was to conquer not only Greece but the entire Mediterranean world. (Xerxes had already negotiated with Carthage, another great Mediterranean power, to support his invasion. As requested, Carthage was simultaneously attacking Greek cities on Sicily to accomplish that joint objective.) As Xerxes watched the Acropolis glow in fire, he must have surrendered to his pride and wondered if all of the Mediterranean, and even all of Europe, would soon be in his grasp. Spain, Italy, southern France, northern Africa? What glory would be his![24]

As for the Greeks, the great question was, "What next?"

The Greek fleet had taken up a defensive position at Salamis, just across a narrow strait from Athens, close enough that Themistocles and his sailors could have watched Athens burn.

With most of the Greek leaders having evacuated to Salamis, a great debate ensued, one that lasted several weeks. Finally, Themistocles convinced his fellow countrymen to fight, convincing them that the only hope they had was to defeat the Persians there and then.

Like a Thermopylae at sea, Salamis was to be their last stand.

By this point in mid-September, Xerxes also faced a crucial decision. His army had quite effectively destroyed the crops of the Grecians as they marauded through the countryside, leaving him totally dependent on his ships for resupply. The Greeks at Salamis were fully capable of harassing or destroying his resupply vessels. Worse, the weather in the Mediterranean was chancy even in the summer; now that it was September, it would only get worse.

His current situation was simply not tenable.

He too decided to stand and fight—and not only to fight, but to engage the Greek navy in a decisive battle that would rid him of the threat for good.

Athens, Greece

THEMISTOCLES KNEW HE and King Leonidas had been betrayed at least twice and maybe many times more. Someone—it had to be a Greek—had told the Persians about the goat trail at Thermopylae. And the former Spartan king, Demaratus, had been seen among the Persians. Who knew what treachery he had committed with Xerxes, what information he had told him of the peninsula, the Spartan soldiers and their training, the local populace, the roads, the water sources and terrain.

Too many Greeks had proven willing to sell their countrymen or lay down their arms. Entire cities had joined with Xerxes, driven by greed or fear. Surely the mighty Xerxes had come to think poorly of his countrymen, expecting a traitor at every turn.

Which was an expectation that Themistocles now planned to take advantage of.

• • •

The Greek stood proudly before the king. He wore the battle dress of a soldier, and he stood tall and firm. He claimed to be a valued servant to Themistocles, even a close friend, and Xerxes watched him carefully, looking down from his mighty throne. Behind him, the ruins of the Acropolis still smoldered. They had been smoldering for days. The Greek held his ground, his eyes bright and unblinking, as if he had no fear.

"Say it again!" Xerxes commanded.

"The men of Themistocles are in disarray," the Greek repeated. Though it ground against his soul to say it, he found the words came surprisingly easy, for most of what he said was true. "Many don't want to fight you, at least not right here and not right now. They have seen your mighty army. Your splendid navy. Their small victories at sea have not brought them comfort. They know what is in store. Some have attempted to escape from Salamis, and many others plan to escape soon. Even Themistocles has threatened to take the two hundred ships of Athens and leave. He talks of sailing away and starting a new colony far from the reach of the mighty Xerxes and your fearful army." The Greek's voice fell almost to a whisper. "Some of the men at Salamis . . . maybe even many . . . would join you, Lord Xerxes, if they saw an appropriate reward."

The men of the court of Xerxes listened. Most of his commanders smiled.

Xerxes looked around, seeing the eagerness on their faces. It was what they had expected, what they had been waiting to hear. The

Greeks were worn and weary. They had sent their best men, given their best battle, and but a few of them had lived. The hordes of Persians had run throughout Greece, taking Athens by storm, burning their holy mountain, cradle of their gods. The Greeks must have watched the fires, smelled the smoke, seen their abandoned city filled with Persian warriors. Though they had won a battle or two at sea, they must have known that they had no real hope of defeating the Persians, not as hopelessly outnumbered as they were.

The shah of Persia raised a hand, motioning for a servant. The man drew near, listened to the master, nodded, and turned around. Moving almost at a run, he went to an ivory-inlaid box, extracted a large map, and laid it at the master's feet. Xerxes pointed at it with a golden scepter, looking at his naval commander. "Salamis is but a few miles off the coast," he said. "Themistocles has his entire navy anchored there."

"Yes, lord, he has hidden his ships out of sight . . ." the commander bent and touched the map . . . "here, behind this small island."

Xerxes looked at the map and thought. "The channels between the mainland and Salamis are very narrow."

"Very narrow, lord."

No one spoke. The commander knew not to interrupt his master with such a look on his face. And the Greek spy had already said everything he had been told to say.

Xerxes moved silently around the chart, always staring down, his dark eyes bright and thoughtful, his face calm. "Very narrow channels," he repeated. "So when they try to flee, they will have to exit through either the channel on the west or to the east. If we divide our forces, we can guard both means of escape. If we position our best naval forces here," he indicated toward the western channel, "we can stop the Greeks from escaping to the west. The Egyptians proved themselves very worthy at the battle of Artemisium. Send them there. At the same time, we will position other naval squadrons to attack and keep them from fleeing to the east."

The naval commander thought, then nodded. There were great risks in dividing his forces, he knew, but it seemed like a reasonable plan. And even if it weren't, there was no way he was going to argue with the king.

Xerxes looked around at his commanders, all of whom were itching for a fight. "Wait until dark," he commanded, "then send the Egyptian ships to cover the western channel of escape. Position our other forces on the east. Tell them to row into position and wait there. Keep their oarsmen at the ready. I care not how cold or tired or hungry they become. Tell them if they let *a single* ship escape, I will have that captain's and his oarsmen's heads! I want to destroy them all, you understand that? Not a single Greek ship survives!"

The commander nodded, his head low.

Xerxes looked at the top of his head and smiled. "Tomorrow, this war is won," he said.

The orders given, the Persian commanders prepared their ships and men for battle. Night came and they slipped into the channel, their oars forming white lines of wake that were barely illuminated by the moon.

Soon after the dark had settled, the Greek traitor slipped away as well. Before midnight, he was back at the camp of Themistocles, giving his report. His reward for such bravery was worth the personal risk that he had taken, for Themistocles awarded the loyal slave not only his freedom but also great wealth.

Early in the morning, as the sun was just beginning to turn the eastern horizon gray, Themistocles walked among his battle-ready ships. The truth was, he had understood, even from the very beginning of the Persian invasion, how it would more or less unfold. He knew that Athens would eventually be taken and so had ordered its evacuation well before the battle at Thermopylae. He knew that the primary benefit of his action at Artemisium was to learn what he needed to know for a decisive confrontation at Salamis. Still, he could hardly believe his good fortune. The Persians, believing the words of his planted spy, had chosen to split their forces, an unimaginably foolish thing to do! The *only* advantage the Persians had was their superior numbers. Once they split their naval forces, they threw that advantage to the wind!

So it was that, as morning broke, he stood upon the beach and pictured in his mind where the Persian forces now lay. The Egyptians were far to the west and no threat to him any longer—not for a time, at least. The other Persian ships were lined up in almost single file, ready to attack through the narrow channel to the east.

The gods had given just what he had asked for, which was only a level battlefield.

The next morning, on September 20, one month after the fall of Thermopylae, the battle began.

Expecting a great victory and wanting to see it for himself, Xerxes had ordered his gold throne positioned on a high point overlooking the Salamis Channel. The sight of his powerful fleet made his heart skip a beat. Though the number of ships he still commanded had been reduced—many had been lost in previous battles or storms at sea—he still looked upon a mass of sails. Many hundreds. Maybe still a thousand! Lined up to enter the channel, his ships were packed so close together they looked like ants on a trail. And what did the Greeks have to stand against him? On the high side, his commanders had estimated the Greeks might have between three and four hundred ships. Being so outnumbered, the Greeks would be destroyed.

The Final Battle

The exact details of what happened that fateful day are not certain. One historian has said of the battle that "despite its momentous importance, Salamis must be regarded as one of the worst-documented battles in the whole history of naval warfare."[25] But the following seems to be generally agreed upon.

Xerxes ordered his fleet into the channel from the east, a narrow enough body of water that the fleet had to deploy strung out in a long line. As they entered the channel, they saw about fifty Greek ships under sail, apparently trying to escape to the west.

The Persians might have assumed that these were the last of the Greek ships. Surely the others had escaped to the west during the night and even now were being destroyed by the Egyptians!

But the truth was very different. The rest of the Greek fleet was still hidden behind the small island off Salamis.

Encouraged by the sight of what appeared to be the last of the fleeing Greeks, the Persians continued up the channel after them.

From behind the island, more Greek ships appeared. Perhaps these were the last of the cowards running?

The Persians entered farther into the narrow channel.

Suddenly, a third group of Greek ships emerged from behind the island. But these did not run! They struck at the flank of the Persian fleet, now well strung out. Then, as if on signal, the Greeks at the far west of the channel suddenly turned and attacked the Persians from the front.

The Persians were trapped. Unable to maneuver in the narrow channel, their ships began to run into each other. Pressed from the front and the side by the Greeks, and from the rear by their own ships, mass confusion ensued.

The Greeks quickly circled the mass of Persian ships. Working together, they attacked at will, picking them off one by one.

All of this unfolded as the mighty king of Persia watched from his throne atop the hill. It is believed that his courtiers were assigned the task of keeping track of which Persian captains fought and which ones fled.

Xerxes' fleet included a contingent of Phoenicians, believed to be the greatest sailors of their time. Several Phoenician captains were forced to run their ships aground. Foolishly, they made their way to Xerxes, who had them beheaded on the spot.

One description of the last of the battle reads:

> A vast mass of Persian ships—many of them badly crippled, with trailing spars and cordage, oars broken off short, timbers sheared or sprung by those terrible bronze-sheathed rams, went streaming away past Psyttaleia towards Phaleron. The water was thick with corpses and wreckage.[26]

Mercifully, the night eventually came.[27]

• • •

From the records, it appears that about forty Greek triremes had been destroyed, against two hundred Persian ships. Those numbers, however, did not reflect how much the Greeks had inflicted in both physical destruction and psychological damage to the Persians.

In fact, the Persian fleet was in now in dire straits. Most definitely, it was badly demoralized. The Phoenicians, humiliated by the defeat at the hands of the Greeks and angry at the treatment of their captains by Xerxes, revolted and left. The remainder of the navy attempted to repair their ships and look for replacements for lost crew members, but their hearts were never in it.

Xerxes was in a deadly predicament. He understood how badly his navy had been beaten. He also understood that September was moving on and soon it would be impossible to count on shipping safely across the Aegean Sea. Remembering how dependent he was upon the critical bridge at Hellespont, he worried that the Greeks might destroy it, leaving him with no way to retreat to Asia.

Having little option, Xerxes sent his navy home. Shortly thereafter, he followed, accompanied by a large force for his own protection, returning to his capital in Susa. He left behind the bulk of his army under the command of his cousin, instructing him to carry on the occupation of conquered Greece.

Little did he know that his conquest would be of short duration.

One year later, the Persians were defeated at the Battle of Plataea. Led by the Spartans, the Greek army mustered a unified force of perhaps seventy thousand men, the largest ever assembled in Greek history. The unity that they displayed, while unusual, was not so remarkable in light of what they had learned at Thermopylae and Salamis. Throughout the battle, they fought with the confidence of winners, while the Persians' memory of Thermopylae and Salamis was very different.

The same day that the Persian army was defeated at Plataea, Xerxes' navy suffered a decisive defeat at Mycale, across the Aegean Sea. The survivors of the Persian army hurried back across the Hellespont.

It would be the last Asian army to invade Europe for many centuries.[28]

Why It Matters

The Greeks won the great war. Some have declared that fact to be a miracle in and of itself, especially in light of the deceit of so many Greeks and Greek city-states. Many of the Greeks were cowards. Many had their loyalty easily purchased. Some have suggested that even the religious icons at Delphi, those oracles who supposedly revealed the will of the gods, had been bought off by Xerxes and told to send unusually dire or misleading messages. Political in-fighting between city-states and within the political structure continually weakened the cause.

Simply put, there is no way to paint all of the Greeks as noble and brave and full of high purpose, which makes the story even more remarkable. And it puts those true heroes of this extraordinary victory in an even more exalted light—King Leonidas and Themistocles in particular.

But it must be understood that the most important element of the Greeks' victory had little to do with their military success. What mattered most was not the fact that a brave and freedom-loving people struggled against a tyrant and won—though that message is of great consequence. Far more important was the survival of the Greek city-states so that they could continue the development of a belief in the importance of the individual, self-government, reason, and all of the advances in the arts and sciences that came from adoption of those values.

The Persians, for all their grandeur and might, left very little to the world of lasting value. Theirs was a static society with one goal: the maintenance of an absolute, theocratic state. Had the Persians been victorious, the world would have been very different.

As one historian has said:

> Against this monolithic opposition the Greek achievement stands out all the more clearly, an inexplicable miracle. We sometimes take it for granted that democratic institutions should have evolved in the city-states from Solon's day onwards, reaching their apogee in the Persian Wars and the

fifty years which followed. Nothing could be further from the predictable course of events. Free scientific enquiry, free political debate, annually appointed magistrates, decision by majority vote—all these things ran flat counter to the whole pattern of thought in any major civilisation with which the Greeks had to deal.[29]

When Alexander the Great and his army spread the Greek ideas of knowledge and self-government throughout the Eastern Mediterranean and to the East, they became the dominant culture of that part of the world. Later, the Romans carried the Greek culture even farther, spreading the Greeks' love of learning and recognition of the individual and self-government to what is now Europe.

The invaluable mixture of these values, along with those of the Jewish faith and Christianity, made the Western world what it is today.

That much is indisputably true. Had the Greeks not survived, all of us living now—even though we represent but a tiny fraction of all the people who have lived upon this earth—likely would not have the fruits of freedom that we enjoy today.

Middle Eastern scholar Bernard Lewis claims that "the accessibility of Hellenistic culture, Jewish religion and Roman polity all helped to prepare the way for the rise and spread of Christianity,"[30] and that

> the Roman State and the Christian Churches were profoundly affected by Greek culture. Both of them contributed to its wider dissemination. . . . In their religion, too, the early Christians were concerned with philosophical subtleties of a kind that had long preoccupied the Greeks, but had never much troubled either the Romans or the Jews. The Christian scripture, the New Testament, was written in a language . . . unmistakably Greek. Even the Old Testament was available in a Greek translation, made centuries earlier in the Greek-speaking Jewish community of Alexandria.[31]

Such assistance, influence, and help would not have been there had Thermopylae and Salamis not happened:

> We may have forgotten, that had Greece become the westernmost province of Persia, in time Greek family farms would have become estates for the Great King. . . . In place of Hellenic philosophy and science, there would have been only the subsidized arts of divination and astrology, which were the appendages of imperial or religious bureaucracies and not governed by unfettered rational inquiry. In a Persian Greece, local councils would be mere puppet bodies . . . , history the official diaries and edicts of the Great King. . . .
>
> . . . We would live under a much different tradition today—one where writers are under death sentences, women secluded and veiled, free speech curtailed, government in the hands of the autocrat's extended family, universities mere centers of religious zealotry, and the thought police in our living rooms and bedrooms.[32]

Such were the stakes in the battles of the Persians over Greece. The development of freedom and self-government hung in the balance.

So it is that, as another essayist has said, "A little of Leonidas lies in the fact that I can go where I like and write what I like. He contributed to set us free."[33]

Notes

1. The Greek historian Herodotus, who is considered the father of history, reported many of the conversations between the former Spartan king Demaratus and the Persian king Xerxes. See Herodotus VII (translated by George Rawlinson), at http://classics.mit.edu/Herodotus/history.7.vii.html. See also Herodotus, *Histories;* "Herodotus," in *Cambridge History of Classical Greek Literature.*
2. Plumb, in *Greeks,* xxi. See also Botsford and Robinson, *Hellenic History.*
3. Cowley, *What If?* 21.
4. Botsford and Robinson, *Hellenic History,* 52, 53–54. See same for general discussion of the city-state, 52–57.

5. See ibid., 84–98, for a discussion of the evolution of Athenian democracy.

6. Ibid., 125.

7. Cowley, *What If?* 18–19.

8. For more information on the Persian Empire, see Curtis and Tallis, *Forgotten Empire.* See also the British Museum at http://www.thebritishmuseum.ac.uk /forgottenempire/persia/later.html.

9. Botsford and Robinson, *Hellenic History,* 127.

10. The ancient city of Troy was located near the southern mouth of the strait. In 334 BC, Alexander the Great and his Greek army crossed the Dardanelles in the opposite direction to invade Persia.

11. See Cowley, *What If?* 24. As with many historical facts, the reports of ancient sources are sometimes suspect. Herodotus was born shortly before the battles of Thermopylae and Salamis, and though a dedicated historian, he did not want to pass up the opportunity to bolster the glory of the ancient Greeks. Modern estimates vary significantly.

12. Bradford, *Thermopylae,* 72.

13. For a full description of the geography of Greece and the weaponry of the two sides, see ibid., 67–74.

14. For a full description of Greek/Persian naval ships and tactics, see ibid., 75–79; Strauss, *Battle of Salamis,* xvii–xxi.

15. For a description of the events leading to the Persian Wars and the events prior to the Battle of Thermopylae, see Botsford and Robinson, *Hellenic History,* 122–39; Bradford, *Thermopylae,* 13–100; Cowley, *What If?* 17–26.

16. The Spartan life is described in Bradford, *Thermopylae,* 58–66.

17. See http://penelope.uchicago.edu/Thayer/E/Roman/Texts/Plutarch/Moralia /Sayings_of_Spartans*/main.html.

18. Many well-known quotes are attributed to King Leonidas before and during the battle at Thermopylae, some of which are depicted here. See Herodotus, *Histories.*

19. See Bradford, *Thermopylae,* 127.

20. See http://penelope.uchicago.edu/Thayer/E/Roman/Texts/Plutarch/Moralia /Sayings_of_Spartans*/main.html.

21. Herodotus, VII.223.3.

22. For a full account of the Battle of Thermopylae, see Botsford and Robinson, *Hellenic History* 139–46; Bradford, *Thermopylae,* 101–53; Green, *Greco-Persian Wars,* 109–53. It should be noted that the dates are best estimates. Most experts agree that the battles of Thermopylae and Salamis occurred in August and September, 480 BC, but the exact days are disputed. We have used those from Bradford, *Thermopylae.*

23. Bradford, *Thermopylae,* 148. See also Green, *Greco-Persian Wars,* 143, 146.

24. For insight into Xerxes' ambition, see Bradford, *Thermopylae,* 171–72. For a

discussion of the Carthaginian invasion of Sicily, see Bradford, *Thermopylae,* 154–62; Botsford and Robinson, *Hellenic History,* 151–54.

25. Green, *Greco-Persian Wars,* 186.

26. Ibid., 195.

27. For information about the events after Thermopylae, including the battle at Salamis, see Botsford and Robinson, *Hellenic History,* 146–50; Bradford, *Thermopylae,* 163–201; Cowley, *What If?* 26–35; Green, *Greco-Persian Wars,* 153–98; Strauss, *Battle of Salamis.*

28. For information about the events after Salamis, see Botsford and Robinson, *Hellenic History,* 151; Bradford, *Thermopylae,* 202–45; Cowley, *What If?* 17–35; Green, *Greco-Persian Wars,* 201–87; Strauss, *Battle of Salamis,* 211–52.

29. Green, *Greco-Persian Wars,* 5.

30. Lewis, *Middle East,* 32.

31. Ibid., 34–35.

32. Cowley, *What If?* 19.

33. Quoted in Green, *Greco-Persian Wars,* 287.

Chapter 3

Miracle at the Bridge

If you are delivered of a child [before I come home],
if it is a boy keep it, if a girl, discard it.
LETTER WRITTEN BY A ROMAN SOLDIER IN
ALEXANDRIA TO HIS WIFE (1 BC)[1]

T he world's quest toward freedom was long and slow in coming.
Many generations passed without seeing much change, the years
slipping by in a state of nearly status quo.

The next significant shift toward a world of freedom entailed, however, a titanic shift. Taking place almost eight hundred years after the
Greeks had chased the Persian army from their lands, this development
would, for the first time in human history, shift the focus from the
Eastern world to the West.

Rome, Italy
AD 300

THEY LIVED MUCH AS THEIR ancestors had lived since the beginning of
recorded history. Nearly all of the major advances in technology, science, medicine, or agriculture would take place in generations yet to
come. The invention of the heavy-wheeled plow was still two hundred

years away, horse collars almost another two hundred years after that, both developments essential to the efficient use of land, leaving most of the entire population one dry summer away from starvation. The answer for most sickness was still a good bleeding, and a constant diet of barley, roots, and wheat left a scourge of malnutrition. Most of their clothes were rough wool that chafed the skin, and the pervasive smell of smoke that permeated their garments acted as a kind of barrier to hold the smell of unwashed skin and perspiration in.

It was a difficult time in nearly every way.

The Jew was only thirty, though he looked much older. But then, everyone did. The world aged one quickly in his day and time, and those fortunate enough to live through adolescence were quickly absorbed in the battle to live to middle age. He had wide teeth and thin hair and a tense face, but he smiled quickly and laughed on occasion, his brown eyes bright and alive. There were men in Rome who had more to complain about, but there weren't many. Yet Josephus seemed almost naively unaware of how difficult his life was. Because of this, he was grateful for every good thing that he received. Every plate of food. Every cup of wine. Every day without harassment. Every night without a Roman soldier slamming on his door.

Over the past year, two of his fellow Christian Jews had been taken away. One had been seized during a worship meeting, his body found crucified beside one of the side roads leading into the city. Forbidden to be removed for burial, his bones were eventually picked dry by the birds. The second man had never been heard from again, his wife and three children left destitute.

Sometimes Josephus had to wonder which was more of a curse: his Jewish fathers or the new religion that he had devoutly accepted into his life. Both of them were great blessings, but those blessings came at a steep price.

Though he was a commoner, he was as successful as a Christian could be. Having developed an extraordinary talent for quick and elegant script, he was paid by the Roman Empire to be a scribe, taking notes from the dozens of contracts, agreements, treaties, or business deals that were made in the senate or by a magistrate every day and putting them into written form where they could be agreed upon and signed. It was tedious work, not appreciated as it should be, but essential to managing an empire such as the Romans had built.

He and his wife had been married for five years—she was just over ten years his junior. Tonight they sat quietly at the small table by the fire. A four-month-old slept in her arms. The small bed beside the table held two other children, both of them younger than four. It was early morning, the sun still an hour from rising on the low hills that lined the east side of the Tiber River (gift of Tiberinus, the river god, one of the many Roman gods that the Christians didn't worship). Though it was early, Josephus knew that time was growing short. The garbage pile would be crowded before the sun was up.

His nephew showed at the half-open door. Josephus nodded to let him in, poured a cup of goat's milk, dropped in a couple of crusts of black bread, and placed it in his hands. The boy downed the food in three gulps, his hunger showing, then waited for any final instructions.

"Go, boy!" the older man told him as he shooed him out the door. "You'll have to run if you are to find anything of worth."

Forty minutes later, the boy was rummaging through the enormous garbage piles that accumulated in the stinking dell outside the massive city walls. Rome, with her million citizens, many of whom were rich and powerful, threw away enough food every day to feed hundreds, and he wasn't alone atop the pile of rotting trash. Digging through the refuse, no longer smelling the rot and decay, he uncovered a string of potato peelings and smiled eagerly. Dropping to his knees, he dug tenderly with his little fingers, not wanting to miss anything. More peelings. Fresh. No more than two days old. He gathered two full handfuls and jammed them into a large pocket on his wool smock, then stood and stepped across the pile again.

Although he was grateful for food, he was there for something else.

Sometimes the wealthy Romans threw away scraps of usable wood. His uncle had tasked him to scavenge the garbage dump, searching for the best pieces, which he would use to build various items of crude furniture: small tables, cribs, beds, and chairs. These he sold to supplement his income, sharing a small portion with the boy.

Flies gathering around his face, the boy suddenly heard a frightening sound. At first, it was so weak it was almost lost in the buzz of the flies and gentle wind, so he cocked his head and listened, holding very still. Yes! There it was again.

The first instinct he felt was a violent urge to run. But he forced himself to stand, his heart leaping to his throat.

Turning his head, he looked to his right. Nothing could be seen. No movement. Now the sound was gone. He almost breathed in relief.

Then he heard the cry again.

Moving carefully, he crawled two paces, then stopped and listened once again. Weak as a bird, the muffled cry sounded once more, closer now. Feeling his way forward, the boy pushed aside the trash.

The infant was very young, no more than a day or two old. Dark-skinned and dark-haired, she squinted at the rising sun and cried. The boy lifted her naked body from the garbage and studied the hungry face. Feeling the touch of human hands around her shoulders, the child opened her eyes and looked at him, sucking hungrily on her tiny fists.

He studied her carefully, counting her toes and fingers, looking in her mouth and eyes and ears. Brushing aside some dirt from her concave belly, he fingered the drying umbilical cord. She settled down and seemed to look at him, then started crying in hunger once again.

It was a strong cry now. Demanding. More forceful.

He looked around in panic. What was he supposed to do, throw her back onto the pile? Cover her with garbage so her cries wouldn't be heard? No! The Romans might have done that, but there was no way that he, a Christian, could. He would have laid down his own life before he would have let her die—such had been ingrained into him from the day he was born. But that didn't change the practicalities of what to do with the child. Who would accept responsibility for the infant? What family needed yet another mouth to feed?

He turned left and right. None of the other scavengers had seen him with the baby. Still frightened, but now more certain, he decided what to do.

Tucking her under his smock, he turned and ran.

And though he didn't know it, the little boy's decision to save the child represented an enormous change that was about to settle on the world.

Why the World Was Ripe to Be Taken

Before we can fully understand the significant impact that Christianity had on the progress of freedom in the world, we need to leap forward fifteen hundred years and examine why the world was so prepared to be influenced by the Western values that had evolved since the birth of Christ.

By the sixteenth century, the foundation for better days in human progress had been firmly put in place, but those days were still a long time ahead.

As Europe commenced a dramatic era of exploration, it is worth noting that the world left behind by Europe's explorers and conquerors was, in many respects, a good place to *get away* from. Europe was a nasty, brutal place. Having just emerged from the era referred to as the Dark Ages, the entire continent suffered from famine, plagues, and never-ending political upheaval. Power was concentrated in a handful of dysfunctional monarchies and institutions, and the day-to-day life of the masses was full of fear and discontent.

There were a few things to commend about the continent, but there was also much to condemn.

It is interesting to note, then, that as these explorers, conquistadors, and missionaries left their European homes to discover, convert, and exploit the lands and peoples of the Americas, Asia, and Africa, they were genuinely surprised at what they found. Though a few of these distant lands contained elements of advanced civilizations, none of them could begin to compare with Europe. When these explorers considered the dreariness of their homelands, they were astonished to learn that, compared with most of what they found, there was something extraordinary about their own culture. This was particularly true in areas of science and technology. As colonization began in earnest, the superiority of European technology, especially in the area of arms and armament, allowed them to subjugate the new lands with relative ease.

In the Americas, the advanced civilizations of the Incas and the Aztecs fell before a mere handful of Spanish soldiers. All of the major powers in Asia and Africa were subdued without much resistance, either colonized outright or thoroughly dominated by European powers.

As time passed, the West increased its influence over these far-flung lands in culture, political systems, and philosophy. As the West evolved its own political and philosophical identity to include personal freedom, self-government, equality, and the rule of law, these concepts were adopted by more and more of the world's distant lands and cultures.

Yet, just a few generations before, the Europeans had *lagged far behind* many of the peoples that they would soon conquer. Just a short time before they began their conquests, the Europeans could not have been favorably compared to the great civilizations of Islam or the advanced peoples of China, India, or the Americas.

What happened to allow the Europeans to leapfrog other cultures?

What allowed the people of the sixteenth-century West to excel in science and technology? Then, having done that, how did they come to embrace a love of freedom, self-government, equality, and the rule of law, principles that would distinguish them from the rest of the world in the most profound of ways?

The simple answer can be found in one word: *Christianity.*

And the story of how Europe became a bastion of Christianity begins with a Roman emperor who lived twelve centuries before the European explorers—and a miracle at a bridge.

We will tell this story in a moment.

But first we must ask if it was good.

For Good or Evil?

It is impossible to overstate the enormously positive impact of Christianity on the West's advancement in technology, wealth, and political thought.

But that is not the popularly understood view. Indeed, it is just the opposite.

If one were to try to gauge the average person's opinion of the role of Christianity in the development of the West, that person would likely say that it was an obstacle that had to be overcome—that religion in general, and Christianity in particular, stood in the way of progress at every opportunity. As just one example that captures this intellectual sentiment, Phillip Jenkins, a noted historian and writer who is considered a moderate voice in evaluating Christianity's impact on world history, wrote: "Between 450 and 650 AD, during what I have called the 'Jesus Wars,' inter-Christian conflicts and purges killed hundreds of thousands, and all but wrecked the Roman Empire."[2]

For more than a generation, sentiments such as this, and many others much more harsh, have been taught in most high school and college history classes, repeated by public figures, emphasized by intellectuals, and accepted as fact by many cultural and media elites.

But in many cases, that assessment oversimplifies what happened. And some of the cases of the most severe criticism simply aren't true.

Professor and author Thomas E. Woods has mustered convincing evidence to establish the overwhelmingly positive role of Christianity (as it was then personified in the Roman Catholic church) during the era after the fall of the Roman Empire. The church offered major contributions in the development of civilization, science, and free governments:

1. It was the Catholic church that was responsible for what has become known as the scientific revolution through its creation of the university system.

2. Catholic priests were pioneers in the fields of geology, Egyptology, astronomy, and atomic theory.

3. Medieval monasteries were responsible for either preserving from classical times (generally accepted as the era of the Greeks and Romans), or initiating on their own, significant advances in agriculture.

4. Medieval monasteries pioneered the use of water power, factories, and metallurgy.

5. The church was pivotal in the preservation of the written words of the ancients—perhaps even literacy itself.

6. Early Christian theology was the foundation of the Western legal system (the rule of law) as well as international law.

7. Christian philosophy led to challenges to slavery in both the Old and New Worlds.

8. And, of great import, the moral code of the West, including belief in the sanctity of human life and marriage, derived from Christian teachings.

Despite these achievements, great negativity has crept into modern thinking when it comes to evaluating the influence of Christianity in human progress. Many contend that religious faith is at the root of most of the world's historical woes, blaming it for poverty, war, atrocities, bloodshed, genocide, slavery, and even the most subtle intolerance or personal bigotry. *How many wars have been fought, how many people killed, in the name of religion?* The question is frequently asked.

Woods responds to this viewpoint:

> That Western civilization stands indebted to the Church for the university system, charitable work, international law, the sciences, important legal principles, and much else besides has not exactly been impressed upon them with terrific zeal. Western civilization owes far more to the Catholic Church than most people—Catholics included—often realize. The Church, in fact, built Western civilization.
>
> Western civilization does not derive entirely from Catholicism, of course; one can scarcely deny the importance of ancient Greece and Rome or the various Germanic tribes that succeeded the Roman Empire in the West as formative influences on our civilization. The Church

repudiated none of these traditions, and in fact absorbed and learned from the best of them. What is striking, though, is how in popular culture the substantial—and essential—Catholic contribution has gone relatively unnoticed.[3]

Another scholar who has devoted much of his career to writing on this subject, Rodney Stark,[4] explains in a number of his works how Christianity affected the development of the West. He argues that it was Christianity's devotion to reason that distinguished it from other religious faiths and allowed its adherents to progress as they did:

> While the other world religions emphasized mystery and intuition, Christianity alone embraced reason and logic as the primary guide to religious truth. . . . [F]rom early days, the church fathers taught that reason was the supreme gift from God and the means to *progressively increase* their understanding of scripture and revelation. . . . Encouraged by the Scholastics and embodied in the great medieval universities founded by the church, faith in the power of reason infused Western culture, stimulating the pursuit of science and the evolution of democratic theory and practice.[5]

Another author, David Brog, argues that the early Christian Jews were the first champions of human rights. For example, even among the most civilized cultures, they were the first—and many times the only—defenders of infants and children.

> The Romans were proud practitioners of infanticide. So were the Greeks before them. Both Plato and Aristotle recommended that the state adopt a policy of killing deformed infants. The Roman philosopher Seneca wrote approvingly of the common practice of drowning abnormal or weak children at birth. The earliest known Roman legal code, written in 450 BCE, permitted fathers to kill any "deformed or weak" male infant or any female infant, no matter how

healthy. Indeed, female babies were the primary victims of Roman infanticide.[6]

Brog goes on to show that the Judeo-Christian values were instrumental in compelling individuals to respect and even to fight for the rights of others, even those outside of their own family, group, or people.[7]

Early Christians campaigned against the totalitarian powers of Roman emperors and European kings. Later Christians would act as emissaries for peace, fighting against the horrors of slavery and for the rights of the "Indians" found in the New World. Women's suffrage found a home in Christian churches. Many of the civil rights movements of our modern time were supported by Christian organizations, and, for generations, Christians have worked to alleviate hunger and disease. Even today, hundreds of millions of dollars are raised and dispensed by Christian charities.

It seems clear, when evaluating Christianity's overall influence on the world, that it has been good. And in very specific ways, particularly its advancing the rule of reason, its influence has been irreplaceable.

Guns, Reason, and the Local Candle Store?

When the European explorers and conquerors began their journeys to the Americas, Asia, and Africa, why did they possess the technological superiority that they did?

Many have argued that the early Western advancements in steel, guns, sailing ships, and agriculture that allowed the early explorers to conquer so many parts of the world were nothing but a lucky draw in the game of human progress. Others argue that the West's main advantage lay in its superior geography or natural resources. Stark responds by pointing out that other civilizations had even greater advantages in natural resources than did Europe. He then asks: Without any natural, geographical, or otherwise environmental advantage, why *did* the Europeans excel in the making of steel, guns, ships, and agriculture?

The answer is this: because the Europeans were more steeped in logic and reason, the critical seedbeds of technological advancement.

How is it that Christianity created a culture that was committed to reason and logic? Part of the answer is found in the fact that "Christian theologians have devoted centuries to reasoning about what God may have really meant by various passages in scripture."[8] This wrestling with scripture, applying logic and reasoning, involved large numbers of Christians over a long period of time and resulted in occasional shifts in doctrine based upon that strenuous exercise of the mind. Regardless of the correctness of the result (that is, the authenticity of the doctrine), it is impossible to deny the impact that this active and incessant reliance on logic and reasoning had inside the Christian faith.[9]

From its inception, it has been accepted within Christianity that it is not necessary to rely upon faith alone in accepting Christian doctrine. For the first time in history, it was allowed that faith in conjunction with reason was an acceptable tenet.[10] For example, Clement of Alexandria, a theologian of Christianity's second century, explained:

> Do not think that we say that these things are only to be received by faith, but also that they are to be asserted by reason. For indeed it is not safe to commit these things to bare faith without reason, since assuredly truth cannot be without reason.[11]

Part of the answer for why the West advanced technologically as rapidly as it did lies in the emergence of capitalism in Europe, the system whereby industry and commerce are controlled not by the government but by the people who operate them to make a profit. Even critics of capitalism must admit that it has resulted in the creation of more productivity and wealth than any other political or economic system in the world.

Capitalism was a system that evolved distinctly and uniquely in the West, its beginnings traced to the large Christian monasteries that sprang up throughout much of Europe. There is no reason that it could not have been the product of the peoples of China, India, or Islam, but for the fact that they did not adopt the Christian beliefs that placed such high value on individual choice and agency.

Christianity led to capitalism. Capitalism emphasized individualism, hard work, personal reward and failure.[12] This allowed for the creation of wealth and economic opportunity, which then led to technological advancements in the West.

Two other things to consider: First, capitalism could emerge only in cultures where individual freedom existed. Such places only existed in the Christian West. The importance of this cannot be overstated.

Second, it was Christianity's devotion to reason and logic that resulted in the pursuit of science and technological advances. Some cultures may have dabbled in scientific discovery in very narrow fields, but it was only in Europe that science truly developed. For example, while other civilizations may have taken baby steps into alchemy and astrology, it was only in Europe that these musings evolved into chemistry and astronomy. The fundamental belief structures of other faiths and cultures, with their focus on mysticism or polytheism, simply did not motivate their followers to develop scientific knowledge, as did Christianity.[13]

Christianity was devoted to an attempt to understand the purpose of God's creations. If God created the world, the Christian asks, for what purpose? If God is bound by certain natural laws, what are they?

Stark explains:

> The rise of science was not an extension of classical learning. It was the natural outgrowth of Christian doctrine: nature exists because it was created by God. In order to love and honor God, it is necessary to fully appreciate the wonders of his handiwork. Because God is perfect, his handiwork functions in accord with *immutable principles.* By the full use of our God-given powers of reason and observation, it ought to be possible to discover these principles.[14]

As a result, the university system that was developed by the Catholic church during the Middle Ages was the place where scientific inquiry was nurtured and reached significant high points:

Historians have marveled at the extent to which intellectual debate in those universities was free and unfettered. The exaltation of human reason and its capabilities, a commitment to rigorous and rational debate, a promotion of intellectual inquiry and scholarly exchange—all sponsored by the Church—provided the framework for the Scientific Revolution, which was unique to Western civilization.[15]

Freedom Was the Fruit

What about the concepts of individual freedom, liberty, equality, self-government, and rule of law? Where did these concepts come from?

"This too was a victory of reason."[16]

The ancients believed that the gods alone determined their lives and personal conduct. It was all fate.

Christians taught that there was such a thing as agency, or free will; that we are responsible for our own conduct; that God rewards and punishes based upon the exercise of our free will, not on fate or luck or whim. This distinctive belief—extraordinarily rare in other world religions—is one of the most fundamental of all Christian beliefs.

It was this belief that led Christians to contend that all should have the right to exercise free will, and that depriving one of the right to exercise free will through slavery was wrong. That is why, by about the tenth century, slavery was almost obliterated in Europe, then eventually throughout the New World colonies as well. This is important to recognize, especially in light of the fact that moral opposition to slavery is not universally the teaching of other faiths.[17]

Belief in the equality of the individual is also a uniquely Christian concept. The message of Jesus Christ was simple: whether male or female, bond or free, Jew, Greek, or Roman, all were equal before God. Christian theologians, following the end of written scripture, also expressed this teaching. For example, one third-century Christian theologian, L. Caecilius Firmianus Lactantius, wrote, "'The second constituent of Justice is *equality*. I mean this . . . in the sense of treating others as one's equal. . . . For God who gives being and life to me wished us all to be equal.'"[18]

Another of the most important foundations for Western political thought is the belief that certain rights are derived from God, not from man. This principle of "natural rights" is most eloquently expressed in the Declaration of Independence. "We hold these truths to be self-evident, that all men are created equal, that they are endowed by their Creator with certain unalienable Rights, that among these are Life, Liberty, and the pursuit of Happiness."

Some contend that this idea was the product of the brilliant political thinkers of the seventeenth century, John Locke being the most masterful and eloquent of them all. But the concept of natural rights dates much further back than that, deriving almost exclusively from original Christian theology.[19] Long before the European philosophers and the Founding Fathers, early Christian philosophers contemplated and wrote about these concepts, exploring agency and the rights of the individual versus the role of government.

Locke's own views on equality and freedom were so thoroughly the result of his Christian beliefs that one commentator suggests that Locke's *Two Treatises of Government* is "saturated with Christian assumptions" and that "Jesus Christ (and Saint Paul) may not appear in person in the text of the *Two Treatises* but their presence can hardly be missed."[20]

The teachings of Christian scripture supported other concepts that became essential foundations of Western political thought, including the recognition of private property rights and limitations on the power of kings. Limiting the power of the monarch results in the ascendancy of the rule of law—that is to say, when the king himself must abide by the rules, everyone else must, and the rule of law is established as supreme.

The most enduring example of the implementation of these religious teachings was the imposition of the Magna Carta on England's King John in 1215. It was the combination of church officials and royalty that forced this document upon the English king. This magnificent document became the foundation for the protection of individual rights, private property, capitalism and free trade, the separation of the church from the government, prohibitions and limitations on the power of kings, and the establishment of the House of Lords, a small but highly significant step toward the creation of a parliament and emergence of self-government and democracy.[21]

Another scholar explains that the nature of the covenant relationship between God and His people is the foundation for the covenant relationship that is known as constitutionalism, making possible the idea that "We the People of the United States" could unite to create a constitution to protect our God-given rights.

This same scholar shows that Christianity is the foundation of the Western legal system that is designed to protect our freedom.[22]

Not Without Sin

In discussing the impacts of Christianity upon the emergence of Western culture, it would be foolish—and painfully obvious—were we not to acknowledge a disappointing historical fact:

Those who professed belief in Christianity were far from perfect. For ages, Christian churches have been the home of many corrupt men and women, and, far too often, sinful conduct has been displayed in the name of Christianity. Too many governments, church officials, and individuals have, in the name of Christianity, been responsible for historical episodes that cannot be called anything but evil. Some professing Christianity have displayed grievous examples of extravagance, lust, gluttony, greed, and every other of the seven deadly sins.

For too long, the Christian church attempted to keep the people under its control by withholding the holy scriptures from them. In the name of Christianity, some scientific and technological advances have been blocked.

The evil to be found in those chapters of history where the church attempted to purify itself through inquisition is well-known. Far too many wars have been waged in the name of Christianity, or a favored sect of Christianity, and millions of innocents have died as a result of those wars.

The mixed history of Christianity has been summarized as follows:

> Christianity, like other faiths, produced double-sided effects, its community often having been made up of healers who killed and killers who healed. In the name of Jesus, believers have engaged in humble acts of mercy and justice. Also in the name of their exalted Lord, Christians have engaged in often violent acts of power and dominion.[23]

Yet while it is true that the professed followers of Christianity have not always been a source of advancing the common good, we should not let this tragic fact blind us to the overwhelmingly positive impact that Christianity has had upon the world.

The Christian Church Was Not the Only Source of Good

It is also true that Christianity is not the only explanation for the rise of Western civilization. The examples of the Greek city-states and the Roman Republic, with their various experiments in democracy, were vitally important to those European political philosophers of the seventeenth and eighteenth centuries who pronounced the philosophical foundations for self-government. Many of the ideas and institutions of these classical giants were adopted by the Europeans, giving them a significant jump start toward modern civilization.

It is also important to acknowledge that Judaism and Islam impacted the development of the West in significant and positive ways:

> Religion defines the foundations of the West. Christianity, meeting at specific times and places with Judaism and Islam, from ancient times to the present day, has formed the basis for Western civilization. The

confrontation between Islam and Christianity brought centuries of strife, the conflict between Judaism and Christianity precipitated an unending debate, full of recrimination. But the three religions that, in unequal proportions to be sure, defined for the West the human situation and determined the goals of the social order also engaged with one another in religious, not only in political, terms.[24]

Those caveats notwithstanding, the irrefutable fact is that Christianity and its biblical teachings created the foundation that led to the establishment of Western civilization and all of the good that has flowed from that civilization.

How, then, did a tiny religion, born in a backwater Asian town in the bowels of the immense Roman Empire, its first members being nothing but a group of humble Jews, become the dominant religion of Europe, then the most influential religion in the world?

To answer this question, we have to talk about the miracle at the bridge.

Rome, Italy
AD 312

HER NAME WAS RUTH. She had been christened after one of the most powerful (and one of the few) women whose presence was made known in ancient scriptures.

Whither thou goest, I will go; . . . thy people shall be my people, and thy God my God.

It was the untold story of her life. She was literally an outcast in her own land.

She had never been told the explanation behind her name. She didn't know—and she would never be told—that she had been rescued from the garbage dump outside the city walls. She didn't know that her birth parents had abandoned her to death. She didn't know how the boy had rescued her that day.

Josephus wasn't unaware of the bitter irony, and sometimes he couldn't help but smile. As a Christian, he had been cast out from the prosperous and tightly knit Jewish community. His wife's family had cast her out on the day that she had been baptized, her new religion anathema to their pagan beliefs. Now they had a child who had been cast away, thrown out with the Roman trash.

Josephus and his family were vagabonds and outcasts, that was sure, and the slums of Rome were most unfriendly to their kind. And though they lived in a neighborhood with some Christians, there were only a few thousand of them, against a city of a million people. The odds were not on their side.

His adopted daughter stood beside the wooden table and watched him work. His writing was small but nearly perfect, and he seemed to recall the words entirely from memory as he wrote them down. She knew enough not to interrupt him, and though more than an hour passed, she stood without moving or saying anything. Finally, Josephus raised his head from the papers, lifted his arms to stretch, then placed his writing tool upon the table. The ink needed time to dry now. He had a few moments to talk.

Ruth looked at him, then down at his work. She could read as well as he could, and she quickly scanned the contract that he was working on. "Is this one complicated, Father?" she asked.

"It is difficult. And important. It must be right."

She looked away, her dark eyes half closed, then turned back to him. "May I ask you something, Father?"

Josephus nodded wearily. It was getting close to sundown. He would have to work by candlelight tonight, something he hardly could afford, for candles were expensive.

"Constantine is fighting through the northern Italian mountains. Is that a good thing for us, Father? Or is his approaching army something that we should fear?"

Josephus stared at the narrow slit in the mortar wall that was the only window on their one-room home. He wanted to tell her something that would give her a reason to be optimistic, but the truth was, he didn't know. After three hundred years of hatred in the good years and deadly persecution in the worst, he didn't want to say anything that would disappoint her if he were wrong.

"There is always hope," he finally answered.

Ruth stared at him with frightened eyes. "Will it be dangerous for us, Father?"

For a long time, he only thought.

For centuries, the Romans had persecuted the Christians as the hounds of hell. Any of them could be taken at any time, for any reason, without any explanation, without breaking any law. He had ancestors who had died in the Roman Colosseum, torn to pieces for no reason other than to provide a good show. Their children lived in terror, afraid to admit to anyone what they were. Having lived this way for generations, it was hard for Christians to believe that the future would somehow change.

Still, they *had* to hope. What else did they have? What else could they give their children? For what other reason did they live?

Making a gesture to the north, he motioned toward the approaching army and the leader that rode before it, a man they called Constantine. The emperor of Gaul was a stranger from the West and unknown to the people in this part of the Empire. Would he conquer or be conquered? What kind of ruler would he be?

"We render unto Caesar what is Caesar's," he finally answered. "We have always been faithful citizens. There is no reason for Constantine to hate us."

Ruth shook her head, sadness in her eyes. In an age and place that disregarded the value of a man, where compassion was scoffed at and reason ignored, the fact that Christians were good citizens had never been enough to save them from Roman rage or persecution.

Her father waited for her to answer. When she was silent, he went on. "At worst, things will remain as they have always been. But it is my hope, and we have been commanded to always hope . . ." he lifted an instructive eyebrow toward her, " . . . that things will get better. I really believe that. Someday they will."

Though only thirteen, adversity had forged Ruth into an extremely perceptive girl, much more a woman than a child, and she seemed unconvinced. "We've been talking of hope for almost three hundred years!" she answered angrily. "How many generations! How many lives lost in hate and dread? Emperors come and go. Cities rise and fall. But one thing is always constant: Christians are hated and persecuted. That seems always sure.

"So, no, Father, although I wish I could share your optimism, I don't believe anything is going to change just because a new emperor might fight his way to Rome to claim the throne."

A Religion Is Born

There are two reasons why Christianity's emergence among the Jews in the Roman-dominated area of Palestine was so important.

First, it was only among the Jewish community that this extraordinary new religion could have survived. Christianity was founded upon the teachings and mission of Jesus Christ, who was a Jew. He ministered and taught almost exclusively among the community of Jews. His first converts were all Jews. The faith was nurtured among a Jewish population that was receptive to its message because they had always looked forward to a Messiah. (It is interesting to note, relative to previous chapters, that had the Jews been dispersed among the Assyrian Empire as their cousins in the kingdom of Israel had been, the birth of a new world religion would likely have been impossible.) Then, in his final instructions to his followers, Christ told them to take the faith to all the world.

Second (in trying to comply with this command), the spread of the new religion was possible because of the infrastructure that the Roman Empire could provide.

> It has been observed, with truth as well as propriety, that the conquests of Rome prepared and facilitated those of Christianity.... The public highways, which had been constructed for the use of the legions, opened an easy passage for the Christian missionaries from Damascus to Corinth, and from Italy to the extremity of Spain or Britain.... There is the strongest reason to believe that before the reigns of Diocletian and Constantine, the faith of Christ had been

preached in every province and in all the great cities of the empire.[25]

Christianity's growth in the early decades (in fact, some argue, in the first centuries) was primarily among the Jewish population that was to be found scattered throughout the Roman Empire.[26] However, its acceptance among the gentile population accelerated as the second and third centuries unfolded.

Though it was first and foremost a religion of Asia and then Africa, eventually it established a presence in Europe. Once there, its membership drew from all walks of life and classes of people. It has long been accepted that Christianity appealed primarily to the poor and the downtrodden, but more recent scholarship indicates that it also had great appeal among the middle and upper classes of Roman society. By the second half of the first century, prominent Christians were found in the aristocracy of Rome. And as its numbers increased, its presence also grew among the more privileged classes throughout other regions within the empire.[27]

As to its rate of growth, in the year AD 40, there were an estimated 1,000 Christian converts. By the end of the first century, there may have been around 7,000. At the end of the next century, the number was in the neighborhood of 217,000. At the time of Constantine, AD 312, there were more than six million Christians in the Roman Empire, which itself had an estimated population of sixty million. Less than forty years later, the Christian population had exploded to an estimated thirty-four million, making Christians the majority in the empire.[28]

The appeal of Christianity depends upon one's perspective, and secular opinions vary widely. Eighteenth-century historian Edward Gibbon, who was not a fan of Christianity, asserts that its growth was due to the "intolerant zeal of the Christians," its appealing doctrine of a future life, the miraculous powers that early Christians claimed to possess, the "pure and austere morals" of the Christians, and the discipline and unity of the Christians and their community.[29]

A modern secular view asserts that Christian doctrine was particularly appealing to the Jewish community, the upper classes of society, and women. Also, its rejection of abortion and infanticide, so common with the pagan population, resulted in a higher birthrate among the Christian faithful than among their neighbors. Finally, its doctrines of charity, community, and hope made it particularly appealing to a people who had to deal with the upheavals wrought by nearly constant natural and man-made disasters—deadly epidemics, revolution, and war—not to mention the everyday horrors of urban life that the vast majority of the population endured during this era in the Roman Empire.[30]

Those of a more pious and Christian-oriented viewpoint would argue that Christianity spread because it represented the truth.

Regardless of the explanation, Christianity spread.

But it did not spread without opposition. Beginning with Stephen, the first of many martyrs,[31] succeeding decades would see periods of intense opposition to this new faith. In fact, not long after the death of Christ, persecution and repression of Christianity became the official state policy of Rome. From that time forward, the empire expended blood and treasure to destroy the Christians and their new philosophies that taught about equality and the inherent worth of man.

Rome, Italy
AD 312

THE LITTLE GROUP OF believers gathered in the narrow courtyard behind Josephus's small home. Old bricks and mud made a high wall around the rock-covered patio, tall enough to hide the meeting from prying eyes. The sun was just going down, and the narrow streets around the slum were crowded with peddlers, soldiers, horses, donkeys, a few goats, a few more craftsmen, shopping mothers, and shouting children—the regular evening crowd. Rome was a vast city, considered the largest and most powerful in the world, and it was always crowded and noisy, especially in the slums. Though it was early evening on the Christian Sabbath, it was just another day of work in Rome.

The handful of Christian believers gathered in near silence. They all knew each other, and although their meetings were often tense, and always guarded, there was a sense of happiness in being with each other once again. It would have surprised an outsider to see the children and young people in the group, for the Christians worshipped as families rather than as comrades. Before the first prayers were offered, Ruth and another child, a boy two years younger, were posted to guard the front door. From where they sat, huddled in the shadows of the narrow window, they could see up and down the crowded street just a few feet outside the door.

They watched carefully, their dark eyes wide and sober. Though they were young, they had been given a great responsibility and they took it very seriously. Ruth kept her eyes moving up and down the street, but she felt that in one way it was a useless gesture. What were they to do if the Roman soldiers came? Run? Fight? None of them had any idea what they would do.

No, that wasn't true. They knew. They would keep silent. They would pray. They would bow and grovel. And hope the Roman soldiers didn't take any of them away.

The Christian voices were just rising in a muffled song when two Roman soldiers dressed in full armor came stalking down the narrow road. These two were new to their local post; Ruth had seen them in the market and commons area only a couple of times before. The crowd scattered like dry leaves before the soldiers, some of the more timid pressing against the brick walls and jumping into doorways to get out of their way. The two men walked together but didn't speak, metal shields slung over their armor-protected shoulders, swords hanging from their sides. They were looking for something, that was obvious, as they paused to check each house and shop.

Ruth pulled back into the shadows. Behind her, the young boy ran to tell the others. Ruth listened for the clang of armor and heavy footsteps of the soldiers drawing near. The house was dark and empty. A puff of night air blew down the smelly street and through her window. She cocked her head and listened.

The Romans stopped right outside the house!

In the courtyard, the Christians stopped their singing. Dead silence filled the air.

A sudden knock of a metal-covered fist upon her door!

She glanced back, terrified. Her father was standing there.

The soldier knocked again, this time more slowly.

Ruth watched in terror as her father walked resolutely toward the entrance. Turning, he shooed her back, gesturing toward the courtyard. "Get back there!" he commanded. The young girl didn't move. "Back! Hide!" her father hissed. Again she didn't move. The soldier slammed his fist a final time upon the door. Her father took a breath, unlocked the bolt, and pulled the door open.

The Romans filled the entire door frame, strong and resolute.

The first soldier leaned into the room. "We have been told there are . . ." He paused, his voice falling. "We heard reports of Christians meeting here!" His face was hard but there was also . . . what was it Ruth saw in his eyes? Uncertainty? Maybe fear? Glancing over his shoulder, the second soldier seemed to slump. No one moved past them on the street. The evening stood still.

The first soldier pushed into the room. The other Roman followed. Ruth's father tried to block them, but, seeing it was futile, he stood aside and let them in.

"Brother?" the first soldier whispered. "Are there Christians meeting here?"

Her father didn't answer.

The other soldier stepped forward. "We want to worship with you, brother. We wish to join your service, for we are Christians too."

Opposition on the Rise

The fact that zealous persecution of the Christians would take place in the Roman Empire is a bit puzzling. For one thing, because of the size of the empire, it included an enormous number of cultures and peoples. Each had their own religion. They worshipped their own gods. Even the Romans worshipped a full array of different deities. All of these various gods, beliefs, and religions were tolerated:

> The policy of the emperors and the senate, as far as it
> concerned religion, was happily seconded by the reflections

of the enlightened, and by the habits of the superstitious, part of their subjects. The various modes of worship which prevailed in the Roman world were all considered by the people as equally true; by the philosopher, as equally false; and by the magistrate, as equally useful. And thus toleration produced not only mutual indulgence, but even religious concord.[32]

Yet, despite the fact that dozens of religions and literally hundreds of gods were worshipped throughout the Empire, Christianity was singled out for persecution. Why Roman emperors, those who had "beheld without concern a thousand forms of religion subsisting in peace under their gentle sway,"[33] would turn murderous against the Christians was a mystery, especially in light of the fact that the Christian faith resulted in members who were almost uniformly passive and obedient and known for superior morals.

Perhaps the best explanation is the Romans concluded that the Roman Christians had turned against their own. After all, these Christians weren't foreigners worshipping a foreign god; no, they were "one of us," Romans who had turned their backs on their own history and traditions, their forefathers, their society's religion. They were essentially a group of apostates.

Making matters even more uncomfortable was the fact that, unlike the Roman pagan religions that involved public sacrifices, community festivals, and elaborate celebrations, the Christians preferred to have private little meetings. What took place in those secret meetings? their neighbors had to wonder. Rumors of hideous human sacrifices and sexual orgies were widespread.[34]

Regardless of the reason for their hatred of the Christians, beginning approximately thirty years after the death of Jesus Christ, martyrdom became a tool of the state that was used against the fledgling religion.

In AD 64, a colossal fire swept Rome. It was rumored that the Emperor Nero, murderer of his own wife and mother, had set fire to the city and then entertained himself while observing the horrible spectacle by playing his lyre and singing.

Nero needed a scapegoat for the burning. The Christians were conveniently selected to serve that role. Under horrible torture, the names of fellow Christians were extracted. A great multitude were subject to crucifixion, some sewn up in the skins of wild beasts and delivered up to dogs to be torn asunder, others used as human torches. Nero offered up his gardens for the location of this mass murder. Tradition says that both Peter and Paul were executed in Rome as part of Nero's assault on Christianity.

After this time of brutal persecution, things improved, at least a little. In the following years, there were a few Caesars who tolerated Christianity; in some cases, members of the royal household were even converted. There was no widely enforced government policy of Christian oppression, a fact that at least minimized the systematic Christian persecution that had been so common during the earlier century.

The Christians were, after all, a tiny minority of apostates beset by irrational beliefs, an irrelevant group who posed no real threat to the mighty Roman Empire. Why should the Romans get too worked up over such a hopeless group of outcasts? They had to be kept in their place, that was sure, but having done that, it was better to ignore them than to make martyrs of them all.

But things were never easy for the unpopular religion, and even during the best of times, private Roman citizens were free to persecute Christians at their will. There were multiple accounts of Christian faithful being killed in Gaul, Carthage, and elsewhere throughout the empire, and in certain areas, pagan citizens would demand that local officials harass the Christian fools.

So it was that generations passed with the Christians living in constant fear, their future always uncertain. Depending upon the Caesar, Christian leaders might be left alone or they might be arrested and sentenced to death.

Darkness Before Light

Then, during the third century, things took a sudden turn for the worse.

In AD 250, Emperor Decius ascended to the Roman throne. Feeling it was necessary to purify the empire of the "superstition" known as Christianity, he ordered the death or exile of the bishops of most of the major cities. Another emperor, Valerian, followed suit a few years later.

The turning point was reached in AD 303, when Roman leaders suddenly awoke to a frightening realization: Christians were increasing in both numbers and influence. As previously noted, by this time there may have been as many as six million Christians, or ten percent of the Roman population. Under the Emperors Maximian and Galerus, an all-out assault on Christianity began. Members of the sect were no longer entitled to protection of the Roman law. Orders were issued that all Christian churches in the empire were to be destroyed; death was ordered for those who met in secret meetings; all of their sacred books were to be burned. Christian citizens were deprived of honors or employment; Christian slaves lost all hope of ever becoming free.

A few years later, Emperor Diocletian set about to eliminate utterly the Christian name. Edicts were sent to local officials to arrest *all* religious leaders. Mass arrests occurred. A number of bishops and other leaders were tortured and executed.

Worse, and with much more far-reaching implications for the Christians, the brutal edicts issued by Roman officials energized the citizenry. Cruel and spontaneous outbreaks of "violent and general persecution" became heartbreakingly common.[35]

For three hundred years, Christians had accepted the persecution with stoic faith. They had not risen in rebellion. They never demanded retribution or revenge. What they did do was preserve "their conscience pure and innocent of the guilt of secret conspiracy or open rebellion. While they experienced the rigor of persecution, they were never provoked either to meet their tyrants in the field or indignantly to withdraw themselves into some remote and sequestered corner of the globe."[36]

This forbearance had served them well. Despite the efforts of the pagan emperors to destroy them, their willingness to serve the empire, as well as their reputation for virtue, law-abiding behavior, and strength of character had brought them considerable goodwill.

Now they were about to be rewarded.

The morning of the Christian empire was about to break.

Outside the Walls of Rome
North of the Tiber River
AD 312

ROMAN EMPEROR FLAVIUS VALERIUS Aurelius Constantinus, soon to be known as Constantine the Great, felt his age in his bones. At forty, he was not a young man any longer. Riding horses hurt his knees. The balls of his feet would ache for the first hour after he got out of bed. The sides of his curly brown hair were turning gray now. Worst of all, he swung his sword with less power than he had twenty years before.

But the figurative sword of power that he wielded was more swift and powerful than it had ever been, a fact that, he discovered, gave him more vigor than he had ever felt before.

He was on the cusp of uniting the empire once again, being crowned not merely Caesar but *Caesar Augustus,* supreme emperor of all Rome.

He turned to Basilius, his military adviser, who had just dismounted from his horse. It was early evening but it had grown dark, the low clouds sucking all the light out of the sky.

Basilius slapped his black horse on the rump and the animal snorted as a military aide pulled its reins to lead it away. A cold wind blew up from across the plains, smelling of moss and river. The two men stared at each other. Both of them smiled. They had been on the warpath for months now. Heat. Cold. Death. Pain. Exhilaration. Weariness. Triumph. Was there any physical feeling or emotion they had not felt since they had taken up arms and started their warring march toward Rome? Yet all that was going to end now. Victory was within their grasp. One final battle, and it would be over. But it wouldn't be easy, and the outcome was certainly not assured. Their opponent (it was difficult to think of a fellow Roman as *the enemy*) was very strong. They were in his homeland. He was fortified and ready.

No, the outcome was anything but assured.

Basilius's face was smudged with smoke and dust, for he had been among the troops, an always dirty duty. He moved toward the emperor, then bent a knee and bowed. Constantine touched his shoulder to lift him up. The two men looked around, finding them-selves alone, all of the other aides and solders staying out of their way. Behind them, the walls of Rome fell into the shadows of the coming night and there were torches along the Milvian Bridge, car-ried by the enemy soldiers who were still marching out to meet them. Unbelievably, Caesar Maxentius had chosen to engage them on the open battlefield—this despite the fact that they had defeated every army he had sent to meet them on their march to Rome.

Constantine nodded toward the massive army that was gather-ing outside the city walls. "He comes out of the city to fight me," he said. It puzzled him. It seemed to him that, given the other Roman emperor's penchant for defeat in open battle, he should have kept his army behind the protection of the city walls.

Basilius frowned, his eyes moving to the gathered army. "It seems our rival had seen a vision," he explained.

The emperor, dressed in battle gear so shiny it still reflected the dying light, chewed on a piece of leathered meat while he waited for his counselor to continue.

"Maxentius has been given an omen . . ."

Constantine stopped chewing. As a longtime disciple of Apollo, he was used to signs and wonders, omens from the gods being inte-gral to his worship. If his opponent had received an omen, he had to take it seriously.

Basilius cocked his head. "Maxentius has been told that an enemy of Rome will perish here tomorrow," he said.

Constantine glanced toward the army that had gathered to fight him on the plains north of the river. "I'm assuming he has concluded that I am the enemy that is to die?"

The aide smiled just a little. "That would seem to be, my Caesar."

"That is why he leaves the safety of his city? Because of an omen he received?"

Basilius shrugged.

"He has yet to send out an army that could defeat me," Emperor Constantine went on, his voice growing indignant now. "Yet he believes he can defeat me when I am but a few miles, a few feet from my objective! He thinks I've fought my way from the far reaches of Britannia, through the mountains of the north, and across the plains of Tuscany, only to be defeated at the very doorstep of my goal!"

"The omen says it is to be, my king."

Constantine nodded toward the bridge. "He must be very confident, for he has put himself in a perilous situation. The river there behind him. My army at his front. No escape besides the Milvian Bridge, all of the others having already been destroyed by his own hand. If his god has counseled him to take this action, I would advise he take up with another god."

Basilius smiled grimly. It was true. It was an untenable military situation, a mistake his leader never would have made.

Constantine seemed to grow more serious. "The empire has been in total disarray for more than eighty years. Twenty-six emperors have ruled in that time, most of them weak and foolish men. When Diocletian split the empire into four, he guaranteed that we would live in chaos, diminished in the eyes of those who seek to bring us harm.

"We cannot stand it any longer. We have to win this battle and settle this matter now. The empire depends upon this. Upon us. My father and his fathers. All are depending on what we do here."

The two men fell silent, Constantine staring into the distance, completely lost in thought. He glanced up, taking in the now dark sky, then turned back to his friend. "Maxentius may have received an omen," he said softly, "but I have seen one too."

Basilius took a deep breath. Something in the emperor's eyes sent a jolt deep into his bones. The silence seemed to deepen. Even the wind stood still.

Constantine seemed to glance toward the sky. "In this sign, you will conquer," he whispered to himself.

A Cross in the Sky

In AD 284, less than thirty years before Constantine found himself outside the walls of Rome, Emperor Diocletian seized control and set about to restore stability to the far-flung reaches of the empire. At the time, its domain was spread from Britain in the west to Syria and Palestine in the east.

After an endless series of struggles, defeats, and disappointments, Diocletian concluded that no one man possessed the ability to rule such a massive kingdom. So he divided the empire, first into two, then later into four, appointing four men to rule over their different parts. This strategy, though it may have seemed good in theory, failed to take into account several harsh realities, including the fact that prideful and powerful men always lust for more power. Indeed, it guaranteed instability and war. Within a few years, six men claimed title to the various divisions. These men, and later their successors, were constantly at war, each trying to establish himself as the *Augustus,* supreme emperor of it all.

Constantine was the son of Constantius, the man Emperor Diocletian had first appointed to rule over Gaul and Britain. When Constantius died, his army insisted on Constantine's ascension. One of the other men seeking supreme authority over the empire was Maxentius, ruler in Rome. Fearing Constantine, he concluded that he had to defeat him and he began to prepare for war.

When Constantine learned of Maxentius's intentions, he decided to strike first. In the spring of 312, he marched his army from Gaul into northern Italy.

Son of a lowly barmaid named Helena (who eventually became a legal concubine), Constantine's unfavorable birth status left him at a disadvantage when it came to the benefits that would usually have flowed to the son of such a great man. He was, however, a natural soldier and leader. His father's army loved him as they had loved his father. The soldiers' support for him as Caesar was a factor that could not be ignored. So it was that the son of a barmaid had been named emperor of Gaul.

By the time Constantine crossed the Alps to confront Maxentius, he had an army of about forty thousand men. They moved quickly south. Three times, Maxentius sent his armies out to meet him. Three times, his armies were defeated. At Verona, an enormous army was defeated, the last remaining barrier between Constantine and Rome.

As Constantine's army approached, Maxentius made a critical error. Despite the fact that they had prepared for a long-term siege, he ordered his army outside of the protection of the city walls.

History records that Maxentius had received an omen, making him overconfident. But Constantine had received an omen as well—actually, two of them.

The day before the battle, he reportedly had seen a vision of a flaming cross in the sky with the words "in this sign, you will conquer." The next morning, he heard a voice that instructed him to place that symbol of Christ on the shields of his solders. He ordered this to be done. (While the Christian soldiers among his army must have received this order with great joy, the pagan soldiers were surely much less enthused.)

Constantine then made a sacred vow—if his army was victorious, he would convert to Christianity.

The two armies faced each other, one under the banner of Christianity, the other under a banner representing the Unconquerable Sun. Though Maxentius's army was twice the size of his, Constantine ordered his men to fan out along the entire line. When he commanded his cavalry to charge, they quickly broke through the opposing line of mounted soldiers. Chaos began to spread through the opposing army.

Constantine ordered his infantry forward. They quickly pushed the enemy back against the river. The battle was beginning to shape up as a slaughter. With no room to retreat, and unable to fight their way forward, the army of Maxentius was trapped. Many of them were drowned; those who remained faced a butcher shop of spears and swords. Realizing that the battle had clearly turned against him, Maxentius attempted to retreat over the narrow Milvian Bridge. Panic ensnared the crumbling army as they turned to follow. Maxentius was pushed into the river, where he drowned, along with a large number of his men.

Constantine had won. The city of Rome was his. His dream of becoming *Caesar Augustus* was within his grasp.

True to his vow, he became a Christian.

Constantine's Conversion: Political or Sincere?

There is no question that this battle was a "turning point in the history of religion."[37] Constantine was now the undisputed emperor of the West. Twelve years later, his army defeated a (once again) larger army of pagans under Licinius, Caesar of the East. With that, Constantine became sole ruler of the entire Roman Empire.

Constantine declared religious liberty for all, inviting his subjects to join him in Christianity.

Soon after, he moved the capital of the empire from the ancient metropolis of Rome to Constantinople, a city he had established and named after himself. Not only was Constantinople the political capital, it also rose to rival Rome for preeminence as the center of Christianity.

The sincerity of Constantine's conversion has long been debated. He certainly didn't live a perfect life after it. His reign was full of the failings of a mortal man bent on retaining power. He also wasn't known for being overly zealous when it came to following Christian ritual, not even being baptized until he was nearing death.

In the years after his ostensible conversion, he continued occasional use of pagan rites and symbols in his ruling. Having worshipped Apollo for forty years, he was slow—perhaps understandably—to abandon a lifetime of ingrained practices. However, as his position of emperor became secure, he became more and more orthodox in his Christianity, dropping almost all of the vestiges of his pagan past.

Regardless of his failings, there is no doubt that Constantine's acceptance of Christianity, and his forbidding of its persecution, opened the door for the new religion's acceptance throughout the Western world. In 325, he united the Christian world by calling for the Council of Nicea, its purpose being to bring unanimity among Christian faithful as to the nature of the Christian Godhead. He was responsible for the construction of many churches, exempted Christian property from taxation (a practice that has continued to this day), and vested much authority in local church leaders. His mother was a devout Christian, and, with his support, she spent considerable time and energy trying to ascertain the locations of holy sites in Palestine.

Summing up the impact of his conversion, it has been said:

> His Christianity, beginning as policy, appears to have graduated into sincere conviction. He became the most persistent preacher in his realm, persecuted heretics faithfully, and took God into partnership at every step. . . . By his aid Christianity became a state as well as a church, and the mold, for fourteen centuries, of European life and thought.[38]

As to whether Constantine was sincerely converted or simply used Christianity as a tool to unite his empire, it is impossible for us to know. But this much is sure: "the fact that Christianity is the dominant faith in Europe today is directly traceable to Constantine."[39]

Rome, Italy
AD 320

RUTH AND HER FATHER stood by the doorway of their small home. The girl was much taller now, and even more beautiful. Her dark hair hung behind her back and her eyes were bright and shining. She looked like a princess—a *Roman* princess—her features thin and elegant. Her father looked at her with great pride, and for a moment his mind flashed back to that day, twenty years before, when his nephew had brought her home, a starving infant taken from the garbage pile.

Staring at her now, he thought in wonder, *And they threw this away!*

She turned to him and smiled, then lifted the small container of white paint. Using a rusted piece of metal, she had already sketched an outline on the wooden post outside the door. She dipped the brush and started painting, each stroke careful and deliberate. Twenty minutes later, a beautiful white cross had been painted on the right side of their door.

Finishing her work, she looked over at her father, who hadn't moved from where he stood. For a long time, they didn't speak. There was too much to say. Too many emotions. Words simply didn't seem sufficient, and so they held their peace.

They didn't have to hide it any longer. They were finally free.

Ruth felt a trickle run down her cheeks. And for the first time in her life she understood that there was such a thing as tears of joy.

What It Meant

Constantine died in AD 337. His fellow Christians may have missed him, but they weren't dependent on him anymore. He had forged the path before him, and others had followed in his way.

After Constantine's conversion, Christianity was adopted as the state religion of the Roman Empire. Within a decade, Christianity had become the majority religion. And though it had yet to face one last episode of persecution under Julian the Apostate, he would be the last of the Roman emperors not to rule under the Christian cross.[40]

One of the crucial results of the spread of Christianity was that the religion developed the strength and depth it needed to survive the brutal future that lay ahead.

The Roman Empire was soon to slide into decline, and then to fall. Following the rise of the barbarian tribes, many of whose names are familiar to us today—the Vandals, Huns, Goths, and Franks—civilization began to crumble. Despite the fact that political stability was being crushed under the weight of civilization's collapse,

Christianity survived. Indeed, not only were the barbarians unable to destroy Christianity, most were eventually converted.

Against later invasions of Vikings, Magyars, Mongols, and Muslims, Christianity continued to serve as the light that turned the minds of men toward the higher aspirations that were essential for a civilized culture to develop.

Looking back, this seems clear: Constantine's vision of the cross in the sky was not only a call for a military victory but a plea for all men to fight against irrationality, injustice, and tyranny.

Had it not been for the son of a Roman Caesar and an innkeeper's daughter, the history of Europe—and the world—would have unfolded very differently.[41]

Notes

1. Quoted in Stark, *Rise of Christianity,* 97–98.
2. Jenkins, "Any Faith Can Become Violent."
3. Woods, *Catholic Church,* 1–2. Dr. Woods is a senior fellow at the Ludwig von Mises Institute and the author of nine books. For another voice supporting the essential role of the Christian church in the saving and growth of Western civilization, see Durant, *Reformation,* 3–6, in which this most eminent of scholars gives credit to the Catholic church for being the chief source of order and peace in the Dark Ages; for resurrecting civilization after the barbarian invasions of Europe; for saving classic culture; for keeping alive the Greek and Latin languages; for training Europe's teachers, scholars, judges, diplomats, and ministers of state; for building universities and providing a home for the intellect; and for providing a moral code and national government.
4. Rodney Stark is a Distinguished Professor of the Social Sciences, Baylor University, as well as the author of numerous excellent books on the history and influence of Christianity.
5. Stark, *Victory of Reason,* x; emphasis in original.
6. Brog, *In Defense of Faith,* 2.
7. See ibid., 53–85.
8. Stark, *Victory of Reason,* 6.
9. Historian Edward Grant said, "What made it possible for Western civilization to develop science and the social sciences in a way that no other civilization had ever done before? The answer, I am convinced, lies in a pervasive and deep-seated

spirit of inquiry that was a natural consequence of the emphasis on reason that began in the Middle Ages" (Woods, *Catholic Church*, 66).

10. Stark points out the irony that Christianity was influenced by the Greeks' commitment to reason, when at the same time it is so clear that Greek philosophers totally failed to influence their own religion. The religious faith of the Greeks fell in line with what most other non-Christian religions believed, that religion totally lacked reason and evidence that it was divine. This acceptance of the unknown, and the belief that it could never be known, denied the Greeks (and subsequent faiths) the motivation to seek to understand the whys and wherefores of their religions. Centuries later, Christianity forged the first bond between reason and faith.

11. Stark, *Victory of Reason,* 7. Gerber of Aurillac, who became Pope Sylvester II (r. 999–1003), is quoted as saying, "The just man lives by faith, but it is good that he should combine science with his faith." Elsewhere he said, "The Divinity made a great gift to men in giving them faith while not denying them knowledge" (in Woods, *Catholic Church,* 23).

12. See Woods, *Catholic Church,* 153–67, for a discussion of the influence of the medieval Catholic church on free markets and economic theory generally.

13. See Stark, *Victory of Reason,* 16–22; Woods, *Catholic Church,* 75–85.

14. See Stark, *Victory of Reason,* 22–23; emphasis in original.

15. Woods, *Catholic Church,* 4.

16. Stark, *Victory of Reason,* xiii.

17. See ibid., 26–32.

18. Quoted in ibid., 77.

19. See ibid., xiii; Woods, *Catholic Church,* 197–202.

20. John Dunn, as quoted in Waldron, *God, Locke, and Equality,* 12. Waldron goes into great detail explaining the role of Christianity in Locke's theories of equality, freedom, ownership of property, and natural rights.

21. Stark, *Victory of Reason,* 79–80. For a full discussion of the role of Christianity in the development of Western political thought and its emergence as the leader in science, technology, and capitalism, see Stark, *Victory of Reason,* as well as two of his other works, *The Rise of Christianity* and *Cities of God.* See also Woods, *Catholic Church.*

22. Neusner, *Religious Foundations,* 3–23.

23. Marty, *Christian World,* 17.

24. Neusner, *Religious Foundations,* ix.

25. Gibbon, *Decline and Fall of the Roman Empire,* 270.

26. See Stark, *Rise of Christianity,* 49–71.

27. See ibid., 29–47. See also Gibbon, *Decline and Fall of the Roman Empire,* 271–73.

28. See Stark, *Rise of Christianity,* 3–27.

29. Gibbon, *Decline and Fall of the Roman Empire,* 238–64.

30. See Stark, *Rise of Christianity.*
31. As depicted in Acts 7.
32. Gibbon, *Decline and Fall of the Roman Empire,* 19.
33. Ibid., 276.
34. See ibid., 276–85, for what historians surmise to be the justifications for intolerance of Christianity in the otherwise tolerant Roman society.
35. Ibid., 308. For general descriptions of the persecutions of the Christian faith, see also Durant, *Caesar and Christ,* 596–619, 646–52; Gibbon, *Decline and Fall of the Roman Empire,* 276–314; Stark, *Rise of Christianity,* 163–89.
36. Gibbon, *Decline and Fall of the Roman Empire,* 381.
37. Durant, *Caesar and Christ,* 654.
38. Ibid., 664.
39. Davis, *100 Decisive Battles,* 82. For information about Constantine and his conversion, see ibid., 78–82; Durant, *Caesar and Christ,* 653–64; Gibbon, *Decline and Fall of the Roman Empire,* 213–36, 376–400.
40. See Gibbon, *Decline and Fall of the Roman Empire,* 423–53.
41. For a brief review of the post-Roman history of Christianity in Europe, see Woods, *Catholic Church,* 9–23. For a more extensive review, see Gibbon, *Decline and Fall of the Roman Empire,* 466–1252.

Chapter 4

The Battle That Preserved
a Christian Europe

*Poitiers was the turning point of one of the most
important epochs in the history of the world.*

NOTED GERMAN HISTORIAN LEOPOLD VON RANKE[1]

On the Eastern Tip of the Pyrenees Mountains
Southern France
AD 732

UNDERNEATH THE VAST, perfectly blue sky, the Pyrenees stretched east and west as far as the eye could see, an unending sea of mountains, their white-capped peaks broken by vertical slabs of black stone. Older than the Alps, cut by glaciers, with multiple peaks above eleven thousand feet, the mountain range extended for more than three hundred miles, forming a natural and nearly impenetrable barrier between what would one day be called France and Spain. From the Bay of Biscay on the west to the Mediterranean Sea in the east, the terrain rose suddenly from gently rolling hills to sharp peaks, beautiful geological formations of granite and limestone.

The two men met in a meadow on the east end of the range. A winding road, really more of a trail, ran at the narrow end of the meadow, the main passage through the mountains on the Mediterranean side. It was early summer, but the air was crisp and cold from the snow that lingered on the peaks above them. They stared at each other without speaking. They were brothers, but it had been years, almost a generation, since they had been together, and they were from two vastly different worlds now. One of them was dressed in eastern garb: dark robes, leather shoes, wool turban, black scarf wrapped around his face, a long beard. The other was dressed like any European laborer: a thigh-length tunic, short-sleeved and cinched with a leather belt, barbarian trousers underneath. His hair was to his shoulders, but he did not wear a beard.

The two men took each other in. Same long noses. Same brown eyes. But that was the end of the similarities, and they did not embrace.

At one time, their father had been a lord, with massive tracts of land on the south range of the Pyrenees Mountains. When the Arab armies had arrived some forty years before, the family had been separated, the father and his older son trapped on the Spanish side, the younger brother and his mother fleeing to her family across the mountains into France.

The brothers had not seen each other since.

Now, after all these years, they met here on their father's lands on the eastern tip of the mountains.

It would be the last time they would be together.

In a short time, one of them would be dead.

• • •

One hundred years after the death of the Prophet Muhammad, a battle for the soul of Europe took place.

It happened thousands of miles from the birthplace of Islam, in faraway Gaul, in what we now call France, a very different part of the world from the Arabian Peninsula where the body of Muhammad was laid to rest. It occurred at a very critical time, for the world had changed much since Islam had risen in the East. In fact, the years between the death of the Prophet and the Battle of Poitiers were some of the most dramatic and remarkable in the history of the world.

The battle itself—one of several in a small war upon which the future of Europe hinged—was hardly noteworthy. Greater battles have been fought, with more magnificent armies and more compelling turns of events—famous wars with legendary heroes, their romantic tales told and retold through the years.

Such is not the case with the Battle of Poitiers.

Few of the men who led this battle are familiar to us now: Charles "the Hammer" Martel. Abd al-Rahman. Not many recognize these names. Who were these men? What were they fighting for? Where did the battle take place? And did the outcome of this battle *really* change the world?

Though many of the details of the Battle of Poitiers are lost to history, this much remains clear: it was here that Europe almost lost its Christian identity. It was here, among the forests and plains of western France, that the future of Christianity was saved. It was here, north of the Pyrenees Mountains, that the Christian defenders stopped the seemingly inevitable spread of Islam into Europe.

But to understand the significance of what happened at Poitiers, we must understand the astonishing rise of the Arab Empire, the desperate Christian defenders who stood in the way of Islamic expansion, and—most important of all—why it was essential for European Christianity to be saved.

Christianity, Freedom, and Islam

Would it have mattered if Europe had become an Islamic state? Islam is, after all, one of the world's great religions and, as with every great religion, it has many admirable traits—its emphasis on family, honesty, and fidelity, to name a few. Indeed, the Five Pillars of Islam are straightforward and clearly honorable:

1. The Testimony of Faith. *La ilaha illa Allah, Muhammadur rasoolu Allah.* There is no true god but Allah and Muhammad is His prophet.

2. The importance of daily prayer.

3. Concern for the poor and almsgiving to the needy.

4. Self-purification through fasting during the month of Ramadan.

5. The annual pilgrimage (*Hajj*) to Makkah (*Mecca*) as a once-in-a-lifetime obligation for those who are physically and financially able to do so.[2]

Given these admirable teachings, is it any wonder that hundreds of millions of people have been blessed by following the precepts of Islam?

Not only are the religious teachings of Islam to be admired, so is much of its history. In the first centuries after it arose from the desert of Arabia, with the possible exception of China, Islam and the nations where it predominated were the most advanced on the earth.

In less than a hundred years, it grew to become the mightiest military power in the world. From the borders of China to the waters of the Atlantic Ocean, the caliphate stretched its mighty sword, reaching from the slopes of eastern Asia to the Black Sea, from the Middle East and Arabian Peninsula across northern Africa to the Iberian Peninsula (which includes most of what we now call Spain). Along the northeastern shores of the Mediterranean Sea, the Byzantine Empire watched helplessly as the age of the caliphs dawned upon their world. To the west of the Byzantine Empire, the fragmented tribes and feeble kingdoms of central and western Europe seemed incapable of stopping the spread of the caliphs.

And it was not just a great military power. The economic influence of the Islamic world stretched across a large portion of the globe, with trading relationships reaching into Asia, Europe, and Africa. These powerful trade associations, along with the hordes of slaves and booty they claimed in battle, provided the caliphate the resources it needed to finance a growing empire.

The Islamic culture also had achieved the highest levels in the arts and sciences. For a time, it led the world in technological and cultural advancements, the West sitting as humble students at the feet of Islam.

After it had absorbed much from the Greeks and the Persians, it took advantage of its expansive reach to borrow from the great, distant cultures of the time. For example, it adopted the use of paper from China and decimals and Indian numerals from India. Its own scientists added to the adopted body of knowledge with significant advances of their own.

But it did not lead the way in cultural or scientific discovery for long.

Soon, the Islamic world began to fall behind the West.

As the West forged ahead in the sciences, technology, cultural advancements, and in the advancements in religious thought that led to the concepts of personal freedom and self-government, the world of Islam seemed to freeze. There were no Islamic nations in which personal liberty became a priority. There were no Islamic nations in which representative government emerged. Throughout the nations of Islam, scientific and technological advances came to an end. Industrialization passed Islamic nations by.

But why would this happen?

After creating a massive kingdom from the sands of the Arabian desert, after spreading its reach across most of the known world and creating an empire that would lead the world in many technological advancements, how could the entire culture come to such a dramatic standstill?

There are a number of explanations:

1. In fundamentalist Islam, there is no law but religious law, the Sharia, or Holy Law of Islam. Sharia law is divine, the word of God. And it is all-encompassing, regulating every aspect of life: civil, commercial, criminal, and religious. As such, to the devout Muslim, the Holy Law of Islam is all the law that is needed. One does not add to or detract from Sharia, for to do so would presume that man knows better than God.

It is, therefore, absurd to think that there would be any need for mortal men to meet for the purpose of creating new law. It is absurd to think that a parliament or a congress or any other deliberative body could better the Holy Law of Islam. This leaves no room in strict Islam for self-government or representative government.

As Scholar Bernard Lewis explains, "In the Muslim perception, there is no human legislative power."[3]

2. The idea of separation of church and state is utterly foreign in Islam. Separation of the religious from the secular is a creation of Christianity and, as such, it is entirely rejected by the Islamic faithful. In Islamic culture, there is no equivalent of "render unto Caesar what is Caesar's and unto God what is God's," for everything necessary to direct the affairs of men is found within the Holy Law.

3. The concept of freedom has a very limited meaning in Islam. Bernard Lewis explains:

> Westerners have become accustomed to think of good and bad government in terms of tyranny versus liberty. In Middle-Eastern usage, liberty or freedom was a legal not a political term. It meant one who was not a slave. . . . For traditional Muslims, the converse of tyranny was not liberty but justice. Justice in this context meant essentially two things, that the ruler was there by right and not by usurpation, and that he governed according to God's law.[4]

This very narrow understanding of freedom and justice meant, essentially, that you were either a slave or you were not. Such a limited understanding of personal liberty made it nearly impossible for a faithful follower of Islam to think it was necessary, or even good, to make laws that guaranteed any further individual freedom. It made it impossible for a faithful follower of Islam to think it was either good or necessary to create a political institution that sought to enhance individual liberty, whether political or economic.

The understanding of justice in the Western world is that all men are entitled to protection under the law. This stands in stark contrast to the Muslim view that justice simply means that one is governed by God's intended rulers and according to God's law.

4. When Islam began, its views of equality were, ironically, viewed

as extremely liberal. At a time when the world was a hostile, brutal, and unequal place, with power and wealth concentrated in the hands of a very few, Islam strongly denounced privilege, elitism, and inequality. In fact, many of the everyday citizens of the Persian and Byzantine Empires who were conquered by Islamic armies found themselves with more freedom and opportunity than they had ever enjoyed before. This was particularly true of Jews and minority Christian groups.

However, as Islam evolved, aristocracy returned. Within a few generations, whatever improvements these people might have enjoyed had entirely slipped away.

More fundamentally, there are three groups of people who would never be equal to Muslim men within Islamic law: women, slaves, and nonbelievers. Islamic law simply viewed these groups as forever less than equal.

Full equality has never been available to women. In fundamental Islamic states, this is as true today as it was in the seventh century. And it likely will never be much different, for there is a deep-seated difference between the beliefs of Islam and Western cultures regarding the role of the sexes. Although it is true that Western pressure has somewhat bettered the treatment of the nonbelievers, it still can be very difficult, and sometimes deadly, to live as a nonbeliever in a Muslim culture today. Of course, slavery has been abolished, but deeply held traditions may still allow for a blind eye to be turned to the trade of women for sexual exploitation.

5. Secular education was never important among the believers of Islam. With the Law of Islam being the final word on both government and the affairs of men, it was accepted that no one but religious leaders needed to be educated. Furthering this lack of interest in secular education, as Islam aged, it adopted the view that "knowledge was something to be acquired, stored, if necessary bought, rather than grown or developed."[5]

As the Renaissance and, later, the technological revolution were beginning to sweep through Europe, in the world of Islam, "independent inquiry virtually came to an end, and science was for the most part reduced to the veneration of a corpus of approved knowledge."[6]

While enormously important advances in science, the arts, technology, and industrialization were taking hold in Europe—advancements that bettered the lives of European citizens in almost every way—the world of Islam refused to adopt them. And how could they, with the feelings that they held? Christianity was a mortal enemy to Islam. For centuries, and in many different conflicts, Islam had become obsessed with a desire to overrun Christian Europe. And because Christianity was the enemy, any advance that might be tainted with Christianity— that had its origin in Europe, for instance—was deemed to be unworthy. The only exception to this rule was in means of warfare, religious authorities declaring that it was permissible to copy weapons and battlefield tactics from the infidels if the purpose of copying these new technologies was to defeat them.

6. Even when they had been exposed to the concepts of freedom, liberty, and self-government, Islamic nations turned their backs on them. As the centuries passed, a few of these concepts have seeped into the mind-set of some Middle Eastern leaders, but even today the ability of Middle Eastern nations to implement such concepts into effective governance is severely limited.

So it is that, despite all of its great qualities, the religion of Islam has proven historically have no tradition of freedom, self-government, science, or economic development.[7]

On the Eastern Tip of the Pyrenees Mountains Southern France

THEY STARED AT EACH other uncomfortably. "I don't understand," the younger brother simply said.

The older brother, the southerner, was slow to answer. "Few of you do," he finally replied.

The younger one was angry. It showed in his eyes and the tone of his voice. "You have joined the enemy."

"No, brother, I *became* the enemy a long time ago."

"You have betrayed our family. Our honor. The memory of our father . . ."

"You know *nothing* of our father," the other spat. He had never betrayed his father and he knew he never would, for honor for his elders ran deep within him now. And though his father may not have understood his actions in this world, in the next world he would. "What do you remember of our father?" he continued. "You were too young, naively hanging on our mother's coat as she dragged you away. You were not yet weighed and measured when you last saw our father. It would be foolish to presume that you could speak for him now."

The younger brother held his tongue. "How could you do this?" he asked again.

"Do what, my brother? What have I done? What do I stand accused of? The world is a complicated place. It is evil and cunning and absurdly brutal. My faith teaches something more. Something better. It gives me hope. It gives *us* hope. It is the only thing that teaches the truths to save us . . ."

"*Save us!* Save us from what? You and your people have devastated a swath of earth that never sees the setting sun! You have trampled and defeated. You have taken slaves and riches. And you do it in the name of religion, as if you were on the errand of your God."

"Your God. My God. It is the same thing, brother. There is no God but Allah and Muhammad is His prophet."

The younger brother waved an inpatient hand. He had heard it all before. Over the past twenty years, since the Arab armies had first started racing across the Pyrenees with their scout parties, always probing for weaknesses, summing up their enemies as they prepared for the main attack, the faith of Islam had become well known through the northern land.

"Save us!" he repeated. "You and your armies are going to save us!" His voice reeked with sarcasm and disdain. The Moors, as the Arab and North African invaders were commonly called, had taken the Iberian Peninsula and built up a kingdom they called Al-Andalus, which meant, as he understood it, "to become green after a drought." But many things were not green now. And the world wasn't any better. He had seen how the conquering army treated their own women, how they treated the young girls they took as slaves. He had seen how they put the stamp of their god upon nearly everything they conquered. And if the invaders brought a new color, it wasn't green, but the red blood of war.

The brothers fell into silence once again.

"You lost your religion," the younger finally concluded. "You sold yourself for nothing but a poll tax and a way to better your position in this world. You gave away your Christ because it was a little easier. To save your lands. Your wealth. Your ambition. You sold your religion for a pot of porridge and nothing else."

The older brother sadly shook his head, his face calm. If he felt anger, he didn't show it, and his voice remained soft and composed. "Some have done that, brother. I would be a fool to deny that sometimes that has been the case. But that is not what changed me, brother. I found a better way. More truth. More light. What you believe isn't wrong, and I don't want to take away from the faith you have. After all is said, we still share much together. The prophets and the testament. Prayer. Faith. Goodwill and giving alms. Much of what we believe is the same. I have only . . . how could I say this . . . taken another step up the ladder. Now I'm reaching down to you, my brother." Here he seemed to pause, his face clouding over quickly. "I'm reaching for you, brother, but *you* must take my hand. You cannot fight against us. You cannot defeat the mighty arm of God. We sweep across the earth because it is His will. We cannot be defeated as long as Allah marches at our guard.

"And yes, we bring truth and we bring mercy, but that is not all we bring. We extend a hand to those who take it—but to the others, you are right, we bring subjection. They become our enemies, the enemies of the one true God."

The younger brother stared at his hands. "Would you really do this, brother? Would you really march into our lands? Will you fight against the cross? Against your brothers and your family? Will you ride with the armies of Islam as they fight their way through all of Europe?" He stopped and exhaled slowly, his breath freezing in the mountain air. "Which side will you fight for? Which side of history will you choose?"

The older brother didn't hesitate. Pushing back his robe, he placed his hand upon his sword. "I have already chosen, brother. We will conquer. We will win. The hand of the caliphs stretches from the jungles of Asia to the Great Sea in the west, five thousand miles of conquest underneath our feet. We have conquered every land that we have ever ridden into. Is there any doubt that we will defeat this land also?

"Your lands, your people, and your Christian God, they are the last to stand against us. But you will not stand for long!"

Who Were the Muslim Invaders?

According to tradition, the man known as Muhammad was born in AD 571 in the oasis town of Mecca in western Arabia.

Throughout the Mediterranean and Middle East, Christianity was the dominant force, and the world into which Muhammad was born had been shaped by this fact. Except for Judaism and Zoroastrianism (the religion of Persia, or modern-day Iraq and Iran), almost all of the pre-Christian religions in the area had disappeared. The Roman Empire had fallen into decay, the western branch having essentially been destroyed—overtaken by a series of invasions by barbarians. The Roman Empire of the East, the Byzantine Empire, with its capital in Constantinople, still prevailed, but it was but a fragment of the once mighty realm. And though Christianity had risen as the predominant religion, it had also reached the point where it had begun to fracture into a number of sects and churches.

The world was not a peaceful place. In the east, the powerful Persian Empire and its unceasing conflict with the Byzantines was the dominant political and military reality of the age. The two empires were at constant war, fighting over territory and control of the trade routes to the east.

Most of the people of the region were under the control of one of these two great empires, the Arabs being one of the few exceptions.

But things were changing quickly on the Arabian Peninsula. The contest between the Byzantines and Persians brought many refugees. The richness of the trade routes brought a great number of foreigners and colonists as well. This influx of new blood unsettled the Arabic society, exposing it to the outside world. The ancient pagan religions of the Arabs were being challenged. Some of the Arabs had already converted to Christianity, especially those living in areas that bordered Christian regions. The Jews, many of them refugees, had expanded their numbers as well, forming a substantial presence in the Arab lands. These peoples introduced new ideas, tools, traditions, beliefs, and technologies into the area. (Interestingly, some of the primary technologies introduced to the Arab people were advances in Roman and Persian military hardware, something they would put to considerable use in the near future.)

Although it was a time of considerable turmoil and change, no one had any idea of how much the future was about to be altered by the birth of the man from Mecca.[8]

•   •   •

At the time that Muhammad was born, the Arabian Peninsula was sparsely populated. The nomads who lived in the desert raised a few sheep, goats, or camels. A handful eked out a living farming the tiny patches of arable land that were available. Their primary loyalty was to one thing, and one thing only: their tribe. This was the exclusive focus of their world. They held little identity as Arabs, virtually no identity as a state or nation, and much of their life—outside of feeding themselves—was focused on raiding richer neighbors for bounty and slaves.

There were, however, some small towns and settlements along the trade routes. Mecca was one of those. At the time, Mecca was experiencing a burst of prosperity due to an increase in the number of caravans along the trade route that ran through it. It also had the benefit of something that was almost unheard of the area: an enduring source of income. Thousands of Arabs would travel to Mecca to worship

Al-Hajura-I-Aswad, the Black Stone, a black meteoritic rock that they believed (and Muslims still believe) was found by Abraham and dates back to Adam and Eve.

When he was about thirty-nine years old, Muhammad received his call to become the last of the Prophets. His message was not complicated: there is one God, Allah; Muhammad was his messenger with the responsibility to pass on God's word; in the life hereafter, we will all be judged and either awarded with a wonderful heavenly home or assigned a burning place in hell.

In the first years of his calling he made but a few converts—first, among his family, then among other townspeople. But spreading his message was not easy in Mecca, and he suffered persecution for, among other reasons, fear that his new religion might harm visitation to Mecca's sacred shrine.

In 622, he fled Mecca and found refuge in Medina, a city some two hundred miles to the north. There he was welcomed and found not only acceptance but also strong believers. It wasn't long before he became ruler of the city.

It soon became apparent that Islam was not just a religion and Muhammad was not just a religious ruler. His followers in Medina turned on the pagans of Mecca, instigating war. Muhammad rode at the head of this army, for he was in fact as much a warrior as a prophet. The war was long and wearisome. After an eight-year struggle, Muhammad prevailed against his home city. The Islamic religion was imposed on the people there. As noted by historian and Middle East expert Bernard Lewis, unlike Moses, who was stopped from entering his promised land, Muhammad conquered his:

> Muhammad conquered his promised land, and during his lifetime achieved victory and power in this world, exercising political as well as prophetic authority. As the Apostle of God, he brought and taught a religious revelation. But at the same time, as the head of the Muslim *Umma*, he promulgated laws, dispensed justice, collected taxes, conducted diplomacy, made war, and made peace. The *Umma*, which

began as a community, had become a state. It would soon become an empire.[9]

In the two years between the time he conquered Mecca and his death in 632, Muhammad's religion and political authority spread throughout much of Arabia.

According to Islam, he was the last of the Prophets. Once he had restored the true, monotheistic faith, it was up to his followers to take it to the rest of the world. The supreme rulers who followed Muhammad, the caliphs, took that responsibility very seriously. In the decades that followed, the Islamic empire was to expand to India and China to the east, to the west through Africa as far as the Atlantic Ocean, and north into Europe.

The speed with which the armies of these Islamic Arabs conquered these many peoples and lands was breathtaking.

Rise of the Islamic Caliphs

In 632, Islam was the religion of no more than a few, largely nomadic Arab tribesmen living in the desert regions of Syria and Iraq. Just one hundred years later, it was the religion of Syria, Iraq, Persia, Egypt, North Africa, Spain, Portugal, Uzbekistan, Turkmenistan, and southern Pakistan. All of these lands came to be ruled by Arab-speaking elites. And as Islam took hold in these subjugated lands, it immediately dominated all other religious faiths. Throughout the Persian Empire, Zoroastrianism all but disappeared. And with the exception of Spain and Portugal, Christianity and Judaism were nearly wiped out in the conquered regions.

It is important to note that, unlike other great conquests in history, the empire of the caliphs was to endure. Even today, with the exception of Spain and Portugal (due to events soon to be described), Islam remains the dominant religion in all of these lands. Further, Arabic is the dominant language in many of these countries.

And though it was true that Muhammad's success in spreading his religion was not entirely because of his military conquests—many converts pledged allegiance because of the appeal of his doctrine as well as his prominent tribal connections—the fact that he used military power to achieve his religious aims was of great importance to his followers:

> Muhammad's military campaigns were, in one sense, the beginning of the Muslim conquests. His example showed that armed force was going to be an acceptable and important element first in the defense of the new religion and then in its expansion. The Prophet's example meant that there was no parallel to the tendency to pacifism so marked in early Christianity.[10]

On the whole, Muhammad's military campaigns and successes made up the bulk of the early accounts of his life, and his military prowess was widely acclaimed by his followers.

Once Muhammad was gone, military conquest became the primary means of spreading his gospel, a pattern that was established soon after his death when a number of Arab Muslims declared their independence of Medina. The reaction of Muhammad's self-proclaimed successors was swift and eager. A large military force was sent to crush the apostates, who were quickly corrected or dispatched.

The battle against the renegade Arabs proved to be a watershed event, for it established a powerful precedent that would be adhered to for generations.

A Call to War

Once the armies of Islam had been set in motion, they were not inclined to stop. Having tasted the sweetness of military victory and impressed themselves with its relative ease, they looked at the world around them and realized that the Roman and Persian Empires were ripe to be taken.

The call to battle went out. The Arab armies went on the march. If there was fighting to be done, and booty to be taken, most of the nomadic tribesmen wanted to be part of it, even if it meant strict obedience to Muhammad's successors in Medina.

But although their military campaigns quickly became a powerful source of new recruits, it was an uneasy battle call for some.

The scriptural basis for the use of military force to spread Islam is somewhat cloudy. There are verses in the Koran that clearly justify, if not demand, the use of force to deal with nonbelievers.[11] But other verses imply a less vigorous approach to the "People of the Book" (Christians and Jews), stating that they are to be spared if they will pay a tax and acknowledge that they are to be second-class citizens and subservient to the believers. For others, including pagans and believers in more than one god, the choices were somewhat less appealing: conversion, death, or slavery.[12]

The seeming inconsistency in the scriptures regarding the use of force upon the nonbelievers was eventually settled by looking at the time period in which the revelations were received. Because the more militant verses were received later, they were deemed to be the controlling verses, leading to justification for Islamic conquest.

Despite the fact that outright forced conversion was not condoned, the penalty for failure to convert—punitive taxes, inferior status, even slavery—resulted, not surprisingly, in mass conversions:

> A frequently cited *hadith* refers to the vast and growing numbers of infidels who were converted to Islam after their defeat and enslavement: "God marvels at people who are dragged to paradise in chains."[13]

Having subdued their own territory, the Arabic forces were hardly satisfied. Indeed, they felt they were just getting started. Arab armies were dispatched to the east and the west. These armies were powerful but apparently not large, estimates of the number of soldiers who conquered Syria being only 30,000, Iraq somewhere between 6,000 and 12,000, Egypt around 16,000.[14] And they traveled light, each man supplying his own food and supplies. Their primary weapon was a three-foot sword with a broad, straight blade, but they supplemented these weapons with bows and arrows and spears to defend against enemy cavalry attacks. Although horses and camels provided mobility, most of the fighting took place on foot, sword to sword.

As one expert on the Islamic conquests, Hugh Kennedy, has noted:

> The early Muslims had no secret weapons, no mastery of new military technology with which to overpower their enemies. Their advantages were simply those of mobility, good leadership and, perhaps most important of all, motivation and high morale.[15]

Although it is difficult to surmise what drove these warriors of Islam, scholars have identified five primary motivations for their military campaigns, most of which are ascertained from early Arab sources:

1. Throughout Arabic culture, war and bloodshed were the greatest source of individual glory and enduring reputation. This long tradition of loving war and bringing slaughter existed long before Muhammad. And yet Muhammad's successors understood that their new religion forbade them from attacking other members of their faith. This created a dilemma, for the Arabs had always thrived on assault and pillage. Without the possibility of attacking their fellow Muslims, bringing war to their neighbors to the east and west became a necessity to vent the Arab tradition.[16]

2. The concept of *jihad* or "holy war" was real. Defenders of Islam who died in battle were martyrs who went straight to paradise. The infidels who died were sent straight to endless fire and hell. Some modern Muslim theologians give *jihad* a meaning of personal spiritual or moral striving; however, Bernard Lewis points out that in the early days of Islam its meaning was clear:

> The overwhelming majority of early authorities, however, citing relevant passages in the Qur'an and in the tradition, discuss *jihad* in military terms. Virtually every manual of *shari'a* law has a chapter on *jihad*, which regulates in minute detail such matters as the opening, conduct,

interruption and cessation of hostilities, and the allocation and division of booty.[17]

And it's significant to note that *jihad* was not limited in geography or to ancient times: "The Muslim *jihad* . . . was perceived as unlimited, as a religious obligation that would continue until all the world had either adopted the Muslim faith or submitted to Muslim rule."[18]

3. Islamic armies considered their efforts to liberate conquered people from their evil religions as a noble cause, for once they were liberated, the conquered people could then convert to Islam. As Lewis says, "The object of *jihad* is to bring the whole world under Islamic law. It is not to convert by force, but to remove obstacles to conversion."[19]

4. Arab armies took great pride in the success of their tribes, which pride quickly evolved into a sense of loyalty to their Arab identity.

5. The incredible wealth accumulated by the early leaders of the Islamic crusade was well chronicled by Arab historians. Throughout their campaigns, those leaders captured an enormous amount of gold and silver, as well as an astonishing number of slaves. This wealth was certainly an additional motivation for their conquest.

War Against the Empires

Once the rebellion among the apostate Arabs had been crushed, the Arab army moved to their first conquest, Syria and Palestine, the very home of Christianity.

The Syrian invasion began in 632. The beautiful city of Damascus soon fell and ultimately was to become the center of the entire Muslim world. Jerusalem fell sometime in 637 or 638. By 640, all of Syria and Palestine were under the rule of the caliph in Medina. After one thousand years of Greek and Roman rule and six hundred years of Christian influence, the area fell under the realm of Islam, and it remains primarily Muslim and Arabic-speaking to this day.[20]

The Byzantine and Persian Empires were next. Both had been greatly weakened by their ongoing wars. Further, the bubonic plague had decimated the region, killing as many as one-third of the population, leaving eerily deserted streets in some locations, making them easily conquered.

To the east, in the area of modern-day Iraq, the Persian Empire came under attack. Known for its wealth, prosperity, and power, the Persian Empire was a broad mix of those following the Zoroastrian, Christian, and Jewish religions. The invading Arab army conquered the last of the Persian lands by 640. As with Syria and Palestine, once the Persian army had been disposed of, if the people pledged to pay tribute to Medina and not to aid the enemies of the Muslims, they were generally left alone.[21]

Next came Egypt. Unlike Syria and Iraq, the ancient and venerable kingdom of Egypt had no Arab populations either on its borders or living in its midst. Indeed, the Muslims knew almost nothing about Egypt, other than that it was a place of great wealth.

Egypt generally, and Alexandria specifically, was the center of Christianity in the entire Roman Byzantine Empire. Unfortunately, it was torn by violent internal strife between independent groups of Christians (known as the Coptic Church, which still survives in Egypt today) and the emperor in Constantinople.

This discord, plus the fact that Egypt had also been afflicted by the bubonic plague (its total population may have been as few as three million), made the nation an easy target. The Arab invasion started in 639. Alexandria, one of the greatest cities in the world, surrendered after a brief siege. All of Egypt fell within two years.

In more than one Egyptian city, the Arabs slaughtered every man, woman, and child. Why they chose to abandon their habit of focusing only on enemy soldiers as targets of wholesale slaughter is not clear. As with Palestine and Syria, a thousand years of Greek and Roman rule came to a decisive end. Egypt became both Muslim and Arabic, and remains so to this day.[22]

And still it continued.

Modern-day Iran was conquered by 651.[23] Further north and east, the Arabs pressed into what are known today as Uzbekistan, Tajikistan, and Kazakhstan. To the south, they pushed into modern-day Pakistan where, interestingly, they defeated an army of Chinese soldiers led by a Korean officer. In all of these distant eastern lands, far from the center of Medina, their religion and influence remains to this day.[24]

West of Egypt, the armies of Islam forged toward the Atlantic Ocean. But conquering all of North Africa proved to be no small task. It is over two thousand miles from Alexandria to the Strait of Gibraltar, and the conquest of this enormous sweep of land would take more than seventy years.

Formerly a rich and prosperous part of the Roman Empire, the population of North Africa had grown sparse. The cities contained great buildings and ruins of some grandeur, but many of the people had left. Those who remained, mostly tribal and nomadic Berbers, proved to be more difficult to conquer than the Romans, who had developed a reputation for abandoning their territory as soon as the Arabs drew close. As the war across the territories of North Africa commenced, the Berbers fought bravely, for they were a proud and independent people fighting to be free. Highly motivated, if not well equipped or highly trained, they accomplished something that had never been done before: the defeat of a Muslim army.

Their victory would be only temporary, however, for the Arabs, sobered and angered by this first defeat in Islamic history, soon gathered a force of forty thousand soldiers (the largest army the Muslims would assemble until their assault of France) and quickly retook the Berber lands.

Two aspects of the North African conquest are particularly noteworthy.

First, the Arab armies took a massive number of slaves. The young Berber girls were deemed to be incomparable and highly prized in the markets of Middle Eastern cities. Hundreds of thousands of slaves were taken, with tens of thousands being sent back to Medina.[25]

The second significant aspect of this conquest was that the initial loss at the hands of the Berbers proved alarming to the Muslims.

Having experienced their first stinging defeat, they resolved never to let it happen again.

The Arab Armies Enter Europe

After decades of war, the Arab army finally reached the Strait of Gibraltar. It is reported that when the first Arab military leader had reached the Atlantic Ocean, he rode his horse up to its belly in the water and, with his eyes aimed at heaven, shouted:

> "Great God! if my course were not stopped by this sea,
> I would still go on, to the unknown kingdoms of the West,
> preaching the unity of thy holy name, and putting to the
> sword the rebellious nations who worship any other gods
> than thee."[26]

The Arab conquerors were not, as this leader feared, to be stopped by this sea, however.

Once the whole of North Africa had been subdued and an Arab settlement established at Tangier, the Arab armies cast their eyes across the waters. They knew their work in the name of Allah was not complete. It was inevitable. Spain had to be taken next.

In 711, the first of the invaders made the easy sail across the Strait of Gibraltar. Shortly after making landfall, they realized that they had arrived at a fortuitous moment, for rebellion was in the works.

Three hundred years had passed since the Visigoth kingdom had driven the Romans from Spain. These had been relatively stable years. However, just the year before, a usurper to the throne had appeared. Upon the death of the Visigoth king, a bitter fight for power had ensued, leaving the kingdom in turmoil.

Seizing the opportunity, and likely aided by the sons of the former king, the Muslims moved quickly to confront the army of the new ruler. Many of those in the area apparently thought it was nothing more than a one-time raiding party. Indeed, many of the local noblemen quickly agreed to peace settlements based upon their belief that the Muslims would not stay.

Such was not to be the case. The armies of Islam were to remain in Spain and Portugal for the next eight hundred years!

By 716, almost all of the Iberian Peninsula was under Islamic control.[27] Within the next two to three hundred years, the vast majority of the people in these conquered lands would become part of the Muslim faithful.

This leads to a very important question: Why did the Islamic conquest around the world prove to be so permanent?

Why were the Muslims able to have such long-lasting impact on the people and the cultures of the areas they brought under their control? The Assyrians couldn't do it. Neither did the Babylonians, the Persians, the Greeks, or the Romans. None of these great empires remained in the areas they conquered for so many centuries. And none of them changed so dramatically the values and religious habits of the people that they ruled.

There are a number of obvious explanations:

The poll tax hefted upon the nonbelievers provided a solid motivation for nonbelievers to convert, as did the reality that all nonbelievers were held to a second-class status. If one had any desire to become a part of the ruling elite, one had to become a member of the faith.

But there was another explanation.

There were great similarities between Christianity, Judaism, and Islam. All of these religions shared a belief in prophets, the writings of the Old Testament, prescribed prayers, and other tenets. If one's faith in Christianity or Judaism was not well founded (keep in mind that in this era, there were no copies of the Bible available to the people), devoid of much foundation in doctrine, inherited rather than personally obtained, it was not much of a leap to convert to a new religion that asserted that it was simply a more perfected form of the old religion, especially if that meant an end of punitive taxation and social inequality.[28]

Regardless of the various motivations for accepting the faith, it is irrefutable that the influence of the Muslim armies on the people that they conquered was unparalleled and permanent.

• • •

Having taken possession of the Iberian Peninsula, a very substantial foothold in Europe, the question then had to be, "Where next?"

Classical historian Edward Gibbon surmised the goal of the Muslim military leader in Spain:

> With a powerful armament by sea and land, he was preparing to repass the Pyrenees, to extinguish in Gaul and Italy the declining kingdoms of the Franks and Lombards, and to preach the unity of God on the altar of the Vatican. From thence, subduing the Barbarians of Germany, he proposed to follow the course of the Danube from its source to the Euxine Sea, to overthrow the Greek or Roman empire of Constantinople, and, returning from Europe to Asia, to unite his new acquisitions with Antioch and the provinces of Syria.[29]

If, as Gibbon suggests here, the Muslim armies had been able to continue their European conquests through France and then move east across the continent, circling through Europe from the Strait of Gibraltar, the caliphs would have controlled almost the entire civilized world.

Was it just a matter of time until this dream of conquering all of Europe was to be fulfilled?

The Arab Army Marches North

Having taken the Iberian Peninsula, the Muslims looked north, knowing they first had to cross the Pyrenees Mountains before they could begin their long march through Europe.

Over the next several decades, raiding parties ventured into what is now southern France. These advance warring parties followed a trail on the east side of the Pyrenees, for the mass of snow-covered peaks to the west made the eastern approach the only practical way into France.

The main assault began in May or June of 732. Christian chronicles say the invading army was in the hundreds of thousands. Arab reports state that the army consisted of eighty thousand Arab and Berber soldiers. More likely, the Arab reports are closer to the truth, but either way, the invading army was enormous. In addition, the Arabs possessed all of the siege equipment they would need to destroy the walled cities and fortresses of anyone foolish enough to stand in their way.

It's also important to note that the Arabs came with their wives, children, and belongings, making it clear that, as with everyplace else they had conquered, they intended to stay in France.

Once they had crossed through the mountain pass, the Muslims found the condition of the French monarchy much to their liking. Although they were all Christians, in the three hundred years since the various Germanic tribes had driven the Roman armies out of Gaul, with a very few exceptions they had never united in language, habits, or government. This left the French kingdoms fragmented, weak, and generally unwilling to join in defense of one another. They were forever engaged in civil wars, as well as constantly forced to defend themselves from the marauding pagan hordes that ventured forth from the other side of the Rhine.

In fact, the political and military condition of the Christian French was eerily similar to what the Muslim armies had encountered in many of their previous military campaigns.

Seeing the obvious opportunity, they marched quickly, following the pattern they had relied upon before: raid and probe the enemy's front lines, take a little territory here and there, loot and burn and destroy in order to determine the military might and will of the enemy, all as a preamble to the major assault.

The Muslims had all of the advantages that had resulted in mighty victories in each of their previous campaigns. Their entire empire was united under one caliph, giving them an enormous infrastructure to support their invading armies. They were commanded by Abd al-Rahman, a brilliant and experienced commander. They had the advantage of momentum and high morale, having experienced a hundred years of unbroken success overrunning the entire Persian Empire and one-half of the Roman Empire. Their soldiers were battle hardened and anxious to avenge their brothers who had fallen. Most important, they sincerely believed that they had the truth on their side. Surely their God meant them to prevail against the unbelievers in Gaul and beyond!

It appeared as if the weakened kingdoms on the north side of the Pyrenees had no hope to resist the army of Islam.

As Gibbon saw it, the French kings had

> lost the inheritance of . . . martial and ferocious spirit; and their misfortune or demerit has affixed the epithet of lazy to the last kings of the Merovingian race. They ascended the throne without power and sunk into the grave without a name . . . ; and the south of France, from the mouth of the Garonne to that of the Rhone, assumed the manners and religion of Arabia.[30]

The armies of Abd al-Rahman ventured forth in all directions. They destroyed cities and looted and pillaged churches and abbeys. They roamed unmolested until they reached the River Garonne, which starts in the center of the Pyrenees Mountains and runs toward the heart of France before turning west to the Atlantic Ocean.

And though the Muslims did suffer an occasional defeat, it wasn't long before they controlled all of the significant cities and a vast amount of the territory in southern and eastern Gaul.

Prince Eudes, the count of Aquitaine, came forth with an army to confront them. He was quickly defeated. He withdrew to the great port city of Bordeaux, but it was overrun and sacked, the churches burned, citizens killed, a treasure of booty and slaves taken. An Arab historian describes the great victory:

> The men of Abderrahman were puffed up in spirit by their repeated successes, and they were full of trust in the

valour and the practice in war of their Emir. So the Moslems smote their enemies, and passed the river Garonne, and laid waste the country, and took captives without number. And that army went through all places like a desolating storm. Prosperity made those warriors insatiable. . . . Everything gave way to their scimetars, which were the robbers of lives. All the nations of the Franks trembled at that terrible army.[31]

All of Europe teetered on the edge. Had it fallen under the hands of the Muslim armies, the future development of freedom and democracy would have taken a decisive turn for the worst.

But to understand the critical turn of events that followed, we need, as Gibbon wrote, to "unfold the events that rescued our ancestors of Britain and our neighbors of Gaul from the civil and religious yoke of the Koran."[32]

The Battlefield of Poitiers
Western France

THE TWO BROTHERS didn't see each other as they stood on opposite sides of the battlefield. But how could they? The mass of men around them were dressed for battle, helmets and mud covering their faces, fear of pain or death clouding their eyes. It would have been hard to recognize some of them if they were standing right before a man, let alone looking across a crowded battlefield.

After days of sparring, the two armies finally faced each other. No one knew how many men there were. Tens of thousands. Maybe hundreds of thousands. It was impossible to know, with the rolling hills and trees. More, realizing that there was no hope of avoiding all-out battle by casting fear of defeat upon their enemy, both commanders had chosen to hide some of their forces, wanting to retain at least a portion of the element of surprise.

The older brother, having brought almost two thousand of his own men to the battle, had a position of honor beside Abd al-Rahman, the commander of the Arab army. He sat on a large horse in front of the mighty army, the other royal commanders at his side.

As he watched, the horde of Christians massed before them. Some of them looked hungry. But they appeared to be prepared for battle. He could see that in their manner. He could hear it in their battle cries. These were men defending their homes and honor. Defending their religion.

That made them dangerous, he was sure.

He wasn't frightened, but he was concerned. The enemy was motivated, and he knew what a difference that could make. Motives could be the tipping point between success and defeat, and there wasn't any secret as to what motivated the two armies that had gathered on this field. One fought for the pride of the victory, for the pure joy of battle, for the riches and glory that only war could bring.

Yes, once they had defeated the inhabitants of Gaul, they would impose their God, for in the end, that was the only thing that really mattered: pleasing Allah, becoming a martyr for his cause, subduing the unbelievers. Such pleasurable thoughts were always in his mind.

But all these things would come in due time.

For the moment, this battle was about the here and now. Booty to make them rich. Booty to feed and reward their armies. Slaves and gold and glory. That was what the Arabs were fighting for today.

The invaders had learned that most of the riches in Europe could be found in the cathedral cities, those urban centers, such as they were, where the great churches had been built. Knowing this, they had already sacked the great church at Saint-Hilaire. Their next objective was the church of Saint-Martin, outside the city of Tours. After that, they would continue: another church, another cathedral, another city targeted and defeated, another step on the long march through Europe as they circled back toward the Middle East.

Only this rough band of insolent Christians stood to stop them. They had to be destroyed.

Soon after the sun had risen, the signal to attack was given. A great cry went out!

Leading his men into battle, the older brother, once a Christian, son of a former Spanish lord, rushed toward the fight. Lifting his sword as he rode, he thanked God for the possibility of being a martyr for His name.

A Hero Stands

After Bordeaux was taken and sacked, the defeated Prince Eudes attempted to engage the Arab army a second time, but suffered an even greater defeat. Desperate, he fled north where he frantically looked for a savior among the frightened and enfeebled ranks of Frankish leaders.

Somewhere in Paris, he met with Charles Martel, a longtime enemy but fellow Christian.

Charles Martel, duke of the Austrasian Franks, was the illegitimate son of the mayor (duke) of the Franks, a position roughly equivalent to that of prime minister. Like all the French monarchs, his king was weakened from constant conflicts, leaving the mayor as the most powerful man in the kingdom.

Charles was experienced in war, for he had spent many of his forty-four years struggling for power in Gaul as well as fighting against the fierce pagans from across the Rhine. Prior to 732, he had fought at least eleven major campaigns or battles, developing a reputation for being a strong and decisive leader, so much so that he earned the nickname "Martel" or "hammer," because "'as a martel [hammer] breaks and crushes iron, steel and all other metals, so did he break up and crush his enemies.'"[33]

Courageous. A noble leader. Experienced at war. Martel was an excellent choice to lead the effort to defeat the invading Islamic forces—except for the fact that he had no standing army. This inconvenient fact was the first obstacle Martel had to overcome.

Although he had no army, Martel did have a core of extraordinarily loyal comrades. Though few in number, they were highly disciplined, motivated, and very well trained. They had spent years with Martel marching on campaigns throughout Europe, and he knew he could count on them to come to his side.

After receiving a full report of the invasion by Abd al-Rahman,

Martel immediately issued a summons to war. This was answered by his loyal comrades in arms as well as soldiers from other regions who were terrified by reports of the ravaging Muslim army.

Martel was well aware that if he failed, there were no other forces able to defend Western Christianity. His soldiers also knew that. This made them a group of highly motivated men.

Martel assembled his small army at a point somewhere south of the city of Tours. There he waited for the advancing Muslim army. While he waited, he made the best of a desperate situation. He positioned his men to take tactical advantage of the rising terrain, made efforts to conceal their numbers, and obscured his intentions as best as he could.

The army of Abd al-Rahman was taking its time in getting to Tours. The Arab leader spent three months raiding and looting, roaming the territory without facing any opposition. But Tours, with its considerable wealth, lured him like a great bear to the smell of meat. As he approached the waiting enemy, Abd al-Rahman readied his men for battle, knowing that he would have to contend with Martel's men before he could continue his march into the cities at the very heart of France.

When Abd al-Rahman first made contact with Martel's forces, he was stunned to find a force that appeared to be well prepared for battle. The main infantry were heavily armed, each man plated in iron armor. As he surveyed the battlefield, he also realized that he had made a significant mistake in allowing Martel to choose the location of the battle. His opponent had been able to conceal his strength in the trees, leaving him to wonder how large the Christian army was. Worse, when the time came, he would have to attack uphill and through the forest.

Maybe for this reason, he did not immediately engage. Instead, he took time to recall scattered elements of his army, gathering all the reinforcements that he could. But he knew he could not wait forever. Unlike the local defenders, his men were not prepared to winter in this part of Europe. They were not accustomed to cold-weather warfare. More, his men were eager to continue the fight, always anxious when he held them at bay.

A couple of days of light skirmishes and scouting followed, each commander feeling the other out. The invaders wanted the Franks to come out and meet them in open battle. Martel would have none of that, knowing that the Arab army would decimate his limited forces. He also understood the advantage that he held on the high ground.

On Saturday, October 25, the two armies finally collided.

Organizing his army across a broad front, Abd al-Rahman ordered the attack. His soldiers mounted a frightening assault, riding to the battle on their horses before dismounting for brutal, sword-to-sword combat against the Christian defenders. Hoping to break the charge, Martel organized his men in a phalanx formation—a large square of defending soldiers.

Standing against overwhelming odds, the army of Martel held.

One account, purposefully poetic in its language, described the Christian position as holding like a "glacial wall."

The Muslims kept up the assault. The Christians still held. Thousands of men died on both sides of the attack. Neither army made any progress. At one point, Abd al-Rahman thrust toward Martel and his personal protectors. The defenders held their ground. All through the day, the sound of war lifted over the French landscape. Exhaustion. Blood. Bodies littered the land, blood congealing red in the autumn dust.

It appeared that the battle might be a standoff when, suddenly, the Muslims began to withdraw.

In a brilliantly executed and yet almost predictable maneuver (all armies seek to outflank the enemy position), a contingent of Christians had flanked the main battle to attack the Muslims' camp to the rear. Caught completely by surprise, the warriors of Abd al-Rahman were forced to retreat to defend their families that remained in their camp, not to mention their captured treasure.

As the invaders began to pull back, Martel ordered a counterattack. A fierce battle took place in the main Muslim camp. Eventually, the counterattack was thwarted and Martel was forced to withdraw. But when the battle had ended, Abd al-Rahman, the great Arab leader, was found among the dead, his body pierced through by a javelin.

That night, unexpectedly—really *inexplicably*—the Muslims abandoned their camp. They left their tents. They left their animals and belongings. They left their beloved loot and slaves. They even left their war gear and siege equipment. Without their noble leader, they abandoned a battle that up to that point had generally been considered at worst a draw. Though they still outnumbered their opponents, and though they certainly had reason to be optimistic of the outcome, they hastily packed up a few essentials and left the battlefield.

The next morning, fully expecting a day of battle, Martel prepared his army for another attack. As the sun rose, the Christians were amazed to find the Muslim camp completely deserted. The enemy had yielded and was in full retreat.

It was Sunday, October 26.

The invaders were on their way back to Spain.

Along the Trail of Retreat
East of the Pyrenees Mountains

HE WAS DYING. He didn't know it yet, or at least he didn't realize that it would come so quickly, but he would see only one more sunrise in this world. And though he would fight it until the moment that he finally closed his eyes, he was beginning to see this was a fight he could not win.

His bowels were infected from the sword that had pierced his side. The bacteria were spreading through his blood now, heading for his lungs and heart.

He lay beside the rutted road, his fellow soldiers marching past him. There was nothing they could do to help him and not many would have been inclined to, even if they could. He wasn't the only man who was dying from the battle, not the only soldier to lie down along the trail, not the last man to realize that he would never again see his home.

The oldest son of the former Spanish lord struggled to breathe, his lungs swelling with liquid. He pulled as deeply as he could, but all he got was a solid gurgle in his chest. He shivered. He was cold. He hadn't been warm since the battle on the plains of France. Wrapping himself in his long robes, he prepared for a long, cold night ahead.

Darkness came. The night grew silent. His horse remained beside him, nibbling on the mountain grass. His fellow soldiers kept on marching through the eastern pass that would take them back to Spain. Soon after midnight, they all had passed. The man closed his eyes and slept.

The sun rose over the rolling plains that stretched toward the Mediterranean Sea. He felt its warmth upon his face and woke slowly. Looking stiffly around, he realized that he was alone now, the other soldiers—as many as were left from the terrible battle—having moved on through the night. His entire body hurt. From his feet to his eyes, he was one knotted ball of pain. His chest shook with every breath. His head swam and he could not focus. His mouth was painfully dry, but his hands were so weak he could barely hold his flask of water. Sometimes he shivered from the cold. Sometimes he was drenched in sweat.

Considering his pain, he remembered something one of his soldiers had muttered to him once. *It is very hard work to die.*

Gathering what little strength he could, he took stock of his supplies. His sword, blood-stained and dirty. A leather pouch of water. A small knife. A couple of pieces of dried goat meat, a few scraps of bread.

Struggling to sit, he looked around him and, for the first time, realized where he was. The green meadow of his father was not far, just a short ride up the trail.

He felt a sudden urge that seemed to consume him with desire. He wanted to be there. To die there. To lay his body down and rest there, upon his family land.

It nearly killed him to pull himself up onto the wooden saddle of his horse. He rode, hunched over, barely breathing, his throat gurgling. It took almost two hours to get there, but the meadow finally came into view.

Stopping at the edge of the trees, he rolled onto the grass.

His brother found him two days later. With nothing but a short prayer, he dug a shallow grave and buried him beside the stream.

He was one of tens of thousands of dead Islamic warriors who were left atop the battlefield or scattered along the trail that led back to Andalus.

Over the next few days, a small number of Muslim soldiers returned. The remains of their brother soldiers were dragged to the meadow and buried beside the first. Islamic law was very clear in this regard. It was strictly forbidden for a believer to be buried beside an infidel. The fear of seeing their brothers buried in a sinful manner motivated the invaders to return to assure that they were placed in a proper grave.

After burying their dead, the Muslim soldiers retreated across the mountain pass and never came back.

The burial ground, along with several others, became a tiny Muslim cemetery and remains so to this day.

The Final Outcome

Martel watched the defeated army retreat toward the Pyrenees Mountains. He considered following but, having become aware of an immediate challenge from pagan Germans attacking his frontier along the Rhine, chose not to pursue the retreating army.

During the retreat, the Muslims took occasion to loot what they could. But they could not do much damage, for they were harassed along the way by the newly reassembled army of Prince Eudes as well as other local forces.

One account of the battle reported massive casualties (375,000) on the part of the army of Islam, with only 1,500 Christians killed. Those figures are justifiably in dispute. What is indisputable, however, is the fact that what seemed to be, up to that time, an unconquerable Muslim army had suffered a resounding defeat. Over the coming years, the Arab invaders would continue to launch occasional looting raids on southern France, but never again would they attempt an all-out assault on Christian Gaul.

In 759, the last of their footholds in southeast France was retaken.

The Muslim army never crossed the Pyrenees again.

As for Charles Martel, his great victory resulted in the rise of the

Carolingians, his own family dynasty. The most famous of his successors was his grandson Charlemagne, "Charles the Great," who united the Franks and other warring tribes under the Holy Roman Empire—a fully Christian empire consisting of most of central and western Europe that survived in one form or another for a thousand years. This proved to be a critical event, for Charlemagne's rule is recognized as an era of renaissance in art, religion, and culture, so much so that he is considered to be the "Father of Europe," responsible for creating a common European identity.[34]

But what would have happened if his grandfather had been defeated?

What would the world be like today if the armies of Islam had conquered all of Europe?

Would Rome, the Christian church, and Western Judaism have been destroyed, much like Zoroastrianism had been destroyed in the Persian Empire under Islamic rule?

Would there have been an early end to the Byzantine Empire?

If the caliphs had been allowed to rule, what would have happened to the future development of Western culture and values, including developments in law, respect for human rights and the individual, and economic and religious freedom?

Without Western influence to safeguard these concepts from their early cradle through to maturity, what would have happened to the future development of self-government and democracy?

Concerning the possible march of the Arab army through Europe, and what that would have meant, Edward Gibbon has suggested:

> The Rhine is not more impassable than the Nile or Euphrates, and the Arabian fleet might have sailed without a naval combat into the mouth of the Thames. Perhaps the interpretation of the Koran would now be taught in the schools of Oxford, and her pulpits might demonstrate to a circumcised people the sanctity and truth of the revelation of Muhammed.[35]

Which is why the Battle of Poitiers—which led to the denial of an Islamic conquest of Europe—was absolutely essential to the development of freedom in our day.

Notes

1. Von Ranke, *History of the Reformation,* 1:5.
2. See http://muslimvoices.org/five-pillars-of-islam/.
3. Lewis, *What Went Wrong,* 101.
4. Ibid., 54.
5. Ibid., 39.
6. Ibid., 79.
7. For a thorough discussion of the limitations of Islam and how it affected the development of personal liberty, representative government, and advances in science and economic development in the nations it ruled, see Lewis, *What Went Wrong.*
8. For information about the status of this part of the world leading up to the birth of Muhammad, see Gibbon, *Decline and Fall of the Roman Empire,* 893–944; Kennedy, *Great Arab Conquests,* 34–45; and Lewis, *Middle East,* 33–47.
9. Lewis, *Middle East,* 53. *Umma* means "Muslim community." Regarding his belief in the importance of warfare in his life, Muhammad is reported to have said, "The sword is the key of heaven and of hell; a drop of blood shed in the cause of God, a night spent in arms, is of more avail than two months of fasting or prayer: whosoever falls in battle, his sins are forgiven" (Gibbon, *Decline and Fall of the Roman Empire,* 919–20).
10. Kennedy, *Great Arab Conquests,* 48.
11. For example, verse 9:5 reads: "'When the sacred months are past, kill the idolaters wherever you find them, and seize them, besiege them and lie in wait for them in every place of ambush; but if they repent, pray regularly and give the alms tax, then let them go their way, for God is forgiving, merciful'" (quoted in Kennedy, *Great Arab Conquests,* 49–50).
12. For a discussion of the revelatory justification for military conquest, see Kennedy, *Great Arab Conquests,* 48–51; Lewis, *Middle East,* 57–58, 233–34. As to the choice between conversion or slavery for the pagan, Gibbon characterizes it thus: "A simple profession of faith established the distinction between a brother and a slave" (*Decline and Fall of the Roman Empire,* 946).
13. Lewis, *Middle East,* 234. A *hadith* is a collection of the sayings of the Prophet Muhammad that constitutes a major source of guidance for those of the Islamic faith.
14. See Kennedy, *Great Arab Conquests,* 57.
15. Ibid., 62.

16. For a discussion of the Arab tradition of attack and pillage, as well as the motivation for the early Islamic soldiers, see Kennedy, *Great Arab Conquests,* 55–65; Lewis, *Middle East,* 57–59, 233–35. Lewis pays particular attention to the traditional meaning of *jihad.*

17. Lewis, *Middle East,* 233.

18. Ibid.

19. Ibid., 234.

20. For a discussion of the conquering of Palestine and Syria, see Gibbon, *Decline and Fall of the Roman Empire,* 947–49; Kennedy, *Great Arab Conquests,* 66–97.

21. See Kennedy, *Great Arab Conquests,* 98–138. Gibbon reports that the tribute imposed on the Persian Empire as a whole (both Iraq and Iran) was two million pieces of gold (see Gibbon, *Decline and Fall of the Roman Empire,* 946–47).

22. See Kennedy, *Great Arab Conquests,* 139–68. For a full discussion of the religious discord that beset the Byzantine Empire, see Gibbon, *Decline and Fall of the Roman Empire,* 815–51, and for its specific impact on the Muslim conquest of Egypt, see ibid., 949–51.

23. See Kennedy, *Great Arab Conquests,* 169–99.

24. See ibid., 225–95.

25. See ibid., 214–15, 222–23.

26. Quoted in Gibbon, *Decline and Fall of the Roman Empire,* 953.

27. For information about the conquest of Spain and Portugal, see ibid., 953–54; Kennedy, *Great Arab Conquests,* 308–19.

28. For a discussion of the reasons for the success of the Arab armies and the conversion motivation and process, see Kennedy, *Great Arab Conquests,* 366–76.

29. Gibbon, *Decline and Fall of the Roman Empire,* 954.

30. Ibid., 964.

31. Quoted in Creasy, *Fifteen Decisive Battles,* 155.

32. Gibbon, *Decline and Fall of the Roman Empire,* 961.

33. Quoted in Nicolle, *Poitiers,* 20.

34. For a full account of the invasion of France and the Battle of Poitiers, see Creasy, *Fifteen Decisive Battles,* 148–58; Gibbon, *Decline and Fall of the Roman Empire,* 964–67; Kennedy, *Great Arab Conquests,* 319–23; and Nicolle, *Poitiers,* 1–88.

35. Gibbon, *Decline and Fall of the Roman Empire,* 964. See also Durant, *Age of Faith,* 461, wherein Durant says that Charles Martel "saved Europe for Christianity by turning back the Moslems at Tours."

Chapter 5

The Mongol Horde Turns Back

Part of Genghis Khan's strategy was calculated massacre:
if a city resisted his armies, once it fell to him—and they always fell—
he had all the inhabitants slaughtered. The chroniclers' reports
of the numbers of dead are staggering.

ROBERT COWLEY IN *WHAT IF*

Five hundred years after the Muslim army had been driven from southern France, another army marched on Europe, this one more savage and dangerous than any that had ever been witnessed on the continent before.

This raging army left nothing but devastation in its wake. Whole cities were destroyed, every man, woman, and child beheaded, their bloody skulls stacked in huge piles outside the city walls. Entire cultures and peoples—some of them highly advanced—were wiped off the earth, their history and societies reduced to the point that they were never heard from again. Indeed, the destructive power of this brutal army would be felt throughout Asia and Eastern Europe for the next seven hundred years, to the point that some modern-day nations are still dealing with its devastating impacts.

Such was the power of the Mongol horde.

In 1236, after raging through China and eastern Asia, the Mongols set their eyes on Europe.

The timing couldn't have been any worse, for the world was at a crossroads that it had never approached before. The Dark Ages were receding. Advances in science, technology, art, agriculture, and law were slowly working their way into the light. More important, the embryonic ideas of individual freedom and representative government were just beginning to take hold, with some European leaders beginning to concede to their people the essential elements of free will.

At this critical time, the threat of civilization devolving into chaos rose once again.

The Mongol army raged in from the Mongolian steppes. Throughout all of Eurasia, city after city fell. With the approach of the vicious army, the future of Western civilization hung in the balance, the outcome anything but assured.

But to understand the grave threat that the Mongol army presented, we must first understand the nature of the Mongol treatment of its conquered peoples and the condition of Europe as its invasion began.

Gurganj (Capital City of the Kingdom of Khwarizm) Central Asia AD 1221

WHAT HAD STARTED as a modest settlement along the western bank of the Amu Darya River had grown into the most beautiful city in the entire kingdom. Dating back to the fourth century BC, when the city was nothing but a small square of mud homes, it had spread south and then west until it covered a large tract of the broad plain.

Thick ramparts with four beautiful gates kept the city safe, the massive Gate of Peace the most beautiful of them all. Across the bridge, the Garden of Amusements lay just outside the city walls. Canals ran up to each gate but then stopped, there being no room inside the crowded city for them to continue any farther. The great palace of *Ma'mun* stood next to the *Hajjaj* gate, its blue-tiled dome reflecting the morning light. Inside the highly fortified city, residential neighborhoods took up most of the space. Interspersed among the rock and brick houses were a magnificent mosque, several lesser palaces, three minarets, and a considerable library. Perhaps most surprising of all the structures were the five large and lively schools, nearly unheard-of for a city of this size.

If anything showed where the people of Khwarizm had placed their faith, it was the presence of the schools.

For generations, the kingdom of Khwarizm had been isolated, surrounded by mountains and rolling steppes. But over the past hundred years it had reemerged as a player in world trade. Having tasted greatness under the Persian Empire, it was striving to touch greatness once again.

But the Mongols were about to ensure that would never be the case.

He was an old man, almost seventy, with three wives, fourteen children, a small patch of land outside the city walls, and a rock home inside. His name was Al-Marwazi. White hair. White beard. Thin frame, with long fingers and a solemn face. Trained as an astronomer, he had achieved a certain degree of fame, but he was a teacher, not a fighter, and certainly not trained in the art of war. It didn't matter. Like everyone else in the city, he was focused on just one thing: this day, the next few hours.

If the city were going to survive, it would be only because of what he and his fellow citizens did right now.

He looked down the line of soldiers waiting atop the city wall. Thousands of them. Tens of thousands, maybe. The archers were nearest the ramparts, their weapons ready. Behind them, more archers, then infantry and bulwark defenders. Some of the men, himself among them, were much too old. And there were far too many boys among the fighters. But again, it didn't matter, not with the danger that was riding toward them from the steppes.

Al-Marwazi stared over the plain and considered the events that had brought the Mongols to their land.

Earlier, the Mongol king had sent a caravan to the city under the guise of soliciting trade. Everyone knew the Mongol traders were really spies sent to scout the best way to attack. Not wanting to give them information, the sultan had ordered them killed.

Then they had prepared for war, for the Khwarizmi were not fools. Most of them knew that, caravan or no, an invasion was inevitable. And the pessimists had been proven right. Within months, the khan's army had moved through the kingdom, destroying every city and small town in its path. The capital was the only urban center of any significance that hadn't already fallen under the Mongol hand.

Being at the back end of the trail of destruction, the people of Khwarizm understood what was headed their way. That was why they were so frightened. Some of the refugees from previous engagements had made their way to the capital, telling of entire cities razed, thousands of beheaded bodies stacked outside the city walls, everything of any value taken, including a frightening number of slaves.

So it was that Al-Marwazi stood upon the walls and watched in terror as the violent Mongol army drew near.

They were a few miles in the distance still, but they were coming, their horses kicking up a trail of dust that betrayed their progress. There were no infantry, only riders, each of them armed for war. Beside each mounted warrior, other horses were herded along the way.

They were coming much more slowly than he would have thought, and Al-Marwazi squinted into the distance. A thousand archers moved forward along the wall, getting ready to stop the assault by sending down the rains of hell.

Looking at the billowing cloud of dust, he knew the archers wouldn't be enough.

He expected to hear the thunder from the horses, but the Mongols had tied rags around their hooves to muffle the sound of the attack. Why they did it, he didn't know. A night or surprise attack, maybe, but not this, a daylight frontal assault. It was just one of many things about the Mongols that he didn't understand.

"Archers!" the military commander cried as the invaders drew closer.

He listened as the thousand archers mounted arrows beside their bows, then turned to watch the army trekking across the dusty plain.

Something caught his eye: a mass of movement running wildly before the horses. Riders on each side kept herding it back into line. He lifted his hand to shade the morning sun. It took a few seconds before he realized what he was seeing.

Hundreds of naked children were being herded before the coming horde!

Al-Marwazi took a sudden breath of utter fear, then clenched his hands, his fist growing tight around his cankered sword.

The Mongols were herding children!

A cry of rage and horror rose from atop the city walls.

A thousand children before the army!

He had to fight the bile down.

They were using children—Khwarizmi children taken from the outer province—herding them before their army to protect them from the arrows that would soon come raining down.

He turned in terror toward the archers, almost falling to his knees. They stood there, their arrows drawn. But not one released an arrow as the Mongols drew ever nearer.

He swallowed hard, his mind racing, drops of sweat dripping into his eyes.

Al-Marwazi had anticipated a day of terror.

But he had *never* imagined this!

The Dark Days of Europe

After the fall of the Roman Empire, Europe descended into a long night of instability and darkness—that era known as the Dark Ages.

In AD 410, Rome was a thriving city of over a million people. By AD 560, it had largely been abandoned, crumbling to a struggling village of a few thousand souls. The beautiful Colosseum had been damaged by earthquake and fire, and would soon be looted for its iron and stone; same for the mighty Forum, as well as all of the other beautiful structures that had made Rome the magnificent city it once had been.

The glory days of the Empire had faded to a distant memory. Gone were the Roman legions that had protected the borders and assured security. Gone were the uniform legal system and empire-wide economy. Gone were the unity, security, and prosperity that the Empire had provided. And the decay of the Empire wasn't limited to the cities. Throughout the countryside, much of the farmland had been abandoned and was returning to nature. The celebrated Roman roads and highway system fell into disrepair. With the destruction of the transportation system, trade and communication suffered.

Rome wasn't the only city forsaken. Urban life throughout the continent had been almost entirely abandoned. Without the capacity to secure sufficient food supplies, and without any protection from the barbarians, the major cities in Europe could not sustain themselves. By the tenth century, there were probably only a dozen or so towns in all of Europe, none of them with a population of more than ten thousand people.[1] Without the support of major cities, safety could be found only in small, often isolated communities centered on a local baron (in England known as a lord) or a monastery.

Barons and bishops had to be self-sufficient, for the communities that surrounded them were typically made up of only fifty to five hundred families, hardly enough to call a kingdom, and rarely enough to defend themselves. Because these rural barons and bishops had their own laws and their own armies (such as they were), it wasn't surprising that the most influential and unifying power within the whole of Europe became the church.

In an arrangement that came to be known as feudalism, small farmers, known as serfs, aligned themselves with a local baron, relying upon him and his knights for protection.[2] Though they were not slaves, these serfs were forced to surrender much of their freedom for protection, a necessary evil in such a hostile world.

The local kings were at the top of the social ladder. But the ladder wasn't very tall. Because they had no standing army, the kings were dependent upon the barons to supply mounted knights, as well as serfs for their infantry. This forced them to negotiate from a position of beggary, and the reality was that they had little real power. The entire continent was riddled with strife, for it was presumed that any other baron's fiefdom was subject to taking if one had the means of doing so. For these and other reasons, war was a constant of the feudal age, every baron claiming "the right of private war," every king "free to embark at any time upon . . . robbery of another ruler's land," until "there was scarce a day in the twelfth century when some part of what is now France was not at war."[3]

And though the church deplored this constant state of war, there was one military campaign that it did support. As discussed in the previous chapter, Islamic armies seized the Holy Land from the Christian Byzantine Empire in 637 or 638. Although Jerusalem was occupied by Muslim forces, it remained a holy city to all Christian Europe. In 1095, Pope Urban II called for Christendom to reclaim the city.

One year later, under the rather uninspired leadership of Peter the Hermit and Walter the Penniless, several hundred thousand commoners set out to retake the Holy Land. Their knowledge of geography and war was not impressive. After mistaking several European cities for Jerusalem, they finally stumbled into Asia, where they were slaughtered by the Turks. Despite this disheartening start, at the urging of successive popes, other Crusades were undertaken. Two hundred years of mortal combat followed until, by 1291, European leaders had sponsored a total of eight individual Crusades. Some of them were successful; most were not. When the city of Acre (now Akko) was recaptured by the Saracens in 1291, the last of the major European strongholds in the Middle East was extinguished.[4]

Even though they did not ultimately accomplish their goal of reclaiming the Holy Land, the Crusades still helped to propel the Europeans forward, many scholars suggest, mainly because they initiated contact with the advanced cultures of Islam. Some contend this is absurd.[5]

Either way, there is no doubt that the era of the Crusades, as well as the five hundred years that preceded them, were some of the most difficult times the people of Europe had been called upon to endure. But as the next century began to unfold, things were starting to change.

After all of the suffering, the Dark Ages were giving way to the light.

The Dawn of a New Age

Throughout the Europe of the thirteenth century, the various kings began to consolidate their power and organize their people into potent and functioning kingdoms. For example, by 1250, the king of France had established a kingdom of influence and authority. Fifty years later, the French monarch was actually powerful enough to stand up to the pope.

For a variety of reasons, feudalism was on the wane. The feudal barons grew weaker. Trade and commerce, as well as banking and industry, were accelerating. Currency was being normalized, a development that aided many commercial endeavors. Economies were growing.

The reemergence of the cities had also begun. By 1200, Paris was the largest city north of the Alps, with a population of one hundred thousand. Other cities with populations of fifty thousand included Douai in northern France and Ghent in modern-day Belgium. London had a population of twenty thousand. The growth of these cities further led to the weakening of the feudal barons, their role as protectors becoming less and less necessary.

Agriculture, too, was going through major changes. The heavy plow was brought into common use. Three-field crop rotation became the norm, the rotation of winter wheat, rye, peas, lentils, and beans significantly increasing production while at the same time keeping the land more fertile. Forests were being cleared, swamps were being drained, and additional lands were being tilled. Fewer people went hungry. Starvation from a local drought or other small-scale natural disaster became less common. Health increased, especially among the young, even if only slightly, as diets were improved.

With more productive crops and better communications, shipping, and roads, opportunities for trading the fruits of a farmer's labors were significantly increased.

For the first time, common people had the opportunity of accumulating a certain degree of wealth: a few animals, scattered pieces of simple furniture, cooking utensils, work tools, maybe even a few pieces of silver. This greater individual wealth also fueled commercial activities.

Science stepped out of the overwhelming shadow of superstition. As the feudal barons grew weaker, more powerful monarchs rose in their place, men who had the reach and resources to bring a semblance of stability to the lands that they ruled.

As one noted historian has said in describing the crucial twelfth and thirteenth centuries:

> While political power centralized during the 12th and 13th centuries, the energies and talents of Europe were gathering in one of civilization's great bursts of development. Stimulated by commerce, a surge took place in art, technology, building, learning, exploration by land and sea, universities, cities, banking and credit, and every sphere that enriched life and widened horizons. Those 200 years were the High Middle Ages, a period that brought into use the compass and mechanical clock, the spinning wheel and treadle loom, the windmill and watermill; a period when Marco Polo traveled to China and Thomas Aquinas set himself to organize knowledge, when universities were established . . . ; . . . Roger Bacon delved into experimental science . . . ; . . . while the soaring cathedrals rose arch upon arch, triumphs of creativity, technology, and faith.[6]

Europe was positioned to emerge from the dark days of the early Middle Ages. And all of these developments were the result of, and the cause for, greater personal freedom and recognition of legal rights.

The age of arbitrary rule and tyranny was truly under siege. Personal freedom and liberty were being experienced in the birthplaces of capitalism—small towns in Italy and northern Europe.

As stability took hold, a sense of security began to permeate much of Europe. With this increase of security, and the confidence that it engendered, the people forged the courage to demand certain rights. And for the first time, the idea that the people *might actually have some rights* was not discarded out of hand. In 1215, the Magna Carta, a magnificent document that was forced upon King John of England, established the relative rights of the church and the barons against those of the king. Though the English monarch was to remain a very powerful man for many centuries, the Magna Carta provided the foundation for the development of constitutional law and individual rights.

The Age of Reason was coming. The political philosophy that embraced a love of freedom, self-government, equality, and the rule of law—which distinguished the West from the rest of the world in a profound way—was in its infancy. But it was alive. And it was growing.

It was a remarkable time!

Another well-respected historian described the importance of this era:

> The economic revolution of the thirteenth century was the making of modern Europe. It eventually destroyed a feudalism that had completed the function of agricultural protection and organization. . . . It transformed the immobile wealth of feudalism into the fluent resources of a world-wide economy. It provided the machinery for a progressive development of business and industry, which substantially increased the power, comforts, and knowledge of European man. It brought a prosperity that in two centuries could build a hundred cathedrals. . . . Its production for an extending market made possible the national economic systems that underlay the growth of the modern states. Even the class war that it let loose may have been an added stimulant to the minds and energies of men. When the storm of the transition had subsided, the economic and political structure of Europe had been transformed. A flowing tide of industry and commerce washed away deep-rooted impediments to human development, and carried men onward from the scattered glory of the cathedrals to the universal frenzy of the Renaissance.[7]

But what if this pivotal century had not been allowed to play out as it did?

What if the European cities had been destroyed, the Church crippled, the population decimated?

What if those ideas and values that would have such a powerfully positive influence upon the world over the next seven hundred years had been eliminated?

What if Europe had fallen victim to the most murderous and violent band of invaders the world had ever seen?

Genghis Khan and His Mongol Hordes

The Mongols were not strangers to Europe.

Their distant cousins, the Huns, contributed to the decline of the Roman Empire when they invaded in the fourth and fifth centuries. These were followed by other cousins, the Magyars, who overran major portions of Europe in 889. By 975, all of these invaders had accepted Christianity and made their home in Hungary.[8]

But the Mongols of the late twelfth and early thirteenth centuries were a very different breed of barbarian from their earlier cousins. Much more aggressive. Much more focused. Much more protective of their own. They were bloodthirsty soldiers who fed on war and conquests.

And they were incredibly successful. Undistracted by the niceties of empire building, they could focus on one thing and one thing only: invasion, with its subsequent subjugation.

As author Jack Weatherford has pointed out:

> In twenty-five years, the Mongol army subjugated more lands and people than the Romans had conquered in four hundred years. Genghis Khan, together with his sons and grandsons, conquered the most densely populated civilizations of the thirteenth century. . . . Genghis Khan conquered more than twice as much as any other man in history. . . . The empire covered between 11 and 12 million contiguous square

miles, an area . . . considerably larger than North America.
. . . It stretched from the snowy tundra of Siberia to the hot
plains of India, from the rice paddies of Vietnam to the wheat
fields of Hungary, and from Korea to the Balkans. . . . The
most astonishing aspect . . . is that . . . his army . . . was com-
prised of no more than one hundred thousand warriors—a
group that could comfortably fit into the larger sports stadi-
ums of the modern era.[9]

To understand the Mongols, we must understand their founder,
the infamous Genghis Khan.

Genghis Khan was born on the steppes of Mongolia in 1162. His
Mongol tribe were nomads who made their livelihood hunting, herding, trading, and raiding their neighbors. His given name was Temujin,
the name of a warrior his father had killed shortly before his birth.
Along the steppes of Mongolia, intertribal war was constant. It seemed
to be the nature of the people, having been bred into them over a millennium of fighting to survive. Because of this, Temujin was reared in
a brutal environment where pillaging, kidnapping, rape, and quick and
cruel death were nothing but a way of life.

His father died when Temujin was a teenager. When his older
half brother attempted to take over the role as head of the household,
Temujin rebelled and killed him. For this, his tribe enslaved him, but it
wasn't long until Temujin escaped.

At some point in his young life, Temujin decided that it was his
fate to unite all of the Mongol tribes into one. Gathering a small clan
around him, he began to war upon the nearby clans.

From the beginning, Temujin proved to be a brilliant leader. He
approached clan leadership in a new way, instituting radical and innovative practices that would serve him well.

For one thing, ignoring all custom and tradition, Temujin did not
rely on family or tribe in deciding who would rule with him. No more
taking care of brothers, cousins, or closest friends. Merit and merit
alone would determine who would rule.

Also, contrary to former practices of the steppe, Temujin instituted a policy wherein members of a defeated tribe were allowed to become full members of his clan. Instead of dispersing or enslaving conquered tribes, he used them to enhance and grow his own horde. Even more daring, he started integrating members of the conquered tribes into his military. To be accepted into his army, all one had to do was pledge loyalty to him.

No more did he raise his own tribe above the others. Instead, he abolished any distinctions between tribes, clans, and families. He ended the caste system whereby some were deemed to come from better or richer or more handsome tribes than others. Many different religions could be found among the tribes of the steppe, including shamanists (who worshipped the sky and mountains), Christians, Muslims, and Buddhists. All were accepted into his new society.

But the relative equality with which he governed his own people did not mean that Temujin was a good or compassionate man. Quite the opposite—he was as brutal and merciless as any man who had ever lived.

Early on, he adopted the policy that anyone who dared oppose him was doomed to an immediate and violent death. He showed absolutely no mercy to any leader who refused to kneel before his sword.

The first Mongol tribe he triumphed over was the Jurkins. After Temujin's quick victory, the members of the Jurkin clan were dispersed among his tribe. (He even took a Jurkin orphan into his family, tasking his mother to raise him.) The leaders of the Jurkin clan, however, were viciously murdered. As an example of his brutality, one leader who had insulted Genghis's younger brother had his spinal cord snapped and then was dragged a short distance from the camp, where he died a slow and excruciating death.

This was not the last time that such a cruel method for killing an enemy would be used:

> Temujin had rid himself of all the leaders of the Jurkin. The messages were clear to all their related clans on the steppe. To those who followed Temujin faithfully, there

would be rewards and good treatment. To those who chose
to attack him, he would show no mercy.[10]

• • •

In 1205, when he was forty-three years old, Temujin completed his
conquest of the last of the steppe tribes, becoming the absolute ruler
of all of Mongolia. His new kingdom was roughly the size of Western
Europe and had a population of about a million people. Naming his
united country *The Great Mongol Nation,* he took upon himself the
title of Genghis Khan.

Just as he had instituted radical practices in the development of his
clan and army, he also brought new thinking to the management of
his kingdom, putting into operation a series of laws that reordered his
new society in ways large and small—for example, ending kidnapping,
outlawing adultery, and setting rules for hunting rights.

One of the most important steps he took was the initiation of the
ceremonial *khuriltai,* essentially a primitive method of popular election. A tribal council would be called regarding any critical piece of
business before the nation: future military campaigns, leadership positions, titles, military strategies, and the like. Because of the important nature of these decisions, a *khuriltai* required the presence of all
senior tribal and military leaders. Once the *khuriltai* had been called,
the Mongol nation had the opportunity, essentially, to vote by either
showing up, which evidenced a vote for the decision of the council, or
not showing up, which meant the vote was "no."

Most important, a *khuriltai* was essential to choose a new khan, or
national leader. Indeed, that fact would prove, as the world would see
some forty years later, to be one of those seemingly small but critical
tipping points that would change the future.

The Invasion of China

With the steppe under his dominion, and as the ruler of a nation
of natural-born warriors, Genghis Khan now faced a new problem.

How could he satisfy the bloodlust of his people? Fulfill their ache for plunder? Keep his army satisfied?

For many years, the Mongols had looked longingly upon the riches of the nation to their south. In that day, they called it Cathay. Today we call it China.

In 1211, following a *khuriltai,* the Mongols decided to invade.

> After this in the Year of the Sheep
> Chingis Khan set out to fight the people of Cathay. . . .
> killing the finest and most courageous soldiers of
>   Cathay, . . .
> slaughtering them along the sides of Chu-yung Kuan
> so that their bodies lay piled up like rotting trees.[11]

The leaders of Cathay did not take the invasion seriously. They were, after all, the masters of a highly advanced and powerful civilization with fifty million people. What risk could a group of illiterate barbarians with only one million people and a small army pose to them?

They learned, to their great regret, that they posed a fatal risk.

Relying on military tactics that fit his soldiers' strength, Genghis Khan swept south, his soldiers carrying only what they needed and no more. Because his army had no infantry, only cavalry, and no supply trains to slow their advancement or maneuvering, they moved with frightening speed. As they moved, they lived off of hunting, looting, and the animals that accompanied them. Not only did they move fast, but they moved far, covering long distances in very short periods of time. To keep their means of mobility fresh, each warrior herded four or five spare horses with him. And, unlike conventional armies of the time, the Mongols fought over a broad front, attacking many targets simultaneously, instilling fear and confusion across the battlefield.

It would have been easy to assume the barbarians were simpleminded soldiers. Such was not the case. Genghis Khan honed trickery and deception to perfection. He used sophisticated means of propaganda to frighten the populace and opposing armies. He exploited ancient rivalries and social strife within the peoples the Mongols were invading, exemplifying the notion of "divide and conquer."

Because he had no experience with such obstacles, his first encounters with walled cities did not go well. However, he quickly learned that the loyalty of Chinese engineers could be purchased. Once he had access to their expertise, he built catapults and siege machines. With each new campaign, the Mongols improved this equipment until the machines became some of the most effective weapons within their army.

Genghis Khan's view of the relative value of the enemy versus a brother's life was not entirely unconventional, but he did seem to take it to a more precise level. In his evaluation, there was no ambiguity or middle ground. The life of a Mongol was precious beyond measure. Every fellow soldier's life was indispensable and never should be wasted.

> Genghis Khan would never willingly sacrifice a single one. . . . On and off the battlefield, the Mongol warrior was forbidden to speak of death, injury, or defeat. Just to think of it might make it happen. Even mentioning the name of a fallen comrade or other dead warrior constituted a serious taboo. Every Mongol soldier had to live his life as a warrior with the assumption that he was immortal, that no one could defeat him or harm him, that nothing could kill him.[12]

The value placed upon the life of a Mongol warrior was signified by the fact that whenever possible, regardless of the distance or the hardship that it might cause, the body of a fallen soldier was sent back to Mongolia for burial.

On the other hand, their enemies were nothing. Be they civilians, warriors, women, or children, the lives of the Mongols' enemies were worth less than that of a dog. Indeed, the only value that enemy lives represented was in the various ways in which they could be used to protect a Mongol soldier or aid the invading horde.

For example, the Mongols had learned early on that they could use the vast numbers of animals found in the steppes for military purposes, herding them in advance of their army to bring confusion and disorder to the defenders. Genghis Khan quickly realized that he could use enemy peasant populations to the same effect. After he had burned their villages, the peasants would be herded ahead of his army to cause confusion and to freeze the enemy forces. Other times, they were herded into the walled cities to eat the food, drink the water, spread disease, and incite rebellion.

But that wasn't the only way that Genghis Khan used enemy civilians to his advantage. Why build a bridge when the bodies of the peasant masses were perfect for filling moats? Why build an earthen embankment when the dead bodies of the enemy could be piled on top of each other and used as stepping-stones to reach above a city wall? After all, enemies weren't human beings, only tools: bodies to be used, herded, manipulated, piled, stacked, or killed for sport.

Is it any surprise that, with such a swift, frightening, and brutal army, Genghis Khan found great success?

Four years after Genghis Khan initiated his invasion of Cathay, the nation was defeated. Zhongdu, the capital city (modern-day Beijing), had been conquered, looted, and burned. Incredible amounts of plunder had been captured and sent back home. Slaves were taken in great numbers, especially from among the craftsmen and professional classes. The population had been terrorized and subjugated. To assure that the peasant population would never return, and to guarantee adequate pastures for his future armies, his men destroyed the farmland, walls, and irrigation ditches of the countryside.

After completing their pillage, his victorious soldiers turned their horses and headed for their homeland. They left behind a decimated vassal state with an obligation to pay tribute. Riding north, they carried with them the wealth and prestige of one of the greatest nations in the world.

Gurganj (Capital City of the Kingdom of Khwarizm) Central Asia AD 1221

THE SOLDIERS WERE exhausted, hungry, bloodied, and nearly delirious with rage.

They had been fighting for weeks now, trapped inside their city. Every passing day did nothing but leave them more famished, more sick, and more hopeless. Their water, what little they could steal at night—it was a terrible error not to have extended the canals through the outer walls—had been poisoned with dead bodies and raw sewage. A rotting corpse, infected with some kind of plague, had been catapulted into the city to spread disease and fear. Every night, fire rained down on the city from the Mongol catapults. Every day brought rocks and boulders.

And these were just a few manifestations of the brutality that lay outside the city walls. This was a new enemy. A new terror. Something they never had seen before. They were completely unprepared to fight them.

Soon, they were going to fall.

Al-Marwazi remembered what it was like to watch the Mongols sweep toward the city. He thought of the children herded before the army, some of them tied to the front of the soldiers' saddles, anything to protect the warriors from the incoming arrows. Thinking back on it, he realized that strategy had done much more than protect the enemy. It had caused so much confusion and hesitation—were their archers *really* supposed to release their arrows?—that the Mongols had been able to ride close enough to mount a devastating attack, getting almost to the gates before being pushed back.

The initial assault had lasted most of the day. Then, just as the sun was setting on the city, the attackers had pulled back. As they set up camp, Al-Marwazi was astounded to see how many of the riders carefully slit veins in the necks of their horses to drink their blood, seemingly all the nourishment they needed for another day of war.

Since that time, the city had been assaulted every night and every day. Fire. Rocks and boulders. An occasional head or corpse thrown in. The city was running out of food now, and casualties were mounting. The women and children spent their days in hunger, their nights huddled in the center of the larger buildings.

Earlier that morning, they had received a depressing report from one of their spies. The Chinese engineers had finished assembling the battering rams that would destroy their city gates.

The end was near now. Everyone knew it. Al-Marwazi. His people. The Mongols. Everyone knew the city was on the brink of destruction. The sultan had tried to negotiate release of the women and children (as well as himself), but it was far too late for that; once an attack had been initiated, the Mongols would never show any mercy.

Al-Marwazi hunched wearily behind the cold rock wall. It was growing dark and he was so tired that he simply couldn't stand. He was old. He was exhausted. He had almost reached the point that he didn't care anymore. He hadn't eaten in three days, and the water was so putrid that even when he forced himself to drink it, he couldn't keep it down. He felt a soft breeze blow in from the prairie. As he sniffed, his stomach retched from the sickening smell of the rotting corpses piling up outside the city wall.

Moving carefully—the Mongols had proven their longbows were deadly up to four hundred yards—he positioned himself to look through the narrow slits in the rampart.

Under the cover of their wooden shields, the Mongols continued piling up the bodies. It had taken the Khwarizmi a while to figure out what they were doing, but eventually they realized that they were building a ramp of dead bodies to breach the city wall.

Chinese assault equipment to break down the gates. A ramp of human flesh to top the outer barricade.

It would be only hours before the Mongols were inside the city walls.

A Civilization Is Wiped Away

The defeat and destruction of China was only the beginning for Genghis Khan:

> But starting from the Jurched campaign, the well-trained and tightly organized Mongol army would charge out of its highland home and overrun everything from the Indus River to the Danube, from the Pacific Ocean to the Mediterranean Sea. In a flash, only thirty years, the Mongol warriors would defeat every army, capture every fort, and bring down the walls of every city they encountered. Christians, Muslims, Buddhists, and Hindus would soon kneel before the dusty boots of illiterate young Mongol horsemen.[13]

His next target was the kingdom of Khwarizm, a thriving empire in central Asia that included much of the area once considered ancient Persia. A Muslim kingdom of immense wealth and advanced culture, colonized almost twenty-four hundred years before, it was purported to have the highest level of literacy in the world. Many of its inhabitants were leftovers from the civilization of Persia, but there were other races and nationalities within the kingdom as well, for it was an open society. Because of its strategic and profitable location along the Silk Road, it was internationally recognized as a rising power in the world. It had more than four hundred settlements and fabled cities of great size. In fact, the capital city of Gurganj was considered one of the most beautiful cities in the world.[14]

If this great kingdom is little known today, it is largely because of what the Mongols did to it.

After his attempt to open up a trading relationship with the sultan of Khwarizm had been violently rebuffed, Genghis Khan decided to go to war. And go to war he did, with a violent and bloody vengeance.

It took only a year for all the major cities of Khwarizm to be destroyed. The sultan was chased onto an island in the Caspian Sea to die. As a further humiliation to the defeated nation, the sultan's mother was sent back to Mongolia to live out the rest of her life as a common slave. Their civilization was wiped out to the point that very little of it is known today.

• • •

Four more years of warfare followed in Central Asia as the Mongols swept across the land. Every nation that they targeted fell before the great Genghis Khan, their victories becoming bloody massacres.

> Part of Genghis Khan's strategy was calculated massacre: if a city resisted his armies, once it fell to him—and they always fell—he had all the inhabitants slaughtered. The chroniclers' reports of the numbers of dead are staggering; 1,600,000 at Harat, in 1220. Rumor reached the Mongol prince Tuli that some had survived there by hiding among the piled corpses, and when he took Nishapur, some time later, he ordered the heads cut off all the bodies. At Nishapur, according to contemporaries, 1,747,000 died.[15]

Everything was plundered. Ancient palaces and temples were defaced, looted, and then abandoned. Entire cities were left empty, many razed completely to the ground, leaving nothing but dirt that was turned to pasture to feed the Mongol horses. As just one example of the devastation the invaders left behind, it's estimated that one-half of the entire population of Hungary and 50 to 80 percent of its settlements were destroyed by the Mongols.[16] Irrigation systems—the underpinnings of agriculture and hundreds of years of civilization—were utterly wiped away, leading to the depopulation of large tracts of land. Terrorist tactics were incorporated to weaken the morale and commitment of the Mongols' enemies. Once a city had been destroyed, a few captives might be released to spread word of Mongol terror and atrocities. These reports often frightened the next city into submitting without even the hint of a fight.

It is reported that one communication from Genghis Khan to peoples in Armenia said:

> "It is the will of God that we take the earth and maintain order" to impose Mongol law and taxes, and to those who refused them, the Mongols were obligated to "slay them and destroy their place, so that the others who hear and see should fear and not act the same."[17]

What They Won

In 1222, after sweeping through Central Asia, the Mongol campaign ended in what is now Pakistan. In a few short years the Mongols had expanded to become one of the largest and most powerful empires in the world.

Genghis Khan had brought almost imponderable wealth to the people of Mongolia. For more than a decade, grand caravans of plundered wealth and slaves had made their way back to the homeland. Silk and gold, pearls and precious gems, exotic woods and leathers, prized metal utensils and knives—those were just a sampling of the plunder. More revealing was the expatriation of highly valued human slaves. Long lines of artisans, professionals, and other experts, along with common and uneducated slaves, were driven to the steppes of Mongolia.

Never could the simple folk of Mongolia have imagined what riches would be theirs as they ascended to become the most powerful nation on earth. However, the aggressive expansion of the empire was about to hit a bump in the road.

In 1227, the great Genghis Khan died.

Three years later, Genghis Khan's third-oldest son, Ogodei, replaced him as the khan by means of a *khuriltai*. After his inauguration, he immediately went about dissipating the wealth that his father had accumulated. He built a new capital. He spent lavishly. He demanded this and that from far-off lands. The kingdom put out far more than it brought in. Having suddenly grown wealthy, the Mongols had become accustomed to a lifestyle that required vast amounts of capital to support it. In a foolish attempt to encourage trade, Ogodei started paying for goods brought to his capital twice as much as they were worth.

Within five years, the riches were gone. The great Mongol empire his father had built was on the brink of ruin. This left Ogodei with only one option: He had to find additional lands to loot.

The Mongols Look West

General Subodei, a great leader in the army, suggested that the Mongols go after Europe.

At the time, very little was known about the lands that lay to the west of Asia. Europe didn't have a reputation as a particularly wealthy area or a flourishing culture, but for a number of reasons it seemed a good target. Among the arguments in favor of invading Europe instead of southern China, or Iraq, or overly hot India, was that in the one brief skirmish against European armies a decade before, those armies had been easily defeated.

The Mongol generals anticipated that the European campaign would last for five years. There was, after all, a vast amount of territory and people to be plundered. Under the brilliant leadership of the great Subodei and two of Genghis Khan's most capable grandsons, they put together an army of fifty thousand Mongol warriors and a hundred thousand soldiers from allied or vassal nations. Well led, eager for booty, possessing all of the engineering skills and military knowledge acquired from decades of war, this was perhaps the best army the Mongols ever assembled. They had vastly superior weaponry. A highly mobile and effective cavalry. Much more fighting experience. Their advantages were overwhelming.

The invasion of Eastern Europe began in 1236.

The city-states and small, isolated kingdoms of modern-day Russia and Ukraine were the first to fall. Despite their best efforts, they simply were no match for Subodei's superior army.

Before a Russian city was attacked, its leaders were sent an envoy with invitations to surrender for the mere price of a tithe, 10 percent of their wealth, plus an agreement to become Mongolian vassals. Very few accepted the invitation. In one particularly proud—if ultimately foolish—example, the prince of Ryazan (a city just outside Moscow) responded to the demand for a 10 percent tribute by writing, "When we are dead, you may have the whole."

The Mongols accepted the offer. Ryazan was razed. Its occupants were killed. The Mongols had it all.

Following the destruction of Ryazan, Moscow and other cities were attacked. All of them were destroyed. Each city was plundered of its wealth. Slaves were taken. The civilian populations were massacred.[18]

Early in the winter of 1240, envoys were sent to the beautiful city of Kiev to demand its surrender. Feeling invincible, this great city of perhaps a hundred thousand occupants killed the khan's envoys and desecrated their bodies—the greatest of any possible insults to the Mongols.

By December the city had been utterly destroyed, so much so that twelve years later a traveler found it to be nothing but a tiny village of a hundred pitiful inhabitants. It would take many generations before Kiev would recover from the impacts of the Mongol invasion. And the larger cities were not alone. Most of the smaller cities and kingdoms throughout Russia were also taken and subdued.

Having accomplished their goals, the Mongols built themselves a new capital, renamed the empire *The Golden Horde,* and settled in for a long stay.

Eastern Europe was now a Mongolian state. Much of it would remain so for many centuries.

Western Europe on the Brink

With Russia plundered, the Mongol army turned their eyes even farther to the west.

Within months of taking Kiev, Subodei sent out scouts to determine the most effective strategy for attacking their next target. He was surprised to find that Europe was completely unprepared to defend itself. It was winter, and civilized Europeans did not fight in the cold.

Maybe if they had realized that the hardened winter soil and frozen rivers were perfect for Mongolian army movement, they would have been more prepared for battle.

Subodei dispatched two armies toward Western Europe, one north and one south. The northern force of roughly twenty thousand soldiers moved across Poland, capturing a host of towns and cities. Finally, the Europeans rode to their own defense. In April, the Mongols met a quickly assembled army of knights from Germany, France, and Poland. As usual, the force of thirty thousand European soldiers outnumbered the Mongol invaders. It didn't matter. The Mongols crushed them, killing or capturing as many as twenty-five thousand of the opposing forces.

To the south, the Mongols ran straight into the teeth of a waiting army.

At the time, Hungary was one of the largest and most powerful of the European empires. Under King Bela, a large army of Hungarians and Austrians were dispatched to meet the fifty thousand warriors of Subodei. Once again, the Mongols relied upon maneuver and superior tactics. Retreating until they had found a spot that they could use to their advantage, they surrounded the Europeans, forcing them to huddle inside a protective camp made of their wagons chained together. At that point, the Mongols began to pelt them with flaming liquids and gunpowder from their catapults.

This was something the European knights had never seen before. Panic set in. Then there appeared a sudden gap in the lines of the Mongolian army. Miraculously, it opened in the direction of their capital of Pest. Seeing their only hope of escape, the Europeans broke through their own defensive structures and made for home. Of course it was a trap. The Mongols waited until the terrified enemies were in full flight, dropping their armaments as they ran, then swooped down and massacred them all.

One report described the scene: "'The dead fell to the right and to left; like leaves in winter, the slain bodies of these miserable men were strewn along the whole route; blood flowed like torrents of rain.'"[19] As many as seventy thousand knights were killed, almost the entire military might of the Hungarian kingdom.

> European knighthood never recovered from the blow of losing nearly one hundred thousand soldiers in Hungary and Poland, what the Europeans mourned as "the flower" of their knighthood and aristocracy. Walled cities and heavily armored knights were finished, and in the smoke and gunpowder of that Easter season of 1241, the Mongol triumph portended the coming total destruction of European feudalism and the Middle Ages.[20]

The Final Blow

The way was now wide open for Vienna to be taken. After Vienna, Rome. With Rome, the Christian church. Then Turin. Paris. Cologne. Finally would be London. Western Europe would, like the rest of the known world, fall under the Mongol sword.

Scouts were sent by the Mongols to determine the best route for an attack on the beautiful and important city of Vienna.

The Christians of Europe knew they were at the mercy of the Mongols. Their armies could not stop them. Their cities could not be defended. The only remaining political force in Europe, Frederick II, emperor of the Holy Roman Empire, was already weakened by a prolonged conflict with the pope of Rome. In all of Europe, there was no other monarch with enough power to field an army with any hope of stopping the Mongols. It was beyond foolish to believe that even Frederick could succeed.

It was now spring. The grass was turning green. Subodei knew it was time to stop and rest his warriors while pasturing his herds.

The Europeans could only sit and wait in fear. They knew that as soon as the Mongol warhorses had been fattened by the summer grass, and their soldiers rested, they would attack again. And they knew from experience that the attack would come at the beginning of the winter, the Mongols' favorite time of year for making war.

Two Deaths Save a Nation

Then, just as winter of 1241 was settling over Western Europe, the situation changed in a sudden and unexpected way.

Four thousand miles to the east, Ogodei, the Great Khan of Mongolia, suddenly died. Shortly thereafter, the only other surviving son of Genghis Khan died as well. With no obvious heir to claim the position of the Great Khan, a *khuriltai* was called to choose a new leader.

Throughout the empire, Mongol royalty immediately turned for home, where various members would fight for the right to be declared the next khan. Many of the officers and leaders of the army returned as well, wanting to participate in the decision as to who would be their next commander.

Suddenly leaderless, and without obvious direction from their capital, the Mongol army withdrew from Western Europe.

It never returned again.

• • •

Upon his return to Mongolia, Genghis Khan's grandson Guyuk was anointed Great Khan. His reign was short-lived; eighteen months later he died. Another grandson, Mongke, took his place.

Maybe because of the presence of several Christians within the royal court, particularly among the wives, or perhaps because there was little evidence of great wealth to be taken, the new khan decided not to send his army back to Europe. Instead, he concentrated on solidifying his hold on Russia, a territory that the Mongols ended up staying in for more than two hundred years.[21]

After stabilizing his newly acquired northern holdings, the new khan sent his armies out once more. But again, he didn't look west. Instead, he sent one army to conquer the Muslims of Baghdad,

Damascus, and Cairo and another to conquer the Sung Dynasty of southern China.

Baghdad was the center of the Muslim world and home of the caliph. As the richest city in the Muslim world, it promised great wealth to the Mongolian conquerors.

When Baghdad fell in 1258, as many as eight hundred thousand of its inhabitants were massacred. To punish the Muslim leaders for attempting to defy them, the Mongols took the caliph and all of his male heirs, wrapped them up in blankets or sewed them up in animal skins, and rode over them with horses.

The conquest took a little longer in China. The Great Khan didn't take the capital of the Sung Dynasty until 1276.[22]

With the conquest of Baghdad and southern China, the Mongols controlled all of the territory from the South China Sea to Western Europe.

It was as large as the Mongolian empire would ever be.

What If?

What if Ogodei had not died in the winter of 1241?

What if the army of Subodei had taken all of Europe, which it certainly could have done with relative ease?

The views of two of the world's most renowned historians are worth considering:

Will Durant: "What saved Christianity and Europe was simply the death of Ogadai. . . . Never in history had there been so extensive a devastation—from the Pacific Ocean to the Adriatic and the Baltic Seas."[23]

Edward Gibbon: "If the disciples of Mohammed would have oppressed her religion and liberty, it might be apprehended that the shepherds of Scythia [Mongols] would extinguish her cities, her arts, and all the institutions of civil society."[24]

• • •

More specifically, the following questions must be examined:

What would have happened to the emerging values of Western culture—including the ideas of freedom and capitalism, which were in their infant stage of development—if the Mongols had invaded?

Had the Mongols ridden into Western Europe, the young and growing European cities would have been destroyed. There would have been no emerging financial centers in the Low Countries, no growing wool centers, both of which proved vital to the emergence of capitalism in Antwerp and Ghent. The role of Paris in developing the West would have been aborted, its great universities ruined. Monasteries throughout Europe, those test beds of innovation and discovery, would not have survived. The embryonic notions regarding representative government left over from the Roman and Greek empires would have disappeared in the fog of history.

And these are just a few examples of how capitalism, science, democracy, and education would have been thwarted.

Perhaps most important, Western Europe would have been robbed of its greatest assets: the minds of the intellectuals, skilled craftsmen, teachers, and leaders upon which all great civilizations must be built. After the Mongols destroyed a city, the most skilled and educated men among the captives were sent back to the steppes. This tactic had an extremely negative impact upon the conquered nation, for it robbed them of their very best people. Once they were gone, all of their expertise was taken with them.

Surely the same fate would have befallen the learned and skilled men of Western Europe.[25] Had that been the case, how long would it have taken for Western culture to be rebuilt?

What would have happened to the Christian church if the Mongol invasion had reached Rome?

During the invasion of Europe, the pope had sent envoys in an attempt to appease the Mongols. The reply he received was sobering. He was informed that the Mongols were vested "with a divine power to subdue or extirpate the nations; and that the pope would be involved in the universal destruction unless he visited in person, and as a suppliant, the royal horde."[26]

Clearly the Mongol leaders had no intention of respecting the church. Like every other conquered leader, the pope would have been forced to bow down to the khan.

In Russia, the Mongols understood that the Christian church could help maintain stability in the region. Because of this, its property and laity were protected. But this protection came at a heavy price. In return for being allowed their continued existence, the church advised its people to submit to the Mongolian overlords. Because of this, "a spirit of submissiveness was developed in the people, and opened a road to centuries of despotism."[27]

Some argue that the Russian peoples have never recovered from this attitude of submission. It is, at least in part, an explanation for why the Russians tolerated the absolute reign of the czars while the rest of Europe evolved toward representative government and the love of individual rights and freedom. It also helps explain why the Russian people were so submissive to a communist dictatorship for so long.

Would centuries of Mongol domination and church collaboration in Western Europe have affected the European mind-set any differently? Is there any reason to believe the Europeans would have had a better outcome than their Russian or Muslim counterparts? Indeed, those two empires that were conquered by the Mongols provide ample evidence of what might have been the fate of Western Europe.

Before the Mongols appeared on their borders, both the Russian and Muslim empires had reached a zenith of wealth, prosperity, and enlightenment. Neither of them recovered after the Mongols had invaded and occupied their lands.

Descendants of Genghis Khan ruled large nations such as Russia, Turkey, India, China, and Persia for very long periods of time, in some cases for more than seven centuries. In India, they ruled as the Moghuls until 1857. The last descendant of Genghis Khan ruled in Uzbekistan until 1920.[28]

None of these nations developed into democratic or free governments under their Mongol rulers.

Considering all of these facts, it is impossible to believe that Europe, had it been ravaged and depleted by the Mongols, and the miserable survivors shackled with an obligation to pay tribute forever, would have found a way to enter the golden era known as the Renaissance.

It seems impossible to believe that Europe would have continued on the path toward the rejuvenation of art, science, and religion.

Most vital, it is impossible to believe that the political philosophy of the West, which is the very foundation of freedom, would have survived.

Gurganj (Capital City of the Kingdom of Khwarizm) Central Asia AD 1221

EVERY OTHER INHABITANT of the once great city had been either killed or taken. Out of the entire city, he was the only one who had been allowed to live but not enslaved.

After the killing had ended, an unknown number of his fellows had been led away in ropes or chains. And though Al-Marwazi didn't know it, a few thousand of his fellow citizens had fled to the west, slipping away through a breach in the wall and disappearing into the night. They would end up in various locations throughout the Middle East, absorbed into the local culture, never to be identified as Khwarizmi again.

Having looted everything of any value within the city, the Mongols had burned or torn down every building, leaving no riches, no structures, no people or animals.

Which left Al-Marwazi where he was. Alone. The last of his kingdom. Last of his family. Last of his neighbors. Last of his friends.

He stood outside the ruined city walls and wondered why the

khan had let him live. He didn't know. But he wasn't grateful. Looking at the devastation all around him, he realized that sometimes living was worse than death.

With nothing else to do and nowhere else to go, Al-Marwazi lifted a thin stick from off the ground, used it to stabilize himself, then turned and started hobbling toward the nearest village, hoping it had not already been destroyed.

Walking toward the mountains, he took with him all of the culture of his people.

Four days later, it was over.

Both he and his culture were dead.

Notes

1. See Simons, *Barbarian Europe,* 168. This is the source for all our information regarding the decline and then resurrection of cities.
2. "Feudalism was the economic subjection and military allegiance of a man to a superior in return for economic organization and military protection" (Durant, *Age of Faith,* 553).
3. Durant, *Age of Faith,* 571. For a description of the era of the Middle Ages relevant to this episode, see Durant, *Age of Faith,* 552–79; Hay, *Early Middle Ages,* 157–98; Simons, *Barbarian Europe,* 147–72.
4. For a discussion of the Crusades, see Durant, *Age of Faith,* 585–613; Gibbon, *Decline and Fall of the Roman Empire,* 1047–1107; Newark, *Medieval Warfare,* 67–87.
5. The Crusades "appear to me to have checked rather than forwarded the maturity of Europe. The lives and labors of millions which were buried in the East would have been more profitably employed in the improvement of their native country: the accumulated stock of industry and wealth would have overflowed in navigation and trade; and the Latins would have been enriched and enlightened by a pure and friendly correspondence with the climates of the East" (Gibbon, *Decline and Fall of the Roman Empire,* 1107).
6. Tuchman, *Distant Mirror,* 7.
7. Durant, *Age of Faith,* 649. For a full description of the rise of Europe as an economic power and the birthplace of capitalism, see ibid., 614–49; Stark, *Victory of Reason;* Tuchman, *Distant Mirror,* 1–22.
8. The Mongols were related to both the Turks and the Tartars, and they were often called Tartars or some variation of that name.
9. Weatherford, *Genghis Khan,* xviii.

10. Ibid., 45.

11. Kahn, *Secret History,* 146. *The Secret History of the Mongols* was written shortly after the death of Genghis Khan, apparently as a history for his family. Its full translation has been made available only in the last few decades.

12. Weatherford, *Genghis Khan,* 91.

13. Ibid., 85–86.

14. The first scientific study of Kunya Urgench (Gurganj) was undertaken by an expedition from the State Academy for the History of Material Culture in 1928 and 1929. In 1938, V. I. Pilyavsky surveyed the site and measured its monuments. After World War II, Sergei Tolstov's Khorezm Archaeological-Ethnographical Expedition began the first archaeological studies on the site. Between 1958 and 1960, Alexandr Vinogradov, A. Asanov, and I. I. Notkin drew up plans of the monuments and recorded their physical status. Archaeological work partly resumed by the Uzbek Institute of Conservation between 1979 and 1985. The results of these collective efforts can be found at http://karakalpak.com/ancgurganj .html.

15. Cowley, *What If?* 98.

16. See Sugar, Hanák, Tibor, *History of Hungary,* 27.

17. Weatherford, *Genghis Khan,* 111.

18. See Durant, *Age of Faith,* 655–56.

19. Quoted in Weatherford, *Genghis Khan,* 154.

20. Weatherford, *Genghis Khan,* 155.

21. For information about Genghis Khan and his rise and exploits, as well as the Mongol invasion of Europe under Ogodei, see Cowley, *What If?* 93–106; Durant, *Age of Faith,* 655–58; Kahn, *Secret History;* Weatherford, *Genghis Khan,* 3–159.

22. For the history of the Mongol conquests after 1241, see Durant, *Age of Faith,* 338–41; Weatherford, *Genghis Khan,* 160–209.

23. Durant, *Age of Faith,* 658.

24. Gibbon, *Decline and Fall of the Roman Empire,* 1142.

25. For thoughts on the impact of a Mongol conquest of Western Europe, see Crowley, *What If?* 102–5.

26. Gibbon, *Decline and Fall of the Roman Empire,* 1142.

27. Durant, *Age of Faith,* 656.

28. See Weatherford, *Genghis Khan,* xx.

Chapter 6

How the New World Saved the Old

Parvis e glandibus quercus.

LATIN PHRASE MEANING
"TALL OAKS FROM LITTLE ACORNS GROW"

Human progress—especially in regard to the march of freedom—has proven to come in painful cycles, with plenty of stops and spurts along the way. Though there were occasional steps forward, there were also stumbles, sometimes fantastic failures. For those of us who can look upon these failures with the advantage of hindsight, as well as through the prism of our cultural advancement, some of the stumblings may be difficult to understand.

This is particularly true of nations or religious institutions, both of which may fall under exceptionally critical scrutiny. There are a couple of explanations for why this is true: First, though they may seek to represent the ideal, no nation or institution is ever perfect. All cultures and religious institutions are occupied by mere mortals, making them subject to all the frailties of men. And the simple fact that they *do* seek the ideal, ironically, opens them up to charges of hypocrisy and scorn. Second, often these are not only multigenerational but *multimillennial* institutions. Their stories may stretch over thousands of years. During the passing of so many centuries, every nation or institution will have its ups and downs, experiencing high points of moral leadership, but low points of decadence as well.

This being the case, wouldn't it be unfair—and historically inaccurate—to judge a nation or institution on only one episode in its history or during one particular span of time?

In our story, we also have to recognize the difference between the leaders or members of the Christian faith and Christian doctrine. The shortcomings of one may not accurately reflect the value of the other. Indeed, history shows that there have been times when the teachings of Christianity remained an ally to the development of freedom even when the Christian church did not.

All of these propositions can be shown in one example: European culture and advancement.

As stated in the previous chapter, after the darkest of the Dark Ages, much of Europe began to emerge into the light. But that did not mean that its progress was linear or sure. In fact, it is clear that there came a point when the European people and culture were utterly exhausted, seemingly on the verge of ruin.

Such was the situation just before the discovery of the Americas. Some of the leaders of the Christian church had become corrupt. Western culture, as embodied in European civilization, was not heading toward enlightenment, but leaning toward collapse.

The New World literally saved the Old.

Had it not been for the opportunities and advancements created by the discovery of the New World, all of Christianity and Western culture may have crumbled upon itself.

Along the Black Sea's Western Shore
December 1493

THEY CAME FROM different worlds, from different cultures with different attitudes. And their people were heading in opposite directions now, one on the rise, one on the fall.

That was the unseen truth.

But only one of them understood it.

The older man was a Christian from the West, raised in the cold mountains of northern Italy: lily-white with blue eyes underneath heavy brows, a single man who never had any interest in marrying and certainly no interest in having children, a man who could neither read nor write (though he could add an impressive string of numbers in his head), who viewed women as the gate of the devil and had never once in his life held a book or touched scripture, though he was comfortable with a knife or sword. Having lived on a continent of thieves, fools, and beggars, he had been forced to kill a few men along the way, although he hoped most of that was behind him now, with his advancing age.

The other was a young Arab from the East, raised on the hills of Syria: dark-skinned, black eyes, elegant fingers that wrote in beautiful Arabic script. He had been taught to read and write at age five and was familiar with most of the great literary works of the world. In fact, he had helped to translate some of the original Greek manuscripts of medicine and science from the libraries at Alexandria for the benefit of the backward European leaders. With a fine wife (blessing of the good God) and a large brood of dark-eyed children, he loved being home, though he wasn't there very often, for he spent most of his days on the roads that stretched from India to central Europe. He knew as well as anyone the trade routes, security points, mountain passes, desert waterholes, customs, and cultural arrangements along the routes, a fact that had made him rich. Most important, he was a citizen of the Ottoman Empire, which gave him safety in the most dangerous places.

But though the two men came from very different worlds, they had one thing in common, an obsession that drove them with more power than any other thing in the world. Love of gold. Love of the deal.

They sat atop a rounded sand hill only a few hundred feet from the Black Sea. The air smelled of brine and dead fish and cattails. In front of them, the sun was going down. Behind them, at the bottom of the hill, their servants were setting up two camps, separated by a small stream that dribbled into the great sea. Heavily armed merce-naries stood guard at both ends of the camp. Between them, more than four dozen men worked to stake the tents, pasture the horses, light the fires, and set up the feast—everything that was necessary to make their masters comfortable.

The men sat in silence a long moment, the man from Damascus chewing on a wad of the brown leaf that he always seemed to have with him. The European worked a small knife to trim a piece of dying skin from a wounded finger. He had cut it on a sharp knife three days before (another indication that his reflexes were getting slower) and it had grown red and oozing. His cook had taken a dozen large black ants, used their pincers to force the skin together, then pinched off their heads. The old man knew the wound would heal now, but for the time it had left him feverish and cold.

Pulling at a piece of infected skin, he glanced over at his quiet friend. They had been doing business for almost seven years now, but they didn't trust each other enough to really let their guard down. Business and gold never left any room for trust. And there was something in the air tonight. The Arab seemed very tense.

The Italian watched him chew, then motioned to the packs that the Arab horses had carried for more than a thousand miles. One hundred and forty bags of spice. Enough to keep him well for a year—assuming he wasn't killed or robbed transporting the treasure back to the markets of southern Europe.

The Arab seemed to stare into the distance, his face clouded in thought.

"We have a deal, then?" the old man pressed, fearful the Arab was rethinking the price. Had that been the case, it would have caused a mini-war between the two camps, a battle he was fairly certain he could win, but one never knew. (Were he certain, he would have simply stolen the spice already. Better to take the deal than risk it all on a fight, he had concluded.)

"I am vexed," the Arab finally said.

The old man shrugged. He didn't know what the word meant.

The Arab waited, then tried again. "I am troubled."

The European shrugged once more.

The Arab sniffed the cool evening air. "Things are going to change."

The European simply listened.

"I have talked to many people. Most of them are blind to it, but I am certain it will happen. And it troubles me severely."

The old man gestured in confusion toward the load of well-packed spice. They had inspected each and every bundle. The Arab had counted, tested, and weighed the small nuggets of gold that he would take in payment. Both of them were richer now. With the work being done, all of their men, exhausted from the long march, were happy to drink fresh water from the stream, catch some fish, kill some game, drink some ale, and sleep in their tents instead of under the stars. No one was trying to kill them—at least, not at this moment. Hard winter was being held back on the other side of the mountains and the Black Sea. The sky was clear. Dinner was almost ready.

What was there to be troubled about?

But the Italian had learned a lesson very early in life: *Never underestimate the possibility of doom or failure.* Seeing the tension on the Arab's face, he felt his gut instinctively grow tight.

Exhausted by War

Christian Europe muddled through the Middle Ages, that era generally defined as the years between Constantine and Columbus.[1] Though it endured incessant warfare, feudalism, and grinding poverty, it kept stumbling along. During this period, Europe managed to avoid two potentially devastating invasions—the Muslims in AD 732 and the Mongols in 1241—either one of which would have forever altered its culture and political values, those exceedingly rare and fragile principles that distinctively made Christian Europe *the West.*

It had also survived several lesser but successful invasions. But instead of being destroyed by these invaders, the Europeans had been able to assimilate the aggressors into Christianity, even taking the best from them to enrich their own culture.

By the fifteenth century, however, Europe was exhausted—worn down by violence, constant war, lawlessness, poverty, corruption, and disease.

This fatigue could not have occurred at a less opportune time, for it happened just as the Islamic world, under Turkish leadership, was flexing its muscles in the form of the Ottoman Empire. This great kingdom, sometimes referred to as the Turkish Empire, came into being in 1299. At its height, it extended into three continents and lasted for more than six hundred years.

In the last half of the fourteenth century, the Ottoman Empire began to make significant inroads into that part of southeast Europe known as the Balkans. In 1402, they undertook a siege of Constantinople, the last vestige of the Roman Empire remaining in the East. This city, the single greatest bulwark against Islamic conquest of Eastern Europe, was saved only because of a surprise attack against the Turks by Tamerlane the Great, one of the last of the Mongol conquerors.

Though saved for the moment, Constantinople recognized its exceedingly precarious position. Knowing it couldn't defend itself, it went begging for help from the rest of Europe. None was forthcoming. The Western Catholic church simply refused to allow its kings to aid the Greek Catholics. Such was the brutal tenor of the times, as well as an indicator of the level of corruption among the leaders of the Roman Catholic church.

It was during this interlude that the Islamic rulers of the Ottoman Empire undertook the creation of the *janissaries,* Christian children who had been taken from the people of the conquered Balkans and raised up as soldiers in the Ottoman Empire. These *janissaries* proved to be great warriors, leading to the bitter fact that much of the fighting in Europe was soon to become Christian against Christian.

In AD 1422 the Turks returned to the Balkans, retaking the Peninsula with relative ease. By 1452, Constantinople was under siege once more. Again, the city pleaded for assistance from Western Europe. Again, no help came.

Constantinople fell in May of 1453.

Despite their unwillingness to send assistance, the leaders of the West did not receive this as good news, for they realized that

Constantinople was the major gateway to all of Europe. With the fall of the great city, the door to invasion from the east was kicked open:

> The capture of Constantinople shook every throne in Europe. The bulwark had fallen that had protected Europe from Asia for over a thousand years. That Moslem power and faith which the Crusaders had hoped to drive back into inner Asia had now made its way over the corpse of Byzantium, and through the Balkans to the very gates of Hungary. The papacy, which had dreamed of all Greek Christianity submitting to the rule of Rome, saw with dismay the rapid conversion of millions of southeastern Europeans to Islam. Routes of commerce once open to Western vessels were now in alien hands.[2]

Encouraged by their victory over Constantinople, a prize they had been eyeing for many generations, the Turks reenergized their offensive campaign. Two hundred years of war between Europe and the Ottoman Empire were to follow—two hundred years of battles, conquests, and defeats; two hundred years of death and destruction, fear and reprisal, Europe exhausting its resources in war and self-defense.

Pushing farther into Europe, Turkish armies eventually came to Italy, pillaging within a few miles of Venice, which survived only because it agreed to pay tribute. The kingdom of Naples was then attacked, as well as Otranto, a city on the southern tip of the Italian heel, its Christian archbishop cut in two. "The fate of Christianity and monogamy teetered in the scales."[3]

By 1481, the Islamic tide was stopped—but only for the moment. Forty-five years later, the Turks renewed their effort to "reduce all Europe to the one true faith—Islam."[4]

In 1526, at the invitation of King Francis I of France (who apparently favored the Turkish invaders over his fellow Europeans) and with the encouragement of the Lutherans (indicating the hatred between the emerging Christian sects), the Turks succeeded in conquering

Hungary. Three years later, they undertook a long and bitter cycle of sieges against Vienna, a contest that lasted for another 150 years.

Although they were never able to claim Vienna, the Turks became well established in other parts of Europe. They controlled the Balkans and Hungary and remained there for centuries. With the Turkish navy controlling the Mediterranean Sea, the Ottoman Empire was at the height of its power.[5] It had become, as one contemporary historian described it, "'the present Terror of the World.'"[6]

It appeared that the rise of Islam was, once again, unstoppable.

How Europe withstood the onslaught of the much more powerful Ottoman Empire is one of the great questions of the day. But one thing is certain: it wouldn't have happened without the discovery of the New World.

Along the Black Sea's Western Shore
December 1493

"I DON'T UNDERSTAND IT," the Arab muttered. It seemed that he was growing angry with frustration now. "You come from the most backward civilization that I know of. And I have traveled the world. I know whereof I speak. The pagans on the plains of India are more advanced than you. The yellow skins of Asia have more science than you do! Ninety percent of your people are mere serfs, nothing more than slaves condemned to serve their kings for life. Don't get me wrong; I understand there is glory in serving a good master, but where is the glory in your kings? They are nothing more than weak and prideful monarchs ruling a single forest or famished plat of land. Your religion is in chaos, its leaders whispering and greedy men. You war and you kill and you accomplish little else. You huddle in fear and anticipation of the next catastrophic event. You used to be a greater people—not *great,* mind you, but greater than you are now. Surely, if there are any on the slide of history, it is your people in this day."

The European stared down from the hill. Two of his men were cutting up a beef carcass with a large saw, part of the celebration that would be held tonight. He glanced at the Arab sideways.

The Arab looked at him and continued: "Your lords control you to the point that your daughters must have their permission even to marry. Your unmarried daughters are forced into cloisters where the church must take them or they will starve to death. If your lord sells a swath of land, the serfs go with it, as if you were nothing more than cattle. No . . . as if you were nothing more than goats, for a good cow is worth more than a man.

"Did you know that the Chinese have developed a way to immunize themselves against the Black Death? Do you even know what *immunize* means? They have defeated the Black Death while your people die in hordes. Think on that, my friend! Your people die so quickly they don't have time to bury all the dead."

He checked his tirade, leaving an awkward silence in its place.

"You have made a good trade," the old Italian finally ventured, apparently eager to change the topic. "I look forward to meeting you again next year. The same cargo. The same terms."

The Arab shook his head. This was the last time the men would trade. That was part of the reason he was so angry at how the world was going to change.

"Constant war in Europe," he picked up again, his voice rising with frustration. "Constant hunger. Constant death and disease. You suffer and then you die!

"And yet . . . and yet, I am worried in my heart. This news, it troubles me in ways that I cannot describe. It will change everything. You. Me. The world in which we live. The things we take for granted. Our expectations for our future. Our children will see a world that you and I don't understand. And anyone who doesn't see it is nothing but a fool."

The European sipped from his leather flash, washed his mouth out, and spat. All the time he nodded, as if he agreed.

But the Arab could see the truth: His trading partner had no idea what he was talking about.

An Unchristian Europe

The immeasurable influence of Christianity on the West is undeniable. In addition, the greatness of Christianity, and the overwhelmingly positive role that it has played in the development of freedom and civilization, is also irrefutable. These arguments have been made again and again in this book.

It is ironic, then, that one of the greatest proofs of the truthfulness of these statements is the fact that Christianity was able to survive the corruption that befell the church in the latter centuries of the Middle Ages.

This is worth restating. The fact that Christianity, and more specifically the Catholic church, was able to withstand the level of corruption that permeated its priesthood during this time is more a testament of its strength than a witness of its failure. The fact that it could not only withstand this phase of corruption but correct itself to the point that it was once again able to nurture the cause of freedom is an affirmation of its worth.

Despite the fact that the church was "the chief source of order and peace in the Dark Ages" and "to the Church, more than to any other institution, Europe owed the resurrection of civilization in the West after the barbarian inundation of Italy, Gaul, Britain, and Spain,"[7] it is also clear that the church fell on very bad times in the fourteenth and fifteenth centuries.

From being an influence for great morality and good, as well as one of the world's greatest advocates of order, scholarship, family, and discipline, the church degenerated "into a vested interest absorbed in self-perpetuation and finance."[8]

The church taught that the pope's power came from God. Even if the pope was a great sinner, he had to be obeyed. Because of this, the pope assumed absolute sovereignty over all the kings of the earth, claiming power to install or remove kings and emperors at his will. Several popes created their own armies, their power becoming based on their military prowess rather than their moral leadership.

The logical consequence of political power being *assumed* by the pope was the exercise of competitive and destructive power to *select or manipulate* the pope. For example, during one sixty-eight-year period, the pope was the pawn of France, used almost exclusively as a tool of France's political and military intrigues. (For a time, the home of the papacy was actually shifted from Rome to Avignon, a city in southern France.)

Sadly, during this era, many of the popes were also great sinners. Before he ascended to the papacy, Pope John XXII, vicar of Bologna, was infamous for permitting and then taxing prostitution and gambling. According to his personal assistant, he seduced two hundred virgins, matrons, widows, and nuns. His most persuasive argument for being named pope was that he controlled a powerful army.

The supposedly celibate Pope Innocent VIII celebrated the marriages of his children in the Vatican. Alexander VI had five children prior to becoming pope. Perhaps the most corrupt of all the popes was Rodrigo de Borgia, a dishonest Spanish lord. Installed in August 1492, he obtained the papacy by bribery, threats, and blackmail. A father of an unknown number of children, Borgia instituted policies that would, in the words of Kirkpatrick Sale, encourage "almost continuous and disastrous warfare . . . , open auction of lucrative ecclesiastical offices to the richest and most corrupt . . . , [and] readings of pornography from the papal library."[9]

During what is known as the Great Papal Schism (1378 to 1417), there were two and then three popes, all of whom claimed the authority of the great apostle Peter. This forty-year period of conflict and uncertainty sapped the moral strength of the church, creating more harm to the papacy than all of its other faults, for "the Church was rent in twain."[10]

During this time, the church came to love wealth. And it succeeded in acquiring it.

It became common for church positions to be sold, usually to the highest bidder. Levies were imposed by the church upon the kings, as well as every other level of civic government. By the early sixteenth century, it is estimated that the Catholic church controlled one-third to one-half of the wealth of Germany and as much as three-quarters of the wealth of France, becoming the greatest landowner in all of Europe.[11]

Bribery was rampant in the secular world, and the church was not insulated from such dishonesty. Quite the contrary: everything was for sale in Rome, it being said that there was nothing that couldn't be had if one had enough money. Bribery and corruption became so deeply instilled within the community of the church that the "fattest bribes in Europe were paid at the Roman court."[12]

Perhaps most shocking was the fact that no sin, regardless of how heinous, was beyond forgiveness—if the price was right. The selling of indulgences (payment of a fine in order to release a confessing sinner from guilt or punishment for sins) became a source of great revenue to the church. It also became one of the greatest complaints against the church. In addition, church leaders were frequently paid for saying masses in order to reduce the time a sinner had to spend being punished for his sins.

"No man could say with honesty at the end of the fifteenth century that the supremacy of the Papacy was exercised in the cause of justice, reason, or morality."[13]

And corruption was not the exclusive failing of the upper levels of the church. The selling of indulgences was common with local priests as well. Drunkenness, adultery, gluttony, and sloth were rampant among the friars. It was often asserted that many convents and monasteries were nothing but common brothels.[14]

Pettiness among the local clergy was common. In Paris, a church had been the scene of a fight between two beggars. Because blood had been shed, the church was deemed unclean. The local bishop, "a very ostentatious, grasping man, of a more worldly disposition than his station required," refused to reconsecrate the church until some money had been paid. The beggars could not come up with the sum, so church services were not held for weeks.[15] The bishop's successor prohibited burials in the churchyard until he had been paid a demanded tax.

All of these things led to the perception that the church was corrupt, another failed institution in an exhausted land. Because of the weakness of the church, Christianity itself was viewed as being in steep decline. Indeed, it appeared that Christianity, like so many religions before it, was headed for the dustbin of history, just another religious philosophy destined to fade into oblivion.[16]

Bring Out Your Dead

The fourteenth and fifteenth centuries were a dreadful time in so many other ways as well.

It appeared that human progress had stopped. There had been no new advancements in natural science since before the fourteenth century. Learning and university attendance were in decline. Instead of being engaged in looking to the future and advancing mankind, the educated in society were obsessed with longing for the classical era of the Greeks and the Romans and the study of Europe's pagan past.

More sobering, it was an age of violence, lawlessness, and poverty.

Family feuds and party conflicts were at their height. "From the thirteenth century onward inveterate party quarrels arise in nearly all countries: first in Italy, then in France, the Netherlands, Germany and England."

It's interesting to note that the motives for these conflicts were not economic, but simply the result "of hatred and of vengeance."[17]

Everyone was at war with someone: city against city, region against region, nation against nation, a condition that led to great increases in famine, poverty, and misery.

As Kirkpatrick Sale put it, "death was so daily, brutality so commonplace, destruction of the animate and inanimate so customary— that it is shocking even in our own age of mass destruction."[18]

An example: On August 2, 1492, just one day before Christopher Columbus was to sail on his great voyage, the Spanish king had set a deadline for the banishment of all Jews from Spain. Upon their departure, they were permitted to take only a few personal possessions. All of their real property, gold, and silver was appropriated by the king. It is estimated that between 120,000 and 150,000 Jews were expelled. Many of these families had been in Spain for centuries.[19]

During this time, church leaders undertook the infamous Inquisition, a bloody effort to purify the church through torture and execution.

The authority of the nation-states was weak, with very little respect for human rights. The strong took from the weak. Thievery at the local and national level was the norm. Towns were too poor to have any type of police force, allowing criminals to thrive. No one in Europe escaped the anarchy, including the residents of the British Isles, for, as Will Durant has stated, "Never in known history had Englishmen (now so law-abiding) been so lawless."[20]

The judicial system was pitiable, with widespread cruelty. In the late fifteenth century, England's King Edward IV instituted the use of torture for both the accused and witnesses in judicial proceedings, a practice that continued for two hundred years.[21] One of the most disturbing aspects of such cruelty was the public enjoyment of it. For example, the city of Mons (in modern-day Belgium) bought a convicted man just "for the pleasure of seeing him quartered, 'at which the people rejoiced more than if a new holy body had risen from the dead.'"[22] Another sign of the cruelty of the age was the conscious deprivation of condemned criminals of the rights of church confession.

Poverty was rampant. In Paris in 1422, there were twenty-four thousand empty homes and eighty thousand beggars within an overall population of about three hundred thousand. Hunger stalked the streets, famine a constant possibility.[23] Corn and potatoes were still unknown. Meat was rarely available. Meals were usually nothing but a piece of wheat or barley bread floating in thin soup. Widespread famines throughout France and Spain left hundreds of thousands dead.

The cities had been built up once again, creating an ideal environment for contagions, which meant that if a famine did not destroy a person, any number of diseases likely would. Bubonic plague—the Black Death—roamed throughout Europe. In England, one out of every three people died from the plague, which seemed to return again and again. Hamburg was revisited by the bubonic plague ten times during the fifteenth century alone. And other scourges ran rampant as well: leprosy, scurvy, smallpox, tuberculosis, and influenza.

Girolamo Savonarola, priest and secular leader of Florence in the late fifteenth century, portrayed the dilemma facing Europe: "There will not be enough men left to bury the dead; nor means to dig enough graves. So many will lie dead in the houses, that men will go forth through the streets crying, 'Send forth your dead!'"[24]

A Matching Moral Decay

These abysmal conditions, along with the weakness of—indeed, the contempt for—the church resulted in a general collapse of morality.

> The morality of the people shared in the common debacle. Cruelty, treachery, and corruption were endemic. Commoner and governor were alike open to bribes. Profanity flourished; . . . the most sacred festivals were passed in card-playing, gambling, and blasphemy. . . .
> Sodomy was frequent, prostitution was general, adultery was almost universal.[25]

Another noted historian describes what an extraordinarily depressing time it was to be alive: "A general feeling of impending calamity hangs over all. Perpetual danger prevails everywhere."[26]

Elsewhere he portrays the era:

> Is it surprising that the people could see their fate and that of the world only as an endless succession of evils? Bad government, exactions, the cupidity and violence of the great. . . . The feeling of general insecurity which was caused by the chronic form wars were apt to take, . . . by the mistrust of justice. . . . The background of all life in the world seems black. Everywhere the flames of hatred arise and injustice reigns.[27]

Such hopelessness permeated the writings of the time: the poems, the histories, the songs and ballads, even the sermons delivered from the pulpits. Court poets reflected no hope or happiness, only suffering and misery. Life was bemoaned. Early death was sought. Even contracts and other forms of legal documents were steeped in pessimism.

One poet talked of the enviable state of the childless: "Happy is he who has no children, for babies mean nothing but crying and stench; they give only trouble and anxiety; they have to be clothed, shod, fed; they are always in danger of falling and hurting themselves; they contract some illness and die."[28]

It was accepted that Satan controlled the earth. His devils and sorcerers and witches and warlocks were to be found everywhere. For some, even death brought no relief, for it was commonly believed that no one who had died subsequent to the Great Papal Schism of 1378 would be allowed to enter paradise.[29]

Little wonder, then, that it was assumed that the end was very near.

> The end of the world: the idea was taken quite seriously
> by Europe of the late fifteenth century—not as a mere con-
> ceit . . . , but as a somber, terrifying prediction based solidly
> on the divine wisdom of biblical prophecy and the felt expe-
> rience of daily life.[30]

A good example of the attitude of the time can be found in the *Nuremberg Chronicle.* Published in 1493, it was one of the first printed books in Western history, its purpose being to recount world history down to that age. One would think, considering this groundbreaking accomplishment, that the *Chronicle* would celebrate its significant place in history. Instead, it predicted only further discouragement and despair:

> "Iniquity and evil have increased to the highest pitch."
> . . . Only the wicked will prosper, good men will fall into
> contempt and penury; there will be no faith, no law, no
> justice, no peace, no humanity, no shame and no truth.
> . . . War and civil tumults will spread over the whole world,
> neighboring cities fall to fighting one another, and condi-
> tions become so abominable that no man can lead the
> good life. Then will be fulfilled the whole screed of the

Apocalypse: flood, earthquake, pestilence and famine; crops will not grow nor fruit ripen; the springs will dry up and waters flow with blood and bitterness.[31]

True to its general theme, the *Chronicle* concluded by prophesying the immediate end of the world.[32]

But it was wrong, for just a few months earlier, the world had received stunning news. A previously unknown captain, a sailor named Christopher Columbus, had returned from a voyage across the Atlantic Ocean in which he claimed that he had found land!

Europe would never be the same again.

Along the Black Sea's Western Shore
December 1493

THE OLD MAN SPOKE HONESTLY. "I don't see it," he admitted.

The Arab looked at him. "Walk with me," he said, pushing himself to his feet.

The old man hesitated until the Arab reached out his hand. The European took it and pulled himself up on creaking knees. The Arab turned and started walking north.

"Where are you going?" the older man asked.

"Come with me," the Arab said.

To the north, a rocky buttress pushed against the banks of the Black Sea. It rose sharply against the sky, the gray rock spotted with patches of vegetation. A game trail cut back and forth along the face of the outcropping and the Arab started climbing, using his hands as much as his feet. The older man hesitated at the base of the rock. He glanced over his shoulder to see a couple of his men watching, then started climbing the steep trail. Twenty minutes later, they had reached the top. Winded, the old man bent over to catch his breath, then straightened up and looked around. The view stretched before him: the sea to his back, the dark water an unending pool of blackness that seemed to suck up the failing light. Before him, rolling hills and plains. This was wilderness area, virtually uninhabited by man. Far to the north, he could barely see the outline of the Balkan Mountains that ran through a sparsely populated land. To the south, much too far to see, he knew the great city of Constantinople stood as the gateway between east and west.

The Arab stood with his face to the setting sun. Lifting a hand, he pointed to the western horizon. "Out of the smallest things, the greatest things may be."

The European moved to his side, still panting in labored breath. It took him a moment before his breathing settled down. He was a little put out by the hike, and more frustrated at being made to feel as if he didn't know what was going on. As the older man, if there was to be any teaching, it should have come from him. But he wasn't completely stupid—his age and wealth were a testament to that—and so he didn't speak.

The Arab pointed again. "To the west, two thousand miles, do you know what is out there? Look with me. Don't you see it?" He gestured to the darkening horizon that had just lost the setting sun.

The European looked, then shook his head. All he saw were shadows of hills and trees and the first of the emerging stars.

"Look across the land that we call Greece. Imagine in your mind. Across the Adriatic, to your homeland, then across the Mediterranean Sea. *That* is the focal point of history now, the turning point of our day."

The old man finally understood. "Christoffa Corombo," he muttered softly.

The Arab turned and nodded to him. "Yes. Christopher Columbus. And the thing that he discovered is going to change virtually everything."

The New World

The discovery of the Americas impacted the Old World in enormously important ways, many of which are not well known and maybe even less appreciated.

The Old World was about to become the beneficiary of

unsurpassed amounts of gold and silver, new foods, a supply of timber and furs, and other sources of wealth and economic vitality.

But the most important changes that were about to unfold were not of a material kind. The psychological impact, the effect on the morale of the people, the burst of enthusiasm and energy and optimism that exploded after Columbus's discovery far surpassed any economic benefits.

> The historical perspective of Christendom in 1493 is desperate. Men felt the blankness of the outlook everywhere. . . .
>
> Here comes one of the cataclysms of the human mind. Turning on a few years we find this disillusionment gone, and the world full of explosive ideals, moral, philosophical, cultural, social, religious. The change is complete and astounding. . . . A new envisagement of the world has begun, and men are no longer sighing after the imaginary Golden Age that lay in the distant past, but speculating as to the Golden Age that might possibly lie in the oncoming future. . . .
>
> But the change was complete and astounding, and the foundation of modern ways of thought had been laid.[33]

Another great historian put it this way:

> In a few years we find the mental picture completely changed. Strong monarchs are stamping out privy conspiracy and rebellion; the Church, purged and chastened by the Protestant Reformation, puts her house in order; new ideas flare up throughout Italy, France, Germany and the northern nations; faith in God revives and the human spirit is renewed. The change is complete and astounding.[34]

But why were things so different? Why did the discovery of the New World change Europe in so many dramatic ways?

First, the Reformation began, allowing for the spiritual abuses of the church to be corrected:

The clash of controversy between Catholic and Protestant on the highest matters of faith produced an enthusiasm on both sides which shows that the moral fibre of Europe had tightened up to a surprising degree. . . . Men braced themselves up to face the hard duty imposed by conscience and a sense of spiritual obligation, in a way that had been much rarer in the Middle Ages.[35]

Second, with the size of the known world being instantly doubled, the greatest commercial revolution in history was about to begin:

> The Atlantic nations found in the New World an outlet for their surplus population, their reserve energy, and their criminals, and developed there avid markets for European goods. Industry was stimulated in Western Europe, and demanded the mechanical inventions, and better forms of power, that made the Industrial Revolution. New plants came from America to enrich European agriculture—the potato, tomato, artichoke, squash, maize. The influx of gold and silver raised prices, encouraged manufacturers, harassed workers, creditors, and feudal lords, and generated and ruined Spain's dream of dominating the world.
>
> The moral and mental effects of the explorations rivaled the economic and political results. . . .
>
> All limits were removed; all the world was open; everything seemed possible. Now, with a bold and optimistic surge, modern history began.[36]

The vast amounts of gold and silver found in the New World created great wealth. This infusion of gold and silver also led to the fluidity of currency. This boosted trade, not only within Europe but between Europe and the New World and Asia as well. International markets exploded, leading to vastly increased trade with the Middle East and even farther to the East. India became a noted trader with Western Europe. This surge in trade greatly increased wealth throughout

Europe. In addition, it led to a severely weakened Ottoman Empire, which had held a stranglehold on these important trade routes and associations for many centuries.

Third, new foods from the Americas added to European diets greatly enhanced the health and longevity of the Europeans. Famines became less likely. Droughts became less deadly.

Finally, the New World provided the Europeans with a sudden source of cash crops, specifically coffee and sugar, which they had previously been forced to buy from the Ottomans. Instead of having to import these important commodities, the Europeans were soon able to support their own demand. Shortly thereafter, they started exporting these crops to the Middle East.

Financially weakened and isolated, their invasions thwarted, the Ottoman Empire began to fade as a threat to Europe.[37]

What If?

What if Europe, seemingly exhausted and in a spiral of decline, had never been exposed to the spark of hope that the discovery of the New World created? What if it had remained in its deep and depressing malaise?

Would the Ottoman Empire have overrun all of Europe? If that had been the case, would the New World have eventually been discovered by Ottoman ships, with Muslim sailors and Turkish soldiers? Would the Western Hemisphere, as well as all of Europe, be Muslim, even today?

What would be the status of Christianity in our modern world? Would it even exist, except in small and isolated pockets around the globe? What if Christianity had not been allowed to play the vital role it did in the development of the West, especially in regard to the political and philosophical evolution that led to its unique belief in freedom, individual rights, and equality?

If Europe had continued its precipitous slide, would its people have developed the moral courage to begin the Reformation? Would the word *Renaissance* have the same meaning as it has for us today?

Would Europe have ever mustered the rational energy that was necessary to develop the political and moral philosophy that we refer to as *the West?* Or would the classical Greek ideas of democracy that we inherited, as well as the Roman philosophy of government, been utterly lost in time?

Would Europe, and then the United States, ever have developed into a place where personal liberty was recognized, equality was sought, the rule of law replaced the rule of man, and the original ideas of self-government began?

And without the influence of the United States, what kind of world would we live in today?

• • •

We do not need to find the answers to these questions. The New World *was* discovered. And that changed everything.

Europe was revitalized with hope. It regained its religious faith and confidence. It gathered the fortitude to fight off the Turks. The economic and innovative opportunities created by the discovery of the New World allowed Europe to leap forward in wide areas of trade, science, philosophy, and technology, initiating a new era of wealth and discovery. This period of revitalization then launched the most significant developments ever seen by man in government, law, ethics, philosophy, and liberty.

In short, this period of revitalization allowed Europe to evolve into the home of Western thought and philosophy.

Then, when the time was right and the foundation had been settled, these elements gave birth to the United States.

Along the Black Sea's Western Shore
December 1493

THEY STOOD ATOP THE ROCK. The sun had gone down now and the world had turned dark. Overhead there were too many stars to count, too many stars even to comprehend. The Arab looked at the constellations, then nodded to the Pole Star, knowing the sailor Christopher Columbus must have used it to navigate, just as he and his people did. "The world has opened up," he stated. "Perhaps it has doubled in size. Instantly, there is triple, maybe quintuple, the amount of gold and silver that existed in the world as we knew it just a short while ago. And that is just the beginning. I can feel it. *Can you feel it?* There is something in the air. A new beginning. A new door. It is as if the sky has opened and the hand of God has been seen. We don't understand what is out there, *but everyone wants to know.* There will be a whole new world in exploration. Inspiration. Motivation. Hope. Wealth. *And all of it will go through Europe.* It will lift and sustain your people, even the fools that you are. It will lift you and change you and leave us all behind. I wish I could see another answer, but I know that that's the truth. You will rise. Then we must fall. It is the way it has always been."

The older man shook his head. Even if it was true, he didn't care. All he wanted was to create a hint of security among the chaos that his homeland had become.

The Arab seemed to read his mind. "Have good hope, my friend from Europe, your best days are yet to come. Born again. Risen from the ashes. So many good things are in store."

Notes

1. See Durant, *Reformation,* 230.
2. Ibid., 183.
3. Ibid., 187.
4. Ibid., 704.
5. For information about the Ottoman Empire's invasion of southeastern Europe and its ascent to world power, see Durant, *Reformation,* 175–90, 702–7; Gibbon, *Decline and Fall of the Roman Empire,* 1197–1218; Lewis, *Middle East,* 106–15.
6. Quoted in Lewis, *Middle East,* 115.
7. Durant, *Reformation,* 5.
8. Ibid., 6.
9. Sale, *Conquest of Paradise,* 16.
10. Oman, *On the Writing of History,* 113.
11. See Durant, *Reformation,* 17.
12. Ibid., 18.

13. Oman, *On the Writing of History,* 115–16.
14. See Durant, *Reformation,* 20.
15. See Huizinga, *Waning of the Middle Ages,* 19–20.
16. For information about the status of the Catholic church prior to and during the era of Columbus, see Durant, *Reformation,* 3–25, 213–216; Huizinga, *Waning of the Middle Ages;* Oman, *On the Writing of History,* 110–17; Sale, *Conquest,* 16, 37.
17. Huizinga, *Waning of the Middle Ages,* 13.
18. Sale, *Conquest of Paradise,* 31.
19. See ibid., 13.
20. Durant, *Reformation,* 112.
21. Ibid., 115.
22. Huizinga, *Waning of the Middle Ages,* 15.
23. See Durant, *Reformation,* 71.
24. Quoted in Sale, *Conquest of Paradise,* 34.
25. Durant, *Reformation,* 71–72.
26. Huizinga, *Waning of the Middle Ages,* 20.
27. Ibid., 21.
28. Ibid., 25–26.
29. See ibid., 21.
30. Sale, *Conquest of Paradise,* 29.
31. Morison, *Admiral of the Ocean Sea,* 4–5.
32. For information about the conditions in Europe during the end of the Middle Ages and prior to the Renaissance, see Durant, *Reformation,* 39, 64–65, 72–73; Huizinga, *Waning of the Middle Ages;* Morison, *Admiral of the Ocean Sea,* 3–5; Sale, *Conquest of Paradise,* 28–46.
33. Oman, *On the Writing of History,* 117, 118.
34. Morison, *Admiral of the Ocean Sea,* 5.
35. Oman, *On the Writing of History,* 119.
36. Durant, *Reformation,* 269, 270.
37. For information about the impact of the New World on the Old, see Cowley, *What If?* 813–27; Durant, *Reformation,* 269–70, 752, 755, 849; Lewis, *What Went Wrong,* 15–16; Mann, *1491,* 177; Morison, *Admiral of the Ocean Sea,* 3–6; Oman, *On the Writing of History,* 117–22; Sale, *Conquest of Paradise,* 46.

Chapter 7

The Battle of Britain

*"... victory at all costs, victory in spite of all terror,
victory however long and hard the road may be;
for without victory, there is no survival."*

Winston Churchill

He may have been as young as seventeen. He may have flown, fought, and died without any other member of his squadron even knowing his name—his entire combat experience lasting but a fraction of a day. He may have reported one morning, tossed his bag into the tent, heard the scramble horn go off, jumped into his single-engine fighter, and lifted into the sky.

Fifteen minutes later, he may have been dead.

He was one of "The Few" (there were only about a thousand of them): the pilots of the Royal Air Force (RAF) who battled—and beat—the German Luftwaffe in the air war over England during the summer of 1940. He was one of those young men whose courage in the face of a seemingly unstoppable enemy was set to change the history of the world.

The Battle of Britain was the first military campaign limited entirely to air forces, breaking significant new ground in modern warfare tactics. It also was the largest and longest aerial campaign ever experienced up to that day. It proved to be the decisive tipping point in the Second World War, shaping the future of the world in many critical ways.

One eminent scholar described the Battle of Britain as "the single greatest event in world political history."[1]

Or, as Winston Churchill said, in a quote that is as memorable as the story that it tells, "Never in the field of human combat has so much been owed by so many to so few."[2]

Time would prove that he chose his heroes well.

RAF Biggin Hill
Twelve Miles Southeast of London

HE SAT IN THE COCKPIT, 1,175 horses vibrating in front of him, the enormous Rolls Royce engine pushing back the smell of exhaust and compressed air, its twelve cylinders sucking down his precious fuel. His name was Gilbert Manson, but everyone called him Snap. Seconds before, he had taxied to the end of the runway, but now he had to wait for the leader of his formation to take off. He hated this moment, the final seconds of hesitation while waiting for the signal to go. It was the only time that he was really scared, and his feet were tapping nervously on the metal floor, his gut already rolled into a knot. A drip of sweat stung his left eye. He had slid the cockpit cover closed and it was getting warm, the midmorning sun pouring through the bulletproof glass. Without looking, he reached down and extracted his leather flask for a quick drink, swishing the water around in his dry mouth and then swallowing it down.

The pilot was eighteen, or would be in just a few weeks. (In the situation in which he found himself, it was better to round up.) He had blond hair and green eyes, and, judging by the young women who were attracted to him, he must have been good-looking (or so he had concluded, despite some of the things that his little sister used to say). The Spitfire was fresh as well, having never seen combat. He could smell the factory newness of the fabric on his seat, the clean engine oil, the metal welds that still bore a whiff of sulfur.

And that wasn't all he smelled. If he took a deep breath, he could capture a hint of deep perfume, a special gift from the female WAAF pilot who had delivered the aircraft from the factory just a few hours before.

Pilots were a suspicious lot, and it had to be a good sign, he thought, having such a fresh bird underneath him, let alone one that smelled of roses. Surely the combat gods were going to smile on him today.

Unless, of course, they didn't . . .

Turning in his seat, he glanced back along the smooth lines of the fuselage. The Spitfire was such a beautiful machine. Smooth. Fast. Powerful. It was a bull, not a bronco, all muscle, spit, and power. It climbed like a bat, could take a heavy punch before going down, and, with eight machine guns, give a fistful in a fight. But it wasn't perfect: it rolled like a rock, taking literally all of his strength against the stick to put the fighter on its side, but once it was over, it rolled out smoothly and never shuddered. An aircraft was like a rifle—it had to be steadied before he fired, and the Spitfire was very smooth, making it easier to be accurate with his guns.

Which was good. Really good. Because right now, there were something like 250 German bombers and fighters heading toward him. Sitting in the sweaty cockpit, he was ready to do some damage to those Krauts.

Hearing the fighters in front of him push up their power, the young pilot turned back to face the runway. The first two aircraft in his formation started rolling, staying in line abreast. He glanced around the cockpit quickly, checking his engine instruments a final time. Behind him, fourteen other Spitfires waited to take off, every one of the pilots at least as scared as he was. Some of them, he knew, had already thrown up. He hadn't yet, and wouldn't. Everyone dealt with fear a little differently. Some threw up. Some tapped their feet. Some smoked cigarettes until their teeth were brown. Besides, his greatest fear wasn't dying in a flame of combat, it was bailing out over the cold waters of the English Channel and then freezing to death before he could be found. But he didn't have to worry about that today. Unless all of the German bombers abandoned their targets and turned to run, he would never get that far south.

But even if he did end up in the Channel, he was okay with that. Truth was, he had accepted the knot of fear inside his chest. He had accepted the weariness that seemed to sap him to the very bone.

There was something important going on around him. A brief moment of glory, maybe. He knew that he was part of it, and that made the other things all right.

A Million Reasons Not to Go to War

The Battle of Britain was fought just twenty-two years after the close of World War I, ironically called the "Great War," or the "war to end all wars." Great Britain had been on the victorious side of that bloody conflict, and for the first decade after the war's end in 1918, it felt like it had won. But starting in about 1929, the narrative changed in a dramatic way as the nation began to realize the terrible price that it had paid. With the bitter reality setting in, England stopped feeling like a victor.

This staggering 180-degree shift was generated by a number of sources. A popular London play, *Journey's End,* stunned its audiences with its antiwar theme. Books, many of them personal memoirs by those who had served in the Great War, began to appear, telling of the horror of that war. Newspapers and magazines began to focus on the stories that either had not been told or had not been believed: stories such as the stark truth that sixty thousand young Englishmen had fallen on the first day of fighting at the First Battle of the Somme.

Sixty thousand soldiers! Without gaining an inch of ground!

The antiwar fervor was fed by the grim facts. World War I had resulted in the death of almost one million of Great Britain's finest, with twice that number wounded—this from a nation with a total population of only thirty million people. The war also left half a million widows and an unknown number of children without their fathers.

Such stunning figures simply could not be ignored.

The intensity of the antiwar fervor was remarkable, with pacifism coming into vogue not only in Britain but also throughout much of Europe. One well-known and not unusual example of the attitudes of the time came in 1933 when the Oxford student union approved a resolution that "'this House will in no circumstances fight for King and Country.'"[3] The same year, a victorious Labor Party candidate ran on the promise that he would close all recruiting stations and do away with the army and the air force. He called for England to set the example by demanding worldwide disarmament. And he wasn't the only pacifist candidate to win.[4]

The pacifist wave that rolled over England was also fed by other factors besides the terrible human cost of the previous war. Its time having come and gone, the once-great British Empire was on an irreversible downward slide. After generations of belonging to the most powerful nation in the world, the English found that sad fact difficult to accept. Traditional economic principles were in shambles as the nation found itself in the throes of the worldwide Great Depression. Nearly one-fourth of the workforce was unemployed. In some parts of the country, the unemployment rate was 70 percent. Britain's export industry was dying. Hunger riots broke out. Feelings of betrayal and resentment boiled over, resulting in many symbols of wealth or privilege being attacked. In an embarrassing indication of the nation's steep decline, the venerable British navy found its sailors rebelling as their wages were reduced.

While the ruling elite found imperialism still attractive, the working people were no longer enamored by its cost in money and men, leaving a philosophical vacuum that had to be filled.

In the midst of this political uncertainty, the Communist party emerged as an acceptable alternative, many of England's intellectual elite enlisting in the Communist cause. Russia was held up as a great success story, visitors to Stalin's sadistic empire having been brainwashed into believing that the fairy-tale harmony and prosperity created by the Russian propaganda machine were real.

With the Russian Bear rising up in Eastern Europe, a genuine fear that England might be the victim of a Communist revolution began to dominate the political thinking of the time.

But through this great fear, a ray of hope began to shine.

Unexpectedly, and with astonishing speed, Germany rose as a counterweight to the Communist Bear. Feeding on the seeming success of the Fascist rulers in Italy (though a tyrant, Benito Mussolini did appear to create stability and economic growth), the Fascist movement began to stir in Germany, a desperate country that was suffering not only from the ravages of the Depression but also from the shame of a lost war and the oppressive peace agreement that had followed.

With the rise of Fascism, a man named Adolf Hitler forced himself onto the national stage.

Some in England welcomed the new movement as a bulwark against a Communist wave sweeping over Europe. With a desire for peace at any cost, and the dread of Communism hanging over their heads, French and English leaders decided to befriend any anti-Communist government that might emerge in Germany.

Adolf Hitler was more than happy to oblige them.

Rise of the Reich

At the conclusion of World War I, the victorious Allies had imposed a new government upon Germany in the form of the Weimar Republic, a system that was completely foreign to the German mind-set. Under the best of circumstances, it might have succeeded. Under the desperate environment facing Germany after 1918, it was doomed to fail.

First and foremost, Germany had lost its honor in the Great War, no small matter to a nation where pride was an essential element of the national psyche. While the thought of another war caused the French or English to recoil in horror, many Germans viewed it as the only way to retrieve their national honor.

The costs imposed upon Germany by the Treaty of Versailles (which ended the First World War) were beyond punitive. A sum of more than \$31 billion was demanded in reparations—an impossible amount for the Germans to pay. Severe limits were placed on the German military, which was not permitted to have airplanes, tanks, submarines, a draft, or a general staff. Its total army was limited to one hundred thousand soldiers. Germany's national boundaries were reduced, and it was prohibited from fortifying its western border. Private property held abroad was confiscated. Its five great rivers were internationalized, meaning, essentially, that Germany had lost control over its own waterways.

The victorious Allies seemed intent on totally humiliating the German people.

It was a dangerous thing to do, for, even in defeat, Germany remained the most powerful nation in all of Europe. Its geographical location gave it enormous strategic advantages, and its population exceeded that of either France or Great Britain by more than thirty million people.

With the German people roiling under these oppressive conditions, the stage was set for a sudden and drastic change.

Adolf Hitler's emergence as the leader of the National Socialist Party (the Nazis) was dramatic. In the election of 1928, that Nazi party won only 2.6 percent of the votes. It was viewed then as only a fringe party; no one took it seriously. But the Depression and the decadence of the Weimar Republic led to a dramatic acceptance of the Nazi creed. Just four years later, the Nazis were the largest political party in the country. The president of the Weimar Republic was forced to make Hitler the nation's chancellor. Within months, the evil genius had maneuvered to be granted dictatorial powers by the elected Reichstag. With total authority to make laws, control the budget, and negotiate treaties, Hitler's rise to power was complete.

Only fourteen years after its inception, the Weimar Republic came to a sudden end. Hitler immediately began to ignore the limitations of the Treaty of Versailles. Germany began to rearm. At first it did so secretly. By 1935, it was openly preparing for war.

A Fool's Errand

From 1933 until 1939, a great melodrama unfolded in Berlin and London. While Germany rearmed, Britain engaged in what could only be described as purposeful ignorance, an ostrich with its head stuffed firmly in the sand. When Hitler demanded that Germany be allowed to rebuild its army, navy, and air force, three British prime ministers (McDonald, Baldwin, and Chamberlain) took up his cause, arguing that peace was possible only if Hitler's demands were met.

Most of Britain's other leaders and elites had nothing but praise for Hitler. After a brief visit, former Prime Minister David Lloyd George declared that Hitler had a single-minded purpose: to keep the peace. He happily assured his countrymen that as long as Hitler was Germany's leader, the Germans would never invade any other land. A popular British journalist wrote of Hitler's "'large, brown eyes—so large and so brown that one might grow lyrical about them if one were a woman.'"[5] Church of England clergymen spoke of Nazi devotion to religion and Christianity.

But Adolf Hitler was not a Christian. And he was not religious. He was a pagan and a man whose heart was full of murder and evil.

Fortunately, the pacifists were not the only leaders who had an opinion about the rising German Reich. Winston Churchill understood how evil Hitler really was. He understood the genuine threat that a rising Germany held for the rest of Europe—for the rest of the world. And though he was not the only voice of dissent, he was by far the most eloquent and persistent.

Regrettably, Churchill was not given the same attention and acclaim that Hitler was. While Hitler's crude speeches were met with near delirium, Churchill was "distrusted, disliked—even hated—by those who did not share his conviction that Germany threatened the peace and England must arm to defend her shores."[6] His voice of dissent was even mocked. On one occasion, when addressing students at Oxford University, he stated that England needed to rearm if it was to remain safe in its island home. The laughter and raucous response to his statement grew so intense that he was forced to abandon his presentation.

In Germany, Hitler rebuilt his army and navy and created a powerful air force known as the Luftwaffe. He reinstituted the draft while also building a core of professional and highly capable officers. To pacify the suspicions of his neighbors, he continually declared that Germany would never threaten anyone.

In London, appeasement became the official government policy. It was declared that Germany had the right to rebuild its military might. Many argued that, in order to show its good faith in the peace process, England should unilaterally disarm. Speeches by Churchill pointing out the insanity of such a policy were delivered to a largely empty Parliament chamber. Later in the 1930s, when he spoke of the urgent need to rearm in order to protect their great nation, the response from his political opponents bordered on the absurd. They argued that they favored disarmament because they were realists. One said, "'We deny the proposition that an increased British air force will make for the peace of the world.'"[7]

Hitler's meteoric rise to power, the rebuilding of his military, and England's pacifist stance in the face of the rising threat are well documented:

1935: Hitler renounces the Treaty of Versailles, invokes anti-Semitic laws, and obtains the capacity for air superiority over England.

1936: Germany drives France from the Rhineland; Italy joins Germany in an alliance.

1937: Neville Chamberlain becomes prime minister and establishes appeasement as his official government policy.

1938: Hitler seizes Austria; Churchill proposes an Allied response to Hitler; Chamberlain refuses, saying that it might anger the German leader. At Munich, Chamberlain sells out the Czechs.

1939: Hitler seizes Czechoslovakia; Hitler invades Poland; the Allies (with England and France as the primary members) declare war on Germany.

By 1940, the clash of civilizations had finally come to a head.

On May 10, Germany unleashed a full-scale attack on Holland, Belgium, and France. That same day, Winston Churchill became the prime minister of England.[8]

One Man and One Nation Stand Alone

King George did not want Churchill to be his prime minister. Most within the government and among the nation's elite preferred just about anyone else. His support was tepid even among his own party members. Many assumed that Churchill would quickly fail and that Chamberlain would return to replace him.

But Churchill possessed two rare and precious gifts: first, a clear vision of the great threat that faced the free world; and second, the power of words.

In his first speech to the Parliament as prime minister, he stated with absolute clarity what the new government's goal was:

> I would say to the House, as I have said to those who have joined this Government: "I have nothing to offer but blood, toil, tears and sweat." . . .
>
> You ask, what is our policy? I will say: It is to wage war, by sea, land and air, with all our might and with all the strength God can give us. . . . That is our policy.
>
> You ask, what is our aim? I can answer in one word: It is victory, victory at all costs, victory in spite of all terror, victory however long and hard the road may be; for without victory, there is no survival.[9]

As his own words make clear, Churchill understood that victory was essential for survival. But that didn't change the fact that the war on the Continent was going very poorly. Five short weeks after this speech was given, the French sued for peace.

Great Britain was now the only viable force on earth fighting the Nazis of Germany and the Fascists of Italy.

The day after the French surrendered, Churchill again addressed his nation. He vowed that England would continue the battle, even though they were now alone:

> Upon this battle depends the survival of Christian civilization. Upon it depends our own British life, and the long continuity of our institutions and our Empire. . . .
>
> Hitler knows that he will have to break us on this island or lose the war. If we can stand up to him all Europe may be free and the life of the world may move forward into broad, sunlit uplands.
>
> But, if we fail, then the whole world, including the United States, including all we have known and cared for, will sink into the abyss of a new Dark Age. . . .
>
> Let us therefore brace ourselves to our duties, and so bear ourselves that if the British Empire and its Commonwealth last for a thousand years, Men will still say: "*This* was their finest hour."[10]

The Royal Air Force

At most crucial moments in world history, certain men or women have stepped forward or been called upon to alter the course of history. Certainly, Winston Churchill was one of those men.

But the story of the Battle of Britain[11] is not about a single man. Though he was crucial to the survival of his nation, Winston Churchill would be the first to admit that the Battle of Britain was not about him, but rather about all the men and women of Fighter Command of the Royal Air Force (RAF). And fortunately, despite incessant calls during the 1930s for complete disarmament in the face of Germany's reemergence as a military power, the British military had not been totally dismantled. However, its air force had momentarily bought into a military theory that was decidedly flawed, a dangerous theory that had the potential, by itself, to cause the English to lose the entire war.

The essence of this dangerous military theory was this: Fighter aircraft were no longer a necessity.

In 1932, British Prime Minister Stanley Baldwin embraced the conventional view of military theorists of the time that fighter aircraft could never succeed in stopping big bombers. The theory was best expressed in the phrase, "the bomber will always get through." Because of this, it was believed that the only reliable defense was in having a sufficiently large bomber force so as to deter any enemy from attacking you. As Baldwin warned the House of Commons, "'The only defense is in offense which means that you have to kill more women and children more quickly than the enemy if you want to save yourselves.'"[12]

It was a horrible theory upon which to plan a war.[13] Nevertheless, it was the guiding principle the British used in their (meager, most would argue) preparations to defend themselves.

Accordingly, the bulk of spending on aircraft during this era was on offensive weapons systems—that is, bombers—it being widely believed that money spent on fighter aircraft was money wasted.

There was, however, one man who did not buy into the notion that fighter aircraft were without value. That man was Sir Hugh Dowding, the man who became Air Officer Commanding-in-Chief of RAF Fighter Command when it was created in 1936.

• • •

Following the German army's lightning-fast conquest of France in 1940, the question became not *if* but *when* the invasion of Great Britain would occur.

At least one German general argued that the Germans had already missed their best opportunity, believing the invasion should have taken place in late May, while 250,000 British soldiers had languished helplessly on the beaches at Dunkirk.[14]

Initially, Hitler hesitated to wage war on Great Britain, for he had been led to believe by his visits with former Prime Minister Lloyd George, as well as other British appeasers, that the English wanted peace above all else. His own foreign minister, a man who had once been the ambassador to England and had mingled with the elite of English society, reinforced this view.

Hitler's hope that he could reach a compromise with England was further encouraged in late May when an unofficial inquiry was made by Lord Halifax, the British foreign secretary in Churchill's cabinet. Halifax asked if Mussolini would act as an emissary to find out what peace terms Hitler would be willing to offer the English. This personal initiative by Halifax was not made known to Churchill until May 26. To say the least, the prime minister was not pleased! But Hitler was, and he took the inquiry seriously. Shortly afterward, he gave a speech in which he outlined his plan that if Great Britain would simply agree to let him maintain control of Europe, it would be left alone.

Was Hitler's overture tempting? If Lord Halifax had become prime minister and sought a peace agreement with Hitler, would his nation have supported him? There is evidence that a large segment of Great Britain would have endorsed such a move.

But Churchill refused to entertain such a dangerous and self-defeating notion. He made it clear that as long as he was prime minister, England would not surrender.

Still, Hitler was not convinced. He continued to believe that if he were able to make the British suffer enough, or fear enough, a prime minister more reasonable than Churchill would replace him. Peace, under Hitler's terms, could then be negotiated. Many of his subsequent decisions were apparently based on this belief. In fact, Hitler was so convinced that the English would sue for peace that he continued sending out peace feelers even as the Battle of Britain was being waged.[15]

Invasion Day Set

Notwithstanding Hitler's continued hope for Great Britain's capitulation, on July 16, he issued Directive No. 16, calling for a landing operation against England.

In part, Directive No. 16 read:

> As England, despite her hopeless situation, still shows no sign of willingness to come to terms, I have decided to prepare and if necessary to carry out a landing operation against

her. The aim of this operation is to eliminate the English motherland as a base from which war against Germany can be continued, and, if this should become unavoidable, to occupy it to the full extent.[16]

It was time, Hitler had decided, to take the battle to the British homeland. August 15, 1940, was set as the invasion date.

But his plans for invasion were contingent on two critical, independent considerations. First, in order to allow for difficult landings and the unloading of heavy armaments, the invasion had to occur before the days turned short and weather in the English Channel turned bad—something that usually happened by late September or early October. The second condition was of even greater import: The German air force had to secure air superiority over the RAF.

Specifically, Directive No. 16 indicated that, prior to the land invasion: "The English air force must have been beaten down to such an extent morally and in actual fact that it can no longer muster an[y] power of attack worth mentioning against the German crossing."[17]

German leadership was adamant in this resolve. The invasion could not happen until the Luftwaffe, under its leader, Hermann Göring, had decimated the RAF to the point that it would no longer be able to interfere with the massing of the invasion force, the crossing of the English Channel, or the establishment of a beachhead in England.[18]

Göring assured the other members of the German High Command that his Luftwaffe would make certain the RAF posed no threat to the pending invasion. With this assurance, and Hitler's Directive No. 16 in hand, "Operation Sea Lion" got under way.

The German navy began to assemble a vast armada from every available source in Germany as well as the recently occupied countries. They practiced moving tanks, guns, horses, and men on and off the landing craft. The Luftwaffe began to move nearly three thousand planes forward to the recently secured airfields in France. This was critical, for not only did it shorten the flying time to their targets but it also allowed Messerschmitts to protect the bombers, something these small fighters did not carry enough fuel to do if they had been forced to operate from bases in Germany. Finally, in preparation for taking command of the British military and civilian government, the Gestapo created a list of 2,820 Englishmen who were to be quickly arrested upon the operation's successful conclusion.[19]

With typical German precision, the pieces for the invasion began to fall into place. Göring was then given the green light to destroy the RAF.

Radar, Spitfires, and Hurricanes

Despite a decade of appeasement and talk of disarmament among the political classes, Great Britain had not left itself entirely at the mercy of Hitler's good intentions. The groundwork for a viable defense of its island home had been laid. Among the most fortunate decisions that had been made was the appointment of Sir Hugh Dowding to Fighter Command.

During the previous four years, Dowding had performed a miraculous transformation of the defensive capability of Great Britain by:

- Bringing two new fighter aircraft into service
- Incorporating a new technology known as "radar"
- Creating a means of central aircraft control
- Devising an overall strategy bent on bleeding the German Luftwaffe dry

In each of these efforts, he was met with harsh criticism and opposition. But this man, described as stubborn, humorless, impatient, and completely devoted to his mission, stared his opponents down in every substantial confrontation that took place.

When he took command in 1936, Fighter Command consisted of nothing but a bunch of small biplanes with open cockpits, two guns, and fixed landing wheels—aircraft not much different from those that had been used in World War I.

Despite the prevailing view (held by every major military power in the world) that "the bomber would always get through," Dowding said, "maybe not so." He demanded and obtained the manufacture of two new single-engine fighters whose names would become immortal—the Spitfire and the Hurricane. He insisted that these aircraft be equipped with high-frequency radios so that the pilots could communicate with each other and with their ground controllers, that they have eight guns and a transparent sliding cockpit canopy. He also demanded that the canopy have bulletproof glass to protect the pilots. "I can't understand why Chicago gangsters can have bulletproof glass in their cars and I can't get it in my Spitfires," he reportedly said.[20]

Dowding had previously been assigned to a position in research and development, where he had encouraged experiments in, and then became an early advocate of, the new technology known as radar. As head of Fighter Command, he ordered construction of a line of radar stations along the coast of southern England. The radar masts were two to three hundred feet high, and though the stations were unable to determine the altitude of incoming aircraft or to discern between friendly and enemy airplanes, they proved to be absolutely critical to the upcoming battle. More than 1,400 "observer posts" supplemented these modern contrivances: men and women scattered along the coastline to watch for the approaching enemy the old-fashioned way—with their eyes.

Dowding came to understand that the numbers of his aircraft and the experience of his pilots would always be severely limited. He also understood that his pilots would be facing an overwhelming number of bombers and fighter escorts. Knowing this, he concluded that they couldn't waste time on preemptive patrols or random attacks. Everything had to be controlled and coordinated. It had to be precise. In order to maximize use of his resources, he demanded—again, against great opposition—that all of his fighters be controlled from a central location.

He constructed a large amphitheater in his headquarters. In the middle, he placed a map of southern England, the English Channel, and the northern coast of Europe. Around this map, a dozen or so young airmen and airwomen worked. After receiving reports from their radar and observation posts, these young people (first called "filterers," then the "beauty chorus") would move representations of enemy aircraft as they formed up and flew across the channel.

Dowding's "beauty chorus" had the task of not only monitoring German formations but organizing the fighter squadrons to repel them. The incoming bombers flew at two to three hundred miles per hour, a speed that allowed them to get from mainland Europe to their English targets in only twenty minutes or so. To accomplish a successful intercept, the beauty chorus had to direct the British fighter aircraft to arrive not just at the right place but also at the right time, for precious fuel in the small fighters could not be wasted.

According to Dowding's plan, only small numbers of RAF fighters would attack the oncoming bomber groups. But they would be relentless! As soon as one group of pilots ran low on fuel and ammunition, the next group would be waiting to attack, over and over; the Luftwaffe would receive no mercy or reprieve.

Dowding's overall strategy could best be summed up as a war of attrition. He did not have to win the air battle; he just had to avoid defeat.

Though they would always be outnumbered, enough British pilots had to be kept flying to repel the main German invasion force when Hitler committed to the attack. Better yet, if he was really lucky—or good—Dowding wanted to forestall the invasion until the autumn weather and short days made things too dangerous for it to take place.

To this end, he could never let the Luftwaffe know just how many airplanes he had. He would never attack in large numbers, only constant, small-unit "pinpricks." This would lead the Germans to believe that the RAF was far outnumbered and always near the end of its airplanes. And that, in turn, would lead them to keep coming and coming, losing aircraft (mostly the far more expensive bombers and their four-man crews) at a moderate but steady rate, allowing him to bleed the Germans slowly.

By tightly controlling his fighter squadrons, Dowding made the best use of them. But his strategy also appeared to reinforce the conventional theory that "the bombers will always get through." His strategy left the British people even more vulnerable to bombing attacks, a fact for which he was severely condemned. In the end, however, his war of delay and attrition was the only hand he had.[21]

Higgins Blue Flight
Over Southeastern London

ANOTHER DAY. ANOTHER TWO or three combat sorties. Another frenzy of deadly dogfights. Another dozen of his fellow pilots shot down.

Manson, having survived the Battle of Britain for almost six weeks, was one of the old heads now. He had gone from being called Snap to Lieutenant to the Old Man.

Eighteen years old, and they called him old. Which was kind of funny, because that was exactly how he felt.

The pilot watched his formation leader lift into the air, his commander's wheels tucking tightly into the underside of the wings, the second aircraft right beside him. Manson quickly released his brakes and pushed his throttle forward. The aircraft hesitated half a second before the engine spun up, then almost lurched, pushing him back in his seat. Less than ten minutes later, he was cruising at twenty thousand feet.

Another cluster of German bombers and fighters were flying toward them. The radio controller had told them there were eighty enemy aircraft in the formation, but who really knew?

After realizing that keeping their fighters in a tight V formation was a recipe for death, the RAF had loosened up their tactics, allowing a wingman to fly behind and above the main formation in order to keep an eye out to both sides and below. And that was where Manson was now. The air in his mask was cold and dry. His stomach and bowels felt bloated, an overfilled balloon. The Spitfire wasn't pressurized, which made it painful to stay in the cockpit for very long. By nightfall, after his third exhausting sortie, he would be so sore and tired that he would have trouble even holding up his head. But right now, he felt pretty good. In fact, his heart was racing. He was in a fighting mood. Among the many targets the Germans were coming after, one was surely his home base, and the thought of protecting his own turf added a little emotion to the fight.

The formation circled over London as a female voice gave them a vector to line up on the approaching German bombers. Four miles below, Battersea Park slipped beneath his wing. The water of the tree-lined lake was dark, sitting peacefully among the low buildings and townhomes of the city. He noticed a few sailboats on the water—life went on in London, though surely the boaters must have realized that men were dying in the air above them. He glanced at his formation leader, then back at the lake again. As a child, he used to go fishing with his father at the park. The protective instinct kicked in once again.

Banking gently to the right, the formation leader brought his group of fighters around. That was when Manson saw them. They looked like a cloud of glass, so many glinting windscreens, aluminum wing tops, and spinning propellers reflecting in the sun. There must have been, what . . . thirty Heinkel He 111 bombers, surrounded by a swarm of Messerschmitt fighters, all of them tucked together and heading straight toward him.

His heart skipped a beat, his hands clenching around his stick and throttle. Without thinking, he lowered his seat, partly for protection, partly to line up with his fixed gun sight. Blue One, the flight leader, turned the formation to put them in a position to attack the bombers from the side—called the beam—as well as making it so they could drop onto the Germans from out of the sun. As they closed in, Manson's thumb moved across the button on his stick, switching his guns from *safe* to *fire*.

He dropped out of the sky for the attack, the powerful engine on his Spitfire screaming.

A German 111 came into view and he kicked his rudder hard to push his nose to the right, lining up his guns on the black-and-yellow bomber. His leg began to tremble against the pressure of holding his aircraft canted against the passing airstream. The German aircraft didn't move, flying steadily toward its target. It must have been on its final bomb run, Manson realized, and he knew he had only a few seconds to take the bomber down. Once it had dropped its bombs, it would dive and flee. Worse, its bombs would be on their way to their targets.

Around him, the air was already filling with smoke and screaming fighters, diving bombers and falling bombs, contrails and pieces of shattered metal, a couple of parachutes and greasy fireballs. His radio was full of urgent voices: his wingman, "COME AROUND!" His leader, "BLUE FOUR, WATCH MY TAIL." The female voice of the ground controller, "GROUP SIX, YOUR TARGET IS COMING UP THE THAMES." Another radio telephone controller, "GROUP ELEVEN, WHAT IS YOUR FUEL STATE?" There were other voices, some smooth and some panicked, far too many to keep track of or understand. Closing on his target, he moved his finger over the fire button and shoved the rudder pedal once again while rolling to his right. It took both hands to push the stick over, but he didn't need to control the throttle any longer—from here until the fight was over, he would take every ounce of energy that his engine had to give him. The fighter rolled and the German bomber slipped into his gun sight. The bomb bay doors were already open. He had but a second, maybe two. The small red dot lined up on the fuselage and he fired a short burst. The Spitfire shuddered as almost two hundred .303 rounds fired toward the German bomber. The 111 shook and dipped, then rolled abruptly to its side. Pieces of metal peeled back from the left wing and fluttered through the air. The Heinkel righted itself, spat out some bombs—which fell into each other before they even had time to arm—then flew on a wingtip for a moment before the wing snapped off.

Then he saw the tracers shooting by his cockpit, angry red and yellow bits of light. Instinctively, he jerked back on the stick, pulling the Spitfire's nose into the air, while glancing into his rearview mirror to see the Messerschmitt only two hundred yards behind. But his engine was at full power, he had previously built up airspeed, and the Spitfire was better than the Messerschmitt in the climb. As the German fighter fell below, the words *speed is life!* rushed into his head. How many times had his instructor pilot shouted that in training? Now the lesson had saved his life.

Shifting in his seat, he rolled his fighter over and looked for another German bomber to kill.

The Chicks

There is no doubt that Dowding proved to be a tactical genius. Putting his remarkable foresight aside, as well as the fact that he obtained aircraft, radar, and an operations center, and formulated an ingenious strategy, his supreme resource was what he called his "chicks": the roughly one thousand pilots of Fighter Command.[22] These were dashing, brave, resilient young men, everything one thinks of when considering a Hollywood hero.

But they were also hopelessly outnumbered. And depressingly young. By later summer, the average age of replacement pilots was only seventeen.[23]

By the battle's end, fully one-third of these young men would be dead, severely wounded, or missing in the fight.

The simple fact is, they had volunteered for a desperate battle. Their enemy had the largest and most advanced air force in the world. More critically, the German pilots were far more experienced. Most of them had been flying for years. Many had spent the last few months in battle, honing their combat flying skills, an advantage that is hard to appreciate when it comes to the split-second, life-and-death decisions that pilots face in combat. By contrast, few of the pilots of the RAF had any combat experience at all. Most had been trained by instructor pilots who were not much older and did not have much more experience than they had themselves. When they reached their new squadrons, if they were fortunate, they would receive a few precious hours of flying time to "polish up" before they were thrust into combat.

Little surprise, then, that many of these young RAF pilots were killed in their first few skirmishes.

There would be cases during August and September 1940, when the battle was at its peak, of a young RAF pilot arriving at the squadron to which he had been posted and being rushed straight into a fighter before he had even unpacked his suitcases, and killed before anybody knew his name. Opening the suitcases he had left in the entrance to the mess was the only way for the Adjutant or the Station Warrant Officer to learn who he had been.[24]

There are not many battlefield situations in which the odds were so stacked against one side as was the case with these young RAF pilots fighting over England.

Such was the bravery of "the Few" who saved England and the world.[25]

• • •

At the beginning of the Battle of Britain, Dowding had approximately seven hundred Hurricanes and Spitfires. Across the English Channel, the German aircraft numbered more than three thousand.

But despite heavy losses, Dowding was able to keep a reasonable number of fighters flying through the summer, mainly because of a system he had worked out with Lord Beaverbrook, a close friend of Winston Churchill who had been appointed Minister of Aircraft Production. Lord Beaverbrook, a millionaire publisher who knew nothing about building airplanes but made up for that fact with ruthless drive, managed to keep airplane production and repair at a level that was needed. In fact, the system became refined to the point that Dowding would call Beaverbrook every night and tell him how many replacement planes he would need the next day. The next morning they would arrive, often flown by young female pilots.[26]

Expecting the invasion at any moment, the civilians of England were in a state of constant dread. While they waited, the British organized their local defenses into the famous Home Guard. Expecting a massive bombing of their cities (after all, "the bombers will always get through"), many thousands of young children were evacuated to the countryside.

Churchill pleaded for help from the United States. It was largely denied. Joseph Kennedy, the U.S. ambassador to London, filed frequent reports full of pessimism. Simply put, he believed the Brits were finished.

The Battle Begins

By the time the Luftwaffe had relocated its planes and personnel to forward airfields, it was clear that the original Sea Lion invasion date of August 15 was not going to work. Hitler reset the date for September 15. But he did so extremely reluctantly, for he and his senior staff knew they were taking a great risk. Short days. Bad weather. Those two factors were always on their minds.

With the September date set, the Luftwaffe had only a few months to remove the RAF as a threat. The pressure on General Göring grew more intense.

The preliminaries for the main air battle began in July.

The first thing the Germans had to do was to test the British defenses. To accomplish this, they sent small formations to bomb the coastal towns and shipping assets.

As the first of these attacks against the British homeland commenced, Dowding fell under intense pressure to scramble large numbers of his fighters and really take it to the Germans. But he remained determined and disciplined, sticking to his strategy of deception. He relied on smaller but constant fighter attacks, even if that meant that more of the bombers did get through.

In July, he lost 145 fighters but shot down 270 German planes. More important, his tactics succeeded in giving the Germans the impression that the RAF did not have large numbers of Spitfires and Hurricanes. *If they had more fighters, they would have used them!* the Germans believed. By the end of July, German intelligence told Göring that the Brits were operating with three hundred, maybe four hundred fighters at best. He was assured, and in turn assured Hitler, that once full-scale bombing began, the Luftwaffe would make short work of the undermanned RAF.

Göring called for the first all-out attack on August 13. In typical Nazi fashion, the event was awarded a flashy name—*Eagle Day.*

In an attempt to soften up the RAF prior to the main strike, critical airfields and radar stations were attacked the day before. Upon landing, German pilots reported that they had destroyed three RAF airfields. (Though the airfields had suffered some damage, most were grass runways that could be repaired quickly with shovels and bulldozers. All were back in operation the next day.)

More important, the German pilots reported they had shot down seventy British fighters. In fact, they had destroyed only twenty-two.[27]

But Göring didn't know this. Again, relying on intelligence estimates that the RAF had only three to four hundred fighters, and with the reported loss of seventy aircraft in the "softening up," the Germans were elated. Surely, Eagle Day would result in overwhelming losses for the British air force.

The day proved to be far less dramatic than its name implied. Bad weather prevented the overwhelming blitz that had been planned. Rather, the Luftwaffe engaged in a series of badly coordinated, hit-and-miss attacks that inflicted very little damage. At the end of the day, the Germans had lost thirty-eight aircraft; the RAF, thirteen fighters. Again, the Germans rejoiced, being told by their returning aircrews that they had reduced the RAF fighter force to only two or three hundred aircraft.

In reality, Dowding had 647 fighters left.

August 15 turned out to be momentous. The Germans launched so many aircraft that at times the "beauty chorus" was completely swamped: in the south, a hundred struck in the late morning, more than seventy at noon, more than two hundred in the early afternoon, three hundred and then four hundred in the late afternoon, seventy in the early evening. One hundred fifty additional planes struck in northeast England. The attacks took their toll. Airfield after airfield was bombed and bombed again. Finally realizing how critical radar was to Dowding's strategy, the Germans focused on the radar stations. They also sent up enough fighter escorts to inflict considerable losses to the

RAF defenders. Generally outnumbered three to one, the RAF pilots were forced to fly sortie after sortie—three, four, sometimes five in a day. Upon running out of fuel or ammunition, if their airfield was under attack, the exhausted pilots had to find an alternate place to land. Again and again, bone-weary ground crews scrambled to resupply the pilots and send them up again.

The resulting destruction by the German attacks? An unknown number of radar stations taken out of commission, considerable damage to many RAF airfields, a bomber factory set ablaze, thirty-four British airplanes destroyed, a long list of miscellaneous targets damaged.

But the Germans had paid a heavy price. Seventy-five of their aircraft had been shot down.

Upon landing, the German pilots reported that they had downed 101 RAF fighters. At this point, Göring became seriously concerned. If his pilots were destroying so many British planes, how did the RAF keep materializing in such numbers as to be able to destroy so many of his aircraft? He realized there was much more work to be accomplished before the September 15 deadline that he had promised the Supreme Leader of the Reich.

Bunker 47
Provisional HQ, Operation Sea Lion
Along the Northwestern Coast of France

THE COMMANDER-IN-CHIEF of the infamous German Luftwaffe had flown in from Berlin earlier that morning. From the moment that his personal transport had touched down, Göring had ranted and raved to everyone he encountered: the driver of his car, the major who had offered to carry his briefcase, the young woman who had brought him coffee—all had tasted of his wrath.

But most of his rage had been centered on the *Jagdfliegergerfuhrer,* the poor soldier who had the misfortune to brief him on the ongoing battle over England. In Göring's eyes, the briefing general, commander of Fighter Air Command, was one of many officers who had betrayed the German people by not fulfilling the Führer's commands. But the men of the fighter and bomber commands were not alone. His intel officers had clearly dropped the ball. They were incompetent fools or outright liars; either way, he would string them up! He was getting enormous pressure from the Führer—the kind of pressure that some men were going to have to die for—and he had no intention of taking all of the heat himself.

He had promised the Führer!

It was time to set things right.

He scanned the list of the previous day's attrition numbers, the thing that had demanded his presence on the shores of France. Flipping through the sheets of paper, he scowled. It had been one of the single bloodiest days in the campaign so far. Dozens of heavy bombers and an unknown number of fighters killed or missing. No one knew for certain yet, the numbers were still coming in.

He sat back and shook his head. Too many bombers and fighters going down. Too many experienced pilots killed. He *needed* this equipment. For that matter, he needed these men. The Führer was already talking about his next conquest, the invasion of Russia, a nation they currently called an ally. It would be an enormous undertaking, for Russia was a massive country, three times the size of Europe, with tens of millions of people Stalin was ready to throw into the fight.

Yet here he was, with his Luftwaffe still stuck in France, working on an operation that was bleeding him dry.

He stared at the general who was in command of *Jagdgeschwader,* the Hunting Wing, the men who were responsible for protecting his bomber forces. So far, he had lost the fight against the RAF fighters. "Where is Churchill getting all of these aircraft?" Göring demanded.

The officer paused a moment. Did he dare to tell the truth? "We believe, sir," he finally started, "that we are beginning to make a difference. We believe that, with a few more—"

"With a few more what?" Göring shouted while lifting out of his chair. He was a large man, thick in the chest and shoulders, with wavy hair, a handsome face, and very determined eyes. But his features were hard and tight now, his lips pulled back in a snarl. "You believe *what,* General Udet, that with a few more hundred of our fighters shot down, a few more hundred of our bombers, Churchill will surrender? He is laughing at us now!" Göring jabbed an angry finger toward the Channel. "He is laughing while he destroys the greatest air force in the world. He's laughing while the Führer suffers. Is that acceptable to you?"

The general kept his eyes upon the Luftwaffe Supreme Commander, his back straight, his shoulders square. He was one of the finest officers in the world's finest fighting corps. He had been selected, trained, and challenged, and his pride was true and deep.

"Is that acceptable to you, General Udet?" Göring repeated with a hiss.

"No, sir, it is not."

"Then what are you going to do about it, Udet?"

The other man finally broke his eyes away.

Göring let him suffer a moment, then stood up and walked briskly to the front of the briefing room. "Let me help you, General. Let me tell you what we're going to do."

The *Jagdgeschwader* stepped away from the briefing table.

Göring turned to the other aviation officers. "We've finished adequate testing on the radio bombing," he announced.

The Fight Goes On

With no choice but to continue the bombing, the Germans kept coming.

On the sixteenth of August, 250 German aircraft hit in the morning. Another 350 bombers attacked in the afternoon. At one point, every one of the available RAF fighter squadrons within the southeast fighter group was engaged in the terrible struggle.

On the eighteenth, more than 250 German planes attacked in an early morning raid. Another wave came in the afternoon. Two more raids came after that. By the end of the day, the Germans had lost seventy-one aircraft. Twenty-seven British fighters had been shot down.

If the RAF had had the luxury of matching the German forces one for one, they would have been ecstatic with the kill-to-loss ratio. But they didn't. Dowding was running out of pilots. Far too many were being killed.

To meet the urgent need, he reduced yet again the time allotted to train a pilot. This meant that the young men showing up to fly the Spitfires and Hurricanes were even less prepared. More and more of the new pilots were lost in their first skirmish. The mortality rate climbed higher, leaving them down more pilots.

And the conditions for the young pilots were absolutely brutal:

> Combat was physically exhausting for even the strongest of fighter pilots, requiring enormous effort from limbs that were stiff with cold, as well as constant, almost superhuman alertness, split-second reaction to danger, and complete physical indifference to rapidly building g forces and stomach-churning changes of direction . . . with your mouth dry from breathing oxygen; your eyes smarting from the fumes of gasoline, oil, and exhaust seeping into the cockpit and from staring into the sun; and the radio pouring into your ears a constant tumult of static, orders, warnings, and awful cries of pain and despair. All this in the knowledge that you were sitting behind . . . many gallons of high-octane fuel that could turn you into a blazing torch in seconds, not to speak of hundreds of rounds of ammunition, while somewhere from above and behind you another nineteen- to twenty-year-old might already be swooping down on you from out of the sun to . . . end your life in a burst of fire lasting less than a second.[28]

But sometimes death did not come in such a merciful second. Sometimes it came in a more horrible way: "Many WAAFs who served in ground control remember to this day hearing through their earphones the screams of young men trapped in a flaming cockpit, unable to slide back the canopy because their hands were too badly burned."[29]

On some days, the skies over southern England were completely filled with contrails. To the citizens below, whose lives were going on in almost normal fashion, the sight must have been surreal:

> Occasionally they looked up from what they were do-
> ing at the maze of contrails in the blue sky, or more rarely,
> saw an orange flash and a puff of black smoke as an aircraft
> was hit, and from time to time watched a parachute slowly
> descend, and wondered whether it was one of theirs or one
> of ours. . . . People grew accustomed to having the war drop
> in on their lives suddenly and unexpectedly—literally out of
> the blue—as bombs, pilots, aircrews, empty cartridge cases,
> flaming fragments of damaged aircraft, and even whole air-
> planes streaming smoke, flames, or white clouds of glycol,
> descended on them out of the sky.[30]

For the Germans, most of the planes being shot down were the larger bombers with four-man crews. This meant that not only were they losing far more aircraft than the RAF, they were losing crew members by a multiplier of four. Further, most of their losses were occurring over England, which meant that those who bailed out were being taken captive. (Both sides suffered equally when they bailed out over the cold waters of the English Channel, where the likelihood of dying of hypothermia was very high.)

Still, despite the constant attacks upon the Brits and the enormous losses that the Germans were experiencing, despite the best efforts of the mighty Luftwaffe, the most powerful air force in the world, despite Göring's threats and rants and pleadings, little progress had been made.

On August 18, Hitler reluctantly postponed Operation Sea Lion until September 17.

The Battle Becomes More Fierce

By mid-August, the Germans had adopted the new strategy that Göring had briefed his commanders on.

Relying on a recently developed technology involving radio beams, the German Luftwaffe was able to undertake night bombing of military industrial targets with some degree of accuracy. The ability of the RAF to defend against these night attacks was severely limited. With this new capability, the Germans commenced a twofold strategy of bombing airfields during the day and industrial targets at night.

Despite this growing threat, Dowding remained convinced that he still had but one objective: to keep enough of his chicks alive so as to delay the invasion until the end of September. He had to persevere for just a few more weeks.

But it was becoming less and less certain that his pilots could hang on.

• • •

Through the remainder of August and the first week in September, the conflict raged with growing intensity. During the day, all forward airfields were possible targets. During the night, major cities such as Portsmouth, Liverpool, and Birmingham were being blasted.

On August 31, Dowding's fighter command had its heaviest single-day losses: thirty-nine fighter craft shot down and fourteen pilots killed. In turn, the Germans lost forty-one of their airplanes. On September 1, 450 German aircraft hit the airfields again. Frightfully, and for the first time, the British lost the same number of aircraft that the Germans did that day.

The RAF was dying, whittled away by the overwhelming number of German aircraft, the constant waves of attacks, the loss of experienced pilots, and the sheer mind-numbing exhaustion that all of the flyers were forced to endure:

> Pilots were so tired that one of them landed, then fell forward and slumped over his controls—his ground crew assumed he was dead, but when they ran to his aircraft they discovered he had merely fallen asleep with the engine still running. . . . Ground personnel were numbed by the ceaseless bombing—ground crews refueled and rearmed their

aircraft under fire, carrying on with their work even when bombs were exploding nearby; young women dragged unexploded or delayed-action bombs off the runways with tractors, apparently oblivious of the danger.[31]

Some squadrons had fewer than one-half of their allotted pilots. Their airfields were being destroyed. Shovels and bulldozers could not keep up with the damage. Hangars for repairing aircraft were being obliterated. Huts where the exhausted pilots ate and slept had been smashed. By September 6, "Fighter Command had approached the breaking point. . . . At last the Germans were in grasping distance of the first precondition for the invasion—the systematic destruction of Fighter Command's ability to maintain control of the airspace over the Channel, England south of the Thames, and Dover."[32]

With the British RAF against the ropes, the Germans could have—and should have—pressed their advantage. They could have finished off the RAF. That being accomplished, the invasion of the British mainland could have commenced.

But though they held the clear advantage, the Germans didn't advance their cause. And the reason why is worth noting.

Blitz 37
A German Heinkel He 111 Medium Bomber Over Southeastern England

"CLIMB!" THE DORSAL GUNNER screamed into his oxygen mask. He was watching a pair of RAF Hurricanes move onto his tail, lining up like racing lions chasing down a slower prey. His guns had overheated and the ventral gunner was already dead, leaving them defenseless against the attacking Hurricanes. "Climb! CLIMB! JINK RIGHT!" the gunner screamed again.

It was too late. The Hurricanes started to fire. He watched a white-hot tongue of tracer bullets stream toward him, a terrifying line of death. His gut tightened up so hard he had to swallow down the contents of his stomach. The line of death reached out to kill him. "CLIMB!" he screamed a final time.

Instead, the Heinkel pushed over and dove toward the clouds. The gunner felt himself lifting weightless off his seat, his seat belt the only thing that held him from floating to the top of his gunner's cabin and smashing his head. The bomber screamed down, wind picking up around it, accelerating like a falling piece of steel toward the cloud layer five or six hundred feet below. The two Hurricanes gave chase. The bright moon and stars illuminated the soft layer of clouds as they came rushing up. The pilot pushed the nose over even more and the gunner was weightless once again. The aircraft had accelerated well beyond its redline, he could tell. Wind was screeching through the metal welds, and more than a few rivets along the fuselage had popped off. For a moment, the gunner had to wonder what terrified him more: the Hurricanes with their eight machine guns or the thought of his aircraft falling apart in midair. He glanced back again, his eyes wide. The Hurricanes were falling back. Then suddenly, POOF! they were gone. The blackness of the night turned instantly to a soft gray as the layer of clouds swallowed them up. Then he felt the violent g-forces push him back into his seat as the pilot struggled to level off. His head fell against his chin. His vision narrowed. His arms, suddenly the equivalent of sixty pounds apiece, fell against his gun. The nose of the aircraft climbed and wobbled, then fell level. The gunner swallowed and checked his tail. No Hurricanes. No enemy fighters. They were hidden in the clouds.

Of course, they would not be alone. How many other German bombers were flying around in here?

The aircraft wobbled and started climbing, the pilot searching for clear air once again. As little light as the moon and stars had provided, it was far better than the total darkness that had swallowed them inside the clouds.

Looking down, the gunner saw a trickle of blood dribbling along the metal floor. The other gunner was dead, his head almost completely shot off. The aircraft smelled of gas and oil and blood. He tightened his mask against his face, breathing the pure oxygen, and closed his eyes.

Forward, in the cockpit, the pilot had gone for almost forty seconds without taking a breath. He concentrated on his flight instruments, rudimentary though they were, fighting to keep the aircraft level while flying inside the clouds. The navigator/bombardier sat to his right, his eyes scanning across the cockpit instruments. "Looks good," he said, though he really didn't mean it. He was so disoriented, he didn't know up from down. The aircraft could have been pointing straight toward the ground and he wouldn't have recognized it. The pilot saw the blackness of the clouds begin to grow thinner and finally took a breath. Seconds later, they popped out atop the clouds. He leveled off again, keeping the bomber just above the stratus. The layer was perfectly smooth, and he pushed the nose until his aircraft was barely above the clouds. The navigator looked around, struggling to get his bearings while waiting for the spinning inside his head to settle down.

For a long moment, no one spoke. It felt like no one breathed. They had cheated death again. But she was a jealous pursuer. She wouldn't give up, they knew.

"I've got nothing on our tail," the gunner said to fill the empty silence. Everyone knew that he hadn't seen any more enemy fighters or he would have been screaming into his mask.

Only a few seconds passed before the pilot asked, "Where's the target?"

But none of them answered.

Because none of them knew.

• • •

Military campaigns can turn for many different reasons. A great general may prove his genius. New weapons may permit new tactics to which the enemy does not adapt. Some battlefield fortunes change due to great acts of valor, others for reasons that are beyond the control of man.

The Battle of Britain swung because a single German aircrew made a small but significant mistake.

Hitler had always reserved the decision to bomb civilian targets, and specifically the city of London, to himself. On this, he was very clear: *No one bombs London until I tell them to!* Such forbearance was not because he harbored humanitarian feelings but because he still believed there was a chance that the English would simply cave. He believed his self-control might convince English appeasers to unseat Churchill. But he knew that the will of even the pacifist would be stiffened if his Luftwaffe attacked purely civilian populations. Göring understood this. All of his pilots understood it too.

Blitz 37
A German Heinkel He 111 Medium Bomber Over Southeastern England

THE THEORY OF NIGHTTIME bombing was pretty simple.

The application of the theory was a very different thing.

In theory, the crew would use the center of a known radio beam to locate their position. Using one of the 360 radials that emitted from a radio transmitter, they could establish their position, even at night or when flying over a solid layer of clouds. The system was clearly in the very early stages of development—so much so that the British hadn't even begun to understand how the German system worked. But even though it was rudimentary and not entirely accurate, it had opened up an entire world of bombing to the Germans that had been closed to them before. Being able to bomb at night gave them the cover of darkness for protection. Yes, if the RAF was lucky, and if the moon was bright, and if their pilots managed to locate the German bombers, they could bring some of them down. But all in all, the mortality rate was pretty favorable when the Germans bombed at night.

Still, as with any new weapon system, there was much that could go wrong. The bomber pilots could make an error. Very common. In the middle of a life-and-death duel in the sky, and with darkness all around them, how many pilots could discipline themselves to follow an invisible and highly suspect radio beam? The radio transmitter on the ground could go down. Very common too. Finally, the navigational equipment on the aircraft could malfunction, or, as had happened with Blitz 37, get shot completely through.

• • •

The crew stumbled through the sky for four or five minutes. They had entirely lost their formation, leaving them alone and undefended over the British skies. To their right, they saw occasional bursts of fire and lines of tracers. The battle was still going on, but they had slipped away from the center of the conflict when they had dipped into the clouds.

Which left them alone . . . defenseless . . . without any friendly fighter escorts . . . low on fuel . . . one dead crewman . . . their aircraft battle damaged . . . the pilot thinking that they were losing fuel . . . a long flight across the deadly English Channel . . . and a bomb bay full of bombs.

The decision was pretty simple.

The clouds below them grew thin from time to time, letting just a hint from the British spotlights shine through. From that, they estimated they were somewhere over the south side of London.

Their target was on the south side of London!

That was good enough for them.

They opened the bomb bay doors and let 1,500 pounds of bombs fall away.

Below them, dozens of houses and family dwellings exploded into deadly flames.

• • •

Five miles to the east, and three thousand feet above the German bomber, a young British pilot saw a flash across the moon. He immediately recognized the Heinkel's unique shape, but it was too far away to catch it. And he was very low on fuel—so low, in fact, that his engine had started to sputter.

That didn't worry Manson much. RAF Biggins was only twelve miles to his left, and he was high enough that he could have glided to the airfield if he had been forced to. Better yet, he knew that his home base had not been hit—the Germans couldn't strike such small targets as runways when bombing at night—so he wasn't worried about where he was going to land.

Still, watching the single German bomber flee, he wanted to give chase. And there is no doubt that he would have if he had only had a little gas.

A Fatal Error

On that fateful night of August 24–25, after making a navigational error, a German pilot accidentally bombed a neighborhood in London.

Churchill had expected that London and his other population centers would eventually be bombed. In preparation for this, he had instructed Bomber Command to be ready to retaliate as quickly as possible. He, of course, had no way of knowing that the Germans had simply erred. Once he got word that the Germans had escalated the war by attacking citizen targets in London, he immediately ordered retaliatory attacks on Berlin.

Hitler—who, critically, had not been told about the inadvertent bombing of London—was outraged when Churchill attacked his German population centers. *So, this was how his hand of goodwill was to be met—with the bombing of Berlin!* Furious, he ordered Göring to begin revenge attacks on London, declaring, "If they attack our cities, we will raze *their* cities to the ground! We will stop the murderous activities of these air pirates, so help us God!"[33]

So it was that, without being given a critical piece of information, and just as the relentless day-and-night bombing of British airfields and military armament factories was ready to bear fruit, Hitler changed his tactics. The Luftwaffe was directed to begin bombing civilian targets, abandoning the only strategy that had any hope of leading them to victory. Bombing assignments started being made not based upon any tactical or strategic considerations, but on Hitler's desire for revenge.

Upon this change in tactics, the outcome of the battle turned.

The attacks against the British cities began on September 7 with three hundred bombers and six hundred fighters.[34] They came back the next day. The next night. The next day and night after that. Dowding's fighters fought the good fight, inflicting major losses on the Germans, but many hundreds of Londoners were being killed every day.

The fact that the Fighter Command continued to offer major resistance was beginning to cause Herr Göring great distress. For weeks, his intelligence officers had been telling him that Fighter Command was down to two hundred planes. Yet, day after day, Spitfires and Hurricanes appeared in the skies to blow his airplanes to pieces, killing his aircrews in numbers that he simply could not sustain.

He was completely bewildered.

They had *not* achieved air superiority over England. They could not protect their invasion force from the obnoxiously determined RAF.

The date for the invasion had to be postponed once again.

The Turn

On September 11, another series of airstrikes were undertaken against London and other major cities: five hundred bombers during the day and two hundred at night. That day, Dowding lost more planes than the Germans did—a very bad sign. Had that trend continued, the tipping point would have fallen to the Germans in a very short time. Of additional concern was the fact that, for the first time, the Germans had been able to partially jam Dowding's precious radar.

September 15 turned out to be a most important day. It was, in fact, the day when the outcome of the battle would finally turn.

Sensing a serious weakening in the RAF Fighter Command, Göring ordered another massive attack. Two hundred fifty aircraft formed up over France. British radar detected the coming attack.

Dowding's instincts told him that it was time to modify his tactics.

Rather than stick to his previous strategy of pinprick but relentless fighter attacks, he ordered Fighter Command to organize a full-scale response. Nothing was held back. Squadron after squadron was sent to meet the German bombers and their fighter escorts.

The number of British defenders waiting for them over the skies of England took the Germans completely by surprise. For weeks, they had been told there was only a handful of fighters left in all of England, yet here they were, fighting their way toward their targets through wave after wave of Spitfires and Hurricanes!

One of the great aerial combat scenes in history played out over the skies of southern England, with more than five hundred aircraft engaged in a giant dogfight. That afternoon, another wave of German aircraft arrived to meet another full response from Dowding's chicks. By the end of the day, sixty German aircraft had been destroyed to twenty-six RAF fighters.

The German leaders were finally forced to face the bitter truth. After losing hundreds of precious aircraft and thousands of highly trained pilots, they had failed. The RAF was not destroyed. Air superiority had not been won. Winter was coming quickly, and they were still unable to protect their invasion forces if they had been commanded to cross the English Channel.

The next day, Hitler ordered the postponement of Operation Sea Lion for an indefinite period.

The Battle of Britain had been lost.

What the Victory Meant

Dowding's measured strategy had worked. Despite their substantial losses, the RAF had survived.

But no one—not Dowding or the people of Great Britain, not Hitler or Göring or any of the German High Command, and, in fact, not even Churchill—realized the enormous implications the victory was going to have.[35]

The course of the entire war had been turned.

Perhaps without even realizing it, in mid-September 1940 Hitler lost the war, defeated by the efforts of perhaps 1,000 young men. Unable to invade and conquer Britain, he would turn against the Soviet Union, sacrificing the

German army, and thereby prolonging his war until, at last, the Americans were dragged into it by the Japanese attack on Pearl Harbor, pitting Germany against three of the most powerful industrial countries in the world. [36]

. . .

World War II would drag on for five long and brutal years. It would be, by far, the most costly war ever fought. As many as fifty million people were going to die.[37] Some say the number of casualties would probably be much higher, except that poor record keeping in Russia and China made the true number impossible to verify. By any measure, the war was a cataclysmic event.

And the suffering of the British people was just beginning. Over the next few months, they would endure the terror of the Blitz, with more than fifty thousand of them dying from the incessant German bombing of their cities and their towns—primarily at night.[38] With no effective way for the RAF to detect and shoot down the German bombers in the darkness, there was little the English could do but suffer through the merciless attacks.

But the fact that Hitler was unable to invade and conquer Britain forced him to turn his madness somewhere else. In one of the great miscalculations in military history, Hitler unleashed his forces against the Soviet Union, sacrificing his own army in the process. An enormous number of German soldiers would die fighting on the Eastern Front. But the advantages Stalin had—primarily his willingness to sacrifice tens of millions of his own people in the war against the Third Reich—proved to be simply overwhelming.[39]

This prolonged Hitler's war until the Americans, having been forced into the conflict by the Japanese attack on Pearl Harbor, were able to organize and apply their military and industrial might. Once the Americans entered the war, the strategic situation changed dramatically. Once the Americans were fully engaged, the outcome was almost inevitable. Short of the Germans developing a nuclear weapon before the Americans did (something they were working on), there was very little that could change the fact that Germany was going to lose the war.

What If?

What if Dowding had not been put in charge of Fighter Command? What if he had caved to the opposition and never developed the Spitfires and Hurricanes that were so critical to defending the British homeland? What if he had never put his faith in radar? What if he had been forced to abandon his overall strategy of a carefully measured response and had turned his fighters loose at every bombing raid? The RAF would have been destroyed. Hitler would have then invaded.

Or what if Great Britain had accepted Hitler's offer for peace? What if they had given him free rein to rule with blood and terror throughout the rest of Europe? Is there any doubt that, eventually, Hitler would have turned his attention back to Great Britain? Cut off from the rest of the world, including from its fuel supply, Britain's ability to defend itself would have been nil.

What if the British had lost the Battle of Britain and their mainland had been invaded? Left with only a handful of half-manned divisions and little equipment (the British Expeditionary Force had been forced to abandon all of its tanks, artillery, and machine guns during the desperate evacuation at Dunkirk), would the English have been able to defend against the most powerful army in the world, an army that had already proven itself by smashing its way through all of Western Europe?

If Great Britain had been defeated, would the United States still have been willing to enter the war in Europe? And even if they had been willing, what would have happened without Great Britain being able to provide the critical staging ground for the U.S. to pre-position the military assets that were so crucial to the monumental task of invading and retaking all of Europe?

Had Great Britain been conquered, America's war against the Germans and the Japanese would have been fought under very different circumstances. The Germans would have been able to use Britain's mighty navy to control the Atlantic Ocean, making it difficult, if not impossible, for the U.S. to supply a war effort in Europe. The Germans were already working on bombers with a range that would have allowed them to bomb the east coast of the United States. They were developing long-range V-10 rockets. They were working on nuclear fission. With Britain gone, there would have been no way for the Allies to disrupt the development of these fearful weapons, as the extensive bombing of Germany from bases in England subsequently accomplished.[40]

What if the Soviet Union had been conquered, something that likely would have happened had the United States, Great Britain, and their allies not been fighting against a major portion of the German forces on the Western Front? Hitler would have controlled all of Europe, the largest, richest, and most powerful continent in the world. How many believe his appetite would then have been satisfied? Would the Near and Middle East have fallen to his hordes? Would India, and then China? Where would he have stopped?

Several frightening scenarios are laid out by Gregg Easterbrook:

> Had Great Britain capitulated in 1940, the United States counterattack against German fascism probably could not have happened, and darkness might reign over Europe still. Alternatively, English capitulation in 1940 might have led to general atomic warfare in Europe, as the United States and Soviet Union attempted to defeat Nazism via the ultimate weapon. Both horrible fates were averted by Britain's determination to keep fighting no matter what the cost; a case in which bellicosity on the part of a democracy turned out to benefit the entire world.[41]

Had any of these events occurred, the history of the world would have unfolded in a very different way.

But the British won the Battle of Britain.

And because of that, billions of people who otherwise never would have enjoyed the blessings of liberty are doing so today.

• • •

Ironically, in November 1940, Hugh Dowding was forced into retirement, largely because of his inability to make the RAF capable of night fighting. But he was not forgotten. At his former headquarters at Bentley Priory there is a bronze plaque that reads:

TO HIM THE PEOPLE OF BRITAIN AND OF THE FREE WORLD OWE LARGELY THE WAY OF LIFE AND THE LIBERTIES THAT THEY ENJOY TODAY.[42]

White Cliffs of Dover
Southeast Coast of England
May 16, 1941

THE BOY AND HIS LITTLE sister stood in the open meadow staring up at the sky, watching the German bombers flying back toward their bases in France. Though the children were young, there was no fear but only hatred in their eyes. Those were the creatures that had so disrupted their lives. Those were the aircraft that had killed a number of their countrymen too large for them to comprehend. But this much they *did* know: Both of their grandparents were now dead.

Their countrymen had survived the great Battle of Britain, then the far more terrifying Blitz, Germany's outright attempt to kill or maim as many British civilians as they could. But it hadn't worked. The English had held. And now, with the war raging in Russia, the Germans had been forced to move on. Throughout the spring, the bombing raids had become much less frequent and less intense. It had been almost a week now since the last German air attack. In fact, things had gotten so much better that their mother had told them that they could soon come home.

As they watched, the German bombers dipped over the cliffs and headed across the open water. Behind them, a single British fighter gave chase. But the bombers were light and fast, and soon they were lost in the fog that hovered over the cold waters of the Channel.

"There they go," the sister muttered.

Her brother nodded but didn't reply.

Both of them were silent for a moment; then they turned to walk away. With a final glance, the boy looked back. The last of the bombers were just fading into the mist, the sound of their mighty engines rolling across the open sea. Though he didn't know it, he was watching history fly away. This was the last of the massive German air attacks that the British were going to see.

Notes

1. Easterbrook, *Progress Paradox,* 329. At this point in history, Great Britain was the only free nation in all of Europe left to resist Hitler's totalitarianism. In the entire world, there were only about a dozen free nations left to fight the combined tyranny of Germany, Japan, and fascist Italy (see ibid., 71).
2. Korda, *With Wings Like Eagles,* 207.
3. As quoted in Manchester, *Last Lion,* 48.
4. Manchester, *Last Lion,* 48.
5. As quoted in Manchester, *Last Lion,* 82. Actually, Hitler's eyes were blue.
6. Manchester, *Last Lion,* 76–77.
7. As quoted in Manchester, *Last Lion,* 126.
8. For an exhaustive account of the era of the rise of Hitler, appeasement in England, and the events leading up to the ascendancy of Winston Churchill, see Evans, *Coming of the Third Reich;* Evans, *Third Reich in Power;* Manchester, *Last Lion.* See also Fisher, *Summer Bright and Terrible,* 64–66, 107–26.
9. As quoted in Manchester, *Last Lion,* 682–83.
10. Ibid., 686; emphasis in original.
11. So named by Winston Churchill in June 1940. See Korda, *With Wings Like Eagles,* 2.
12. As quoted in Korda, *With Wings Like Eagles,* 3. For information about the almost universally accepted view that "the bomber will always get through," see Korda, *With Wings Like Eagles,* 3–4, 18–29; Fisher, *Summer Bright and Terrible,* 15–26, 45–54; Manchester, *Last Lion,* 96–97.
13. This was a pre–nuclear age version of "mutually assured destruction," or MAD, which dominated post–World War II thinking for decades.
14. Germany's thrust into Belgium, Holland, and France had resulted in Allied forces

being trapped on the beaches of Dunkirk in northern France. In a heroic effort, during the last week in May and first week in June, more than 338,000 men were rescued by more than eight hundred civilian and military ships, all while under brutal attack by German aircraft (see Dear, *Oxford Companion*, 312–13). Before the evacuation, German General Milch had urged the Luftwaffe's commander, Hermann Göring, that they should invade England while the bulk of its army was trapped in France. Fortunately, his proposal was not accepted (see Korda, *With Wings Like Eagles*, 134–35).

15. For a discussion of Hitler's belief that Great Britain could be eliminated as a threat through negotiations or a change in leadership, see Bungay, *Most Dangerous Enemy*, 9–13, where the author asserts that had Lord Halifax become prime minister, there is no evidence that the nation would not have followed him if he had obtained a peace agreement with Hitler. See also Korda, *With Wings Like Eagles*, 5–6, 78, 135, 153–54, 198–99, 248–49. An interesting question is whether England's will to fight might have been the same if General Milch's suggested invasion had taken place in May and if there had been German troops in England.

16. http://www.bbc.co.uk/history/events/hitler_plans_the_invasion_of_britain. See also http://rafairman.wordpress.com/2010/07/16/directive-16-eliminate-the -english-motherland/; Dear, *Oxford Companion*, 988.

17. http://www.bbc.co.uk/history/events/hitler_plans_the_invasion_of_britain. See also http://rafairman.wordpress.com/2010/07/16/directive-16-eliminate-the -english-motherland/.

18. The British had a powerful navy that could have helped repel an invasion. However, unless it could receive air protection from the RAF, it would have been at the mercy of the Luftwaffe in the English Channel. In fact, the navy had been forced to move to harbors on the west side of Great Britain, out of range of the German air force.

19. See Korda, *With Wings Like Eagles*, 5; Dear, *Oxford Companion*, 988–89.

20. Fisher, *Summer Bright and Terrible*, 102.

21. For information regarding Dowding's preparations for the Battle of Britain, see Fisher, *Summer Bright and Terrible*, 58–95, 140; Korda, *With Wings Like Eagles*, 15–16, 33–58, 124–25, 150.

22. It is interesting to note that while most of the pilots who fought in the Battle of Britain were from Great Britain, some came from other nations—New Zealand, South Africa, Rhodesia, Jamaica, Palestine, and America, to name a few.

23. See Korda, *With Wings Like Eagles*, 211.

24. Ibid., 87.

25. For information about the RAF pilots and their training and losses, see ibid., 86–87, 124, 142–46, 211.

26. For information about Lord Beaverbrook, who was born in Canada and whose real name was William Maxwell Aitken, see ibid., 130–34.

27. Throughout the Battle of Britain, pilots on both sides reported enemy losses well in excess of reality. Considering the nature of the conflict, with engagements lasting mere seconds, with aircraft flying toward each other at high speeds (three hundred miles per hour), with cloud cover hindering the ability to observe planes for more than a few seconds, it is easy to understand that such overestimates were the result of pilot error.

28. Korda, *With Wings Like Eagles,* 85–86.

29. Ibid., 87.

30. Ibid., 233.

31. Ibid., 253–54.

32. Ibid., 255.

33. Fisher, *Summer Bright and Terrible,* 216; emphasis in original.

34. For information about the change in bombing strategy, see Fisher, *Summer Bright and Terrible,* 211–25; Korda, *With Wings Like Eagles,* 244–50, 256–72.

35. For detailed information about the day-to-day events in the Battle of Britain, see Dear, *Oxford Companion,* 158–63; Fisher, *Summer Bright and Terrible,* 136–236; Korda, *With Wings Like Eagles,* 141–282. For perhaps the most comprehensive analysis of the Battle of Britain, see Bungay, *Most Dangerous Enemy.*

36. Korda, *With Wings Like Eagles,* 282. For information about the Blitz and the RAF's failure to respond to it adequately, see Fisher, *Summer Bright and Terrible,* 239–52.

37. Ambrose, *American Heritage,* 599.

38. Korda, *With Wings Like Eagles,* 283.

39. Accurate records regarding Russian military and civilian deaths in the war are difficult to verify. Estimates of Russian losses range from 17 million (see http://www.worldwar2database.com/html/frame5.html) to 28 million (see http://civilianmilitaryintelligencegroup.com/?p=3337). A 1993 report published by the Russian Academy of Science estimated the total Soviet losses at 26.6 million (Andreev, *Naselenie Sovetskogo Soiuza;* Ellman and Maksudov, "Soviet Deaths in the Great Patriotic War: A Note," 671–80).

40. See Fisher, *Summer Bright and Terrible,* 271–72.

41. Easterbrook, *Progress Paradox,* 329.

42. Korda, *With Wings Like Eagles,* 119. For more information about Dowding and his irreplaceable role in winning the Battle of Britain, see Fisher, *Summer Bright and Terrible;* Korda, *With Wings Like Eagles.*

Conclusion

Where Did Freedom Come From?

Noted American scholar Thomas Sowell relates that once a student asked his professor of history, "Where did slavery come from?"

The professor replied, "You're asking the wrong question. The real question is: Where did freedom come from?"

Dr. Sowell then goes on to explain that "slavery is one of the oldest and most universal of all human institutions. Slavery has existed among peoples around the world, as far back as recorded history goes. . . . It is the idea of *freedom* for the great masses of ordinary people that is relatively new."[1]

How *was* freedom born? And how does it survive?

This book was written to answer those most important questions.

We contend that freedom exists because Christian Europe created an environment where an incredibly rare combination of values—commitment to reason, personal accountability, individual freedom, equality, rule of law, the right of self-government—provided a philosophical nursery that allowed these ideas to take root and then to flourish.

Because of this evolution in human thinking—which took place uniquely in the West, along with a commitment to expend blood and treasure in its defense—billions of people today enjoy the blessing of living free.

History shows that the freedom distinctively found in what we call the Western world did not suddenly emerge out of nothing. This astounding mesh of morals, philosophy, respect for human rights, and understanding of the role of government did not emerge from thin air. It came with a price. And it took a long time. The march of freedom was like a fire in total darkness that smoldered with barely visible embers. From time to time, a breeze might blow to flame it, but then it retreated to an ember once again. Finally, in the form of the United States of America, it burst into full blaze and has served as the beacon of light ever since.

But had it not been for a handful of critical and unpredicted events, freedom would not exist as it does for us today.

If an Assyrian tyrant had not had a change of heart, there would have been no Jewish community in which Christianity could be born.

Had things happened differently at Thermopylae and Salamis, Europe would have been just another domain of Eastern philosophy and culture, leaving no Greek experiments in democracy, no Roman Empire within which these ideas could spread.

If Constantine had not believed that he had seen a cross in the sky, there would have been no Christian Europe, leaving the infant idea of freedom without a friend.

Had it not been for Charles Martel, the death of a Mongol khan, and the bold discovery of the New World, the West would not have survived. Freedom, if it *had* sprouted, would have never found a home.

Finally, were it not for the daring and courage of a handful of British pilots and the vision of their leaders, all of the values cherished by the West would have been extinguished by the catastrophic events of World War II.

We know that we have only scratched the surface in what we have presented here. There are many other events that altered history, many other themes that we could have followed. We have touched upon only a few, and, in the minds of some, perhaps we have not explored some of the most important.

We also recognize that the game of "What If?" can be risky. Our conclusions about what might have been may not have hit the mark.

But in the end, we stand by these assertions: The history of the world has been shaped in critical ways by these major events. This shaping has allowed, in just the last few centuries, the aberration that is the modern West, permitting a tiny sliver of all of mankind to participate in the blessings of freedom that we enjoy today.

The Miracle of Freedom

This book has also made the bold assertion that the existence of freedom is a miracle.

Whether you agree or not with that statement may depend on how you answer this fundamental question: *What is the natural state of mankind?*

What is more natural: Assyrian, Mongol, and Third Reich empires, with their utter brutality and total disregard for individual freedom, or the fact that today many around the world enjoy the extraordinarily rare blessings of living under democratic governments?

What is more natural: oppression of the masses under the hand of tyrants or the fact that many now live under constitutions that guarantee a wide array of individual rights?

If democratic governments are the natural order of men, then why didn't any such governments develop at any other time or place? Why is it that, as Yale professor Robert Dahl has pointed out, even in our modern world, there are only twenty-two nations with a democracy older than fifty years?[2]

In considering this subject, it might help to ask a more specific question: *Is freedom the rule or the exception?*

What does history prove?

Has it always been universally understood that the people of a nation have the right to form the type of government that they choose? Has it been universally accepted that the citizens of a nation have the right to choose who will make and enforce their laws?

Has it been understood that *all* people are born with certain fundamental rights, that those rights include the right to life, personal liberty, and the fruits of one's labor? Has it always been understood that these rights are inherent and unalienable and that they come from God?

Has equality of all been the norm? Is it ordinary to find governments dedicated to assuring justice?

Historically, such attitudes are rare to the point of being almost nonexistent.

For most of human history, the vast majority of people have been without any hope of freedom. For most of human history, people have been ruled by those with more clout, more swords, better guns, stronger armies, the greatest wealth. For most of human history, the order of things has been survival of the fittest, the weak being trampled while the government looks on.

As we have previously noted, in the early half of the nineteenth century, Frederic Bastiat, in his book entitled *The Law,* pointed out that it is injustice "that has an existence of its own."[3]

Even the briefest look at history indicates that this is true. Injustice fills the hearts of men. Injustice and oppression are the natural way of things.

In order for freedom and democracy to survive, injustice must be defeated. It will not simply disappear. It must be cast aside.

And that is exactly what the West accomplished. Over many centuries, at great cost and in fits and spurts, the West purged injustice and laid claim to democracy.

Are We Strong Enough?

If it is true that the existence of freedom is a miracle, then billions of people are living a miracle today. We are living a life that the vast majority of the earth's historical inhabitants could not have imagined, a life they never could have hoped to enjoy.

Do we have proper appreciation of that fact?

Earlier in this book, we quoted Professor Walter Williams's assertion that those who enjoy freedom are, in fact, a "tiny portion" of those who have lived on this earth. He then postulated that some future historian might view the era in which we live as a "historical curiosity." Note the rest of Walter Williams's observation about the fragile nature of democracy: "That historian might also observe that the curiosity was only a temporary phenomenon and mankind reverted back to the traditional state of affairs—arbitrary control and abuse."[4]

Mr. Williams makes a frightening point. Is it possible that this Golden Age of freedom might be viewed in future ages as nothing more than a curious aberration?

If the natural condition of mankind is the absence of freedom, is it possible that all humankind might one day revert back to tyranny?

• • •

Several years ago, one of us had the opportunity to work with Russian military officers in verifying certain requirements of the Strategic Arms Reduction Treaty. This was about ten years after the Berlin Wall had come down, a chaotic and uncertain decade for all the nations that had been members of the former Soviet Union. During this time, the author had the privilege of getting to know some of the Russian military officers on a more personal basis.

At one time, a group of Russian officers were visiting a U.S. military base. After verifying some of the capabilities of the aircraft on the base, the Russian officers took a tour of the local community, met with city leaders, and then went shopping at a local mall.

Late in the afternoon, this small group of Russian officers and their U.S. escorts were on their way back to the military base. Watching the group, the author couldn't help but notice the rather solemn demeanor of one of the Russian officers. This led to a short, and very guarded, conversation regarding the relative benefits and risks of democratic governments.

At the conclusion of the conversation, this Russian gestured around him. "All of my life, I have been lied to," he said.

The author remained silent as the Texas landscape slid by.

"This thing," the Russian said in wonder.

Though he didn't elaborate, the American knew instantly what he meant.

The Russian gestured again to the wonder all around him: the pleasant homes; the constant flow of clean water; the dependable sources of energy; the cars; the free press; the ability of the citizens to gather and speak and write what they wanted; the ability of the citizens to trust that though they may not agree with the outcome, their elections were free and fair; the fact that one did not need to *be* someone or *know* someone in order to succeed; the fact that one did not need to be a member of a certain party, or to not be a member of a certain religion, in order to avoid persecution; the fact that Americans did not fear a knock on the door at night; the fact that most Americans had great hopes for their children and their future—these are what the Russian officer meant by *this thing.*

"I don't know if my people want this enough," he concluded. "I don't know if we are willing to pay the price to claim these . . ." Here he struggled for the right word. "These privileges," he finally said.

Time proved that the Russian officer was prescient, for he showed a deep understanding of his people and the struggles that lay ahead for them. But the same question could be asked of any people in this day.

Do we *want* these things? Will we still *work* to claim these blessings? Will we fight to preserve the miracle of freedom that we enjoy today?

In fact, could the answer to these questions be the thing upon which the future of the entire world depends?

Notes

1. Sowell, *Applied Economics,* 31; emphasis added.
2. See Dahl, *How Democratic,* 43.
3. Bastiat, *Law,* 25.
4. Ibid., vi.

Bibliography

Introduction

Bastiat, Frederic. *The Law*. Irvington-on-Hudson: Foundation for Economic Education, 1998.

Cropper, Maureen L., Yi Jiang, Anna Alberini, and Patrick Baur. *Getting Cars Off the Road: The Cost-Effectiveness of an Episodic Pollution Control Program*. National Bureau of Economic Freedom Working Paper No. 15904, Cambridge, MA, April 2010.

Dahl, Robert A. *How Democratic Is the American Constitution?* New Haven: Yale University Press, 2001.

Haerpfer, Christian W., Patrick Bernhagen, Ronald F. Inglehart, and Christian Welzel. *Democratization*. Oxford: Oxford University Press, 2009.

Hiatt, Fred, "Around the World, Freedom Is in Peril." *Washington Post*, July 5, 2010. http://www.washingtonpost.com/wpdyn/content/article/2010/07/04/AR2010070403849.html.

Long, Hamilton Albert. *The American Ideal of 1776: The Twelve Basic American Principles*. Philadelphia: Your Heritage Books, 1976.

Stark, Rodney. *The Victory of Reason*. New York: Random House, 2005.

Tierney, John. "Use Energy, Get Rich, and Save the Planet." *The New York Times,* April 21, 2009.

Yandle, Bruce, Madhusudan Bhattarai, and Maya Vijayaraghavan. *Environmental Kuznets Curves: A Review of Findings, Methods, and Policy Implications.* Property and Environment Research Center, 2004.

CHAPTER 1
TWO GODS AT WAR

Coogan, Michael D. *The Oxford History of the Biblical World.* New York: Oxford University Press, 1998.

Cowley, Robert, ed. *The Collected What If?* New York: G.P. Putnam's Sons, 2001.

Durant, Will. *Our Oriental Heritage.* Vol. 1 of *The Story of Civilization.* New York: MJF Books, 1997.

Josephus, Flavius. *The Works of Flavius Josephus.* New York: Ward, Lock & Co.

The Interpreter's Dictionary of the Bible. 5 vols. Edited by Keith R. Crim. Nashville, TN: Abingdon, 1976.

Lewis, Bernard. *The Middle East.* New York: Scribner, 1995.

Rizza, Alfredo. *The Assyrians and the Babylonians: History and Treasures of an Ancient Civilization.* Translated by Richard Pierce. Vercelli, Italy: White Star, 2007.

Russell, John Malcolm. *The Final Sack of Nineveh: The Discovery, Documentation, and Destruction of King Sennacherib's Throne Room at Nineveh, Iraq.* New Haven and London: Yale University Press, 1998.

Thiele, Edwin R. *The Mysterious Numbers of the Hebrew Kings.* Grand Rapids, MI: Zondervan Publishing House, 1983.

Van De Mieroop, Marc. *A History of the Ancient Near East.* 2d ed. Massachusetts: Blackwell Publishing, 2007.

CHAPTER 2
HOW THE GREEKS SAVED THE WEST

Botsford, George Willis, and Charles Alexander Robinson. *Hellenic History.* New York: The Macmillan Company, 1969.

Bradford, Ernle. *Thermopylae: The Battle for the West.* New York: Da Capo Press, 1980.

Cowley, Robert. *What If?* New York: G.P. Putnam's Sons, 1999.

Curtis, John E., and Nigal Tallis, eds. *Forgotten Empire: The World of Ancient*

Persia. Berkeley and Los Angeles: University of California Press, 2005. Published in association with The British Museum.

Green, Peter. *The Greco-Persian Wars*. Berkeley: University of California Press, 1996.

Herodotus. *The Histories*. Translation by Robin Waterfield. Oxford, England: Oxford University Press, 1998.

"Herodotus," in *The Cambridge History of Classical Greek Literature*. Edited by P. E. Easterling and B. M. W. Knox. Cambridge: Cambridge University Press, 1989.

Lewis, Bernard. *The Middle East*. New York: Scribner, 1995.

Plumb, J. H. "Introduction" to *The Greeks* by Antony Andrewes. New York: Alfred A. Knopf, Inc., 1967.

Strauss, Barry. *The Battle of Salamis: The Naval Encounter That Saved Greece— and Western Civilization*. New York: Simon & Schuster, 2004.

CHAPTER 3
MIRACLE AT THE BRIDGE

Brog, David. *In Defense of Faith: The Judeo-Christian Idea and the Struggle for Humanity*. New York and London: Encounter Books, 2010.

Davis, Paul K. *100 Decisive Battles*. New York: Oxford University Press, 1999.

Durant, Will. *Caesar and Christ*. Vol. 3 of *The Story of Civilization*. New York: Simon and Schuster, 1944.

———. *The Reformation*. Vol. 6 of *The Story of Civilization*. New York: Simon and Schuster, 1957.

Gibbon, Edward. *The Decline and Fall of the Roman Empire*. New York: Modern Library, 2003.

Jenkins, Phillip. "Any Faith Can Become Violent." *USA Today*, March 19, 2010.

Marty, Martin. *The Christian World*. New York: Modern Library, 2007.

Neusner, Jacob, ed. *Religious Foundations of Western Civilization*. Nashville: Abingdon Press, 2006.

Stark, Rodney. *Cities of God: Christianizing the Urban Empire*. San Francisco, CA: HarperSanFrancisco, 2006.

———. *The Rise of Christianity*. New York: HarperOne, 1997.

———. *The Victory of Reason*. New York: Random House, 2005.

Waldron, Jeremy. *God, Locke, and Equality*. New York: Cambridge University Press, 2002.

Woods, Thomas E. *How the Catholic Church Built Western Civilization*. Washington, D.C.: Regnery Publishing, Inc., 2005.

CHAPTER 4
THE BATTLE THAT PRESERVED A CHRISTIAN EUROPE

Creasy, Sir Edward Shepherd. *The Fifteen Decisive Battles of the World*. New York: Dover Publications, Inc., 2008.

Durant, Will. *The Age of Faith*. Vol. 4 of *The Story of Civilization*. New York: Simon and Schuster, 1950.

Gibbon, Edward. *The Decline and Fall of the Roman Empire*. New York: Random House, 2003.

Kennedy, Hugh. *The Great Arab Conquests*. Philadelphia: Da Capo Press, 2007.

Lewis, Bernard. *The Middle East*. New York: Scribner, 1995.

———. *What Went Wrong*. New York: Oxford University Press: 2002.

Nicolle, David. *Poitiers A.D. 732*. Great Britain: Osprey Publishing, 2008.

Von Ranke, Leopold. *History of the Reformation*. South Carolina: Nabu Press, 2010; reprinted from original Leipzig: Berlag von Dunder and Bumblot, 1881.

CHAPTER 5
THE MONGOL HORDE TURNS BACK

Cowley, Robert. *What If?* New York: G.P. Putnam's Sons, 1999.

Durant, Will. *The Age of Faith*. Vol. 4 of *The Story of Civilization*. New York: Simon and Schuster, 1950.

Gibbon, Edward. *The Decline and Fall of the Roman Empire*. New York: The Modern Library, 2003.

Hay, Jeff. *The Early Middle Ages*. San Diego: Greenhaven Press, Inc., 2001.

Kahn, Paul. *The Secret History of the Mongols*. Boston: Cheng & Tsui Company, 1984.

Newark, Timothy. *Medieval Warfare*. London: Jupiter Books Limited, 1979.

Simons, Gerald. *Barbarian Europe*. New York: Time-Life Books, 1968.

Stark, Rodney. *The Victory of Reason*. New York: Random House, 2005.

Sugar, Peter F., Péter Hanák, and Frank Tibor, eds. *A History of Hungary*. Indiana: Indiana University Press, 1994.

Tuchman, Barbara. *A Distant Mirror*. New York: Alfred A. Knopf, 1978.

Weatherford, Jack. *Genghis Khan and the Making of the Modern World.* New York: Three Rivers Press, 2004.

CHAPTER 6
HOW THE NEW WORLD SAVED THE OLD

Cowley, Robert. *What If?* New York: G.P. Putnam's Sons, 1999.

Durant, Will. *The Reformation.* Vol. 6 of *The Story of Civilization.* New York: Simon and Schuster, 1957.

Gibbon, Edward. *The Decline and Fall of the Roman Empire.* New York: The Modern Library, 2003.

Huizinga, J. *The Waning of the Middle Ages.* New York: St. Martin's Press, 1924.

Lewis, Bernard. *The Middle East.* New York: Scribner, 1995.

———. *What Went Wrong.* New York: Oxford University Press, 2002.

Mann, Charles C. *1491.* New York: Alfred A. Knopf, 2006.

Morison, Samuel Eliot. *Admiral of the Ocean Sea.* New York: MJF Books, 1942.

Oman, Sir Charles. *On the Writing of History.* New York: Barnes & Noble, Inc., 1969.

Sale, Kirkpatrick. *The Conquest of Paradise.* New York: The Penguin Group, 1990.

CHAPTER 7
THE BATTLE OF BRITAIN

Ambrose, Stephen E., ed. *The American Heritage New History of World War II.* By C. L. Sulzberger. New York: Viking, 1997.

Andreev, E. M. *Naselenie Sovetskogo Soiuza, 1922–1991.* Moscow: Nauka, 1993.

Bungay, Stephen. *The Most Dangerous Enemy.* Great Britain: Aurum Press, 2009.

Dear, I. C. B., ed. *The Oxford Companion to World War II.* Oxford, England: Oxford University Press, 1995.

Easterbrook, Gregg. *The Progress Paradox.* New York: Random House, 2003.

Ellman, Michael, and S. Maksudov. "Soviet Deaths in the Great Patriotic War: A Note." *Europe-Asia Studies* 46, no. 4 (1994).

Evans, Richard J. *The Coming of the Third Reich.* New York: Penguin Press, 2004.

———. *The Third Reich in Power.* New York: Penguin Press, 2005.

Fisher, David E. *A Summer Bright and Terrible.* Washington, DC: Shoemaker & Hoard, 2005.

Korda, Michael. *With Wings Like Eagles.* New York: HarperCollins, 2009.

Manchester, William. *The Last Lion, Winston Spencer Churchill, Alone.* Boston: Little, Brown and Company, 1988.

CONCLUSION

Bastiat, Frederic. *The Law.* Irvington-on-Hudson: Foundation for Economic Education, 1998.

Dahl, Robert A. *How Democratic Is the American Constitution?* New Haven: Yale University Press, 2001.

Sowell, Thomas. *Applied Economics.* New York: Basic Books, 2004.

Index